Praise for *You'll Forget This E*

"This courageous, devastating memoir describes the dark side of the adoption fairy tale: the trauma of forced separation of a mother from her child. Engel's story is stark testimony to the failures of an adoption system that is built on coercion, lies, and shame. Highly recommended to those wanting to understand more about the true story of adoption."

—Alice Stephens, author of *Famous Adopted People*

"*You'll Forget This Ever Happened* is gripping and well written. Laura's determination, grit, love, and faith are admirable and genuine. Don't miss this important book."

—Leslie Johansen Nack, author of *The Blue Butterfly*

"Powerful memories wrenched from the soul of one birth mother in the 1960s who was forced by family and society to relinquish her child for adoption. Not only did she never forget what happened, her heart finally healed when she met her adult son, the child she gave away. A true redemption story."

—Julia Brewer Daily, author of *No Names to Be Given*

"Laura Engel tells a heartbreaking story of a young mother—separated at birth from a child she never knew—who finds the courage to confront her guilt-ridden past and seek redemption. In her moving and deeply personal account, the author makes peace with a long-lost son, and ultimately with herself."

—David Sheffield, screenwriter of *Coming to America*

"A searing energy begins on page one and continues to the unflinching final word of Laura Engel's memoir, *You'll Forget This Ever Happened*. Engel's triumph is in her unwillingness to turn away from the hard stuff. Devastating and stunning—alive with attention to the abundance of the heart—this memoir will stay with you."

—Julie Maloney, award-winning author of *A Matter of Chance*

"In her powerful memoir about making peace with the past, Laura Engel brings the hot summer of 1967 to life. That year, seventeen-year-old Laura is sent to live in a New Orleans maternity home with a rotating cast of pregnant teen girls who are assured they will "forget this ever happened" but of course never can. Losing her firstborn son to adoption changes Engel's life but does not crush her spirit. In time, she finds love and a career and creates the family she always wanted, which then welcomes the boy she named Jamie when he contacts her decades later. Engel's transformation from lost girl to grounded matriarch is deeply moving, a story that stays with you long after you reach the last page."

—Eileen Drennen, writer and editor

"In Laura Engel's compelling memoir, we experience the terrible irony framed by the title: she will *not* forget this experience of giving up her newborn son at the age of seventeen as an unwed mother. Engel *cannot* forget––and doesn't want to. And the reader will never forget this finely crafted journey of recovery. Through her narrative, insightful self-revelations, struggles, and willingness to expose her trauma, Engel creates an experience of intimacy for the reader that establishes a soulful friendship."

—Kelly DuMar, author of *girl in tree bark*

"Heart-wrenching but filled with purpose, this book satisfyingly unreels our emotions to the bright sounds of the '60s. Laura's richly detailed story makes us laugh, cry, gasp, and pray for those caught in that cruel time warp that plunged unwed mothers into the lowest, most loathsome level of 'proper' society."

—Linda Bergman, screenwriter, producer, and educator

"Exactly ten years apart, two scared eighteen-year-olds were forced to surrender their newborn sons for adoption in a home for unwed mothers on Washington Avenue in New Orleans. The first was my birth mother, Julie Francis; the second was Laura Engel. For five decades, Engel thought about her son constantly and wondered what had become of him. Then, miraculously, she found him—only to lose him again. *You'll Forget This Ever Happened* is a heartwarming and heartbreaking memoir about a mother's undying love for her son. I couldn't put it down."

—Brooks Eason, author of *Fortunate Son* and *Redemption*

"Laura Engel's memoir reads like a conversation with a best friend, both genuine and familiar. She anchors her story with references to the music, hair styles, and fashions of the 1960s, while unflinchingly sharing her pain and humiliation. When Laura got pregnant at seventeen, the trajectory of her life was altered, and she was not allowed to make any of her own decisions. These experiences left permanent scars that she kept hidden for decades—until a defining moment changed everything. *You'll Forget This Ever Happened* is Engel's story of resilience, of moving forward and building a different life but never, ever forgetting the secret baby she left behind."

—Deborah Reed, coauthor of *The Chamber and the Cross*

"If Anne Tyler had written a memoir about being forced to give up her son for adoption in the 1960s, it would read like *You'll Forget This Ever Happened*. Laura Engel is immediately likable and draws you in with her warmth, but her gorgeous prose immediately transports you to the Deep South in the '60s. As a reader, you'll keep turning page after page; as a woman, you'll want to hug her. This is a brave memoir that'll make you weep happy *and* sad tears."

—Lauren Cross, author of the forthcoming memoir *Mother Nurture*

"Nearly fifty years after giving up her baby, the past finds her. When Laura Engel's son, now grown and with a family of his own, locates her, the journey moves from trauma and despair to joy and a bittersweet, imperfect healing. Engel describes it all with poignancy and honesty. *You'll Forget This Ever Happened* is achingly lovely, written by a woman who knows her heart, makes up her mind, finds her way, and creates life on her own terms."

—Lisa Shapiro, coauthor of *The Chamber and the Cross* and author of *No Forgotten Fronts: From Classrooms to Combat*

"*You'll Forget This Ever Happened* had me hooked from the opening words. I was fully engaged and on the journey with teenaged Laura. Engel paints the details of popular song and the companionship of other girls in such a way that highlights their youth and lack of agency over their bodies or futures. This is an important book, especially today."

—Louise Carnachan, author of *Work Jerks: How to Cope with Difficult Bosses and Colleagues*

"This book is the reason I read. I couldn't put it down and when I did, it stayed with me. *You'll Forget This Ever Happened* is an incredible story beautifully told."

—Lindsey Salatka, author of *Fish Heads and Duck Skin*

"*You'll Forget This Ever Happened* is a powerful, gripping memoir that grabs a hold of you from the first few words and keeps you turning pages to find out what will happen next. Engel travels back in time to when she was a young teen in the Deep South and was all but forced to give up a baby she wanted. She deftly captures her heartbreaking struggle—and explores the way she faced down shame and buried secrets to find herself and her long-lost son. Told with heart and grit, honesty and wisdom, *You'll Forget This Ever Happened* is a poignant read about a mother›s unending love that will stay with you long after you have read the last page."

—Marni Freedman, cofounder of San Diego Writers Festival and author of *7 Essential Tools* and *Permission To Roar*

"With beautiful descriptions and poetic and engaging writing, Engel breathes new life into a long-gone time in the South. This memoir is hard to put down, in the best ways."

—Tracy J. Jones, editor and writing Coach

"Deeply moving, heart-wrenching, and visually alive, this memoir exposes the pain of becoming pregnant at a young age and being forced to give up a child. Ultimately, a story of resilience, forgiveness, and acceptance, with an ending made for a movie."

—Roberta S. Kuriloff, author of *Everything Special, Living Joy*

You'll Forget
This Ever Happened

You'll Forget This Ever Happened

Secrets, Shame, and Adoption in the 1960s

Laura L. Engel

SHE WRITES PRESS

Published 2022
Printed in the United States of America
Print ISBN: 978-1-64742-349-0
E-ISBN: 978-1-64742-350-6
Library of Congress Control Number: 2021919247

For information, address:
She Writes Press
1569 Solano Ave #546
Berkeley, CA 94707

She Writes Press is a division of SparkPoint Studio, LLC.

To Gene
Who believed in me, loved me,
and never let me down
My Forever North Star

Part One

February 1967, Biloxi, Mississippi

Two weeks under house arrest. No school, no friends, completely alone in my personal misery. Steady rain pelted the tin roof for hours. The chill and gloom outside the window paled in comparison to the frosty stillness inside my bedroom.

I picked at the peeling paint on the windowsill above my bed and turned to glance at the copy of my senior class photo on the desk. I spread my hands across my growing middle, asking myself for the hundredth time, *How could I have messed up like this?*

My heart skipped a beat when Mama pushed open the door and tossed a plain white envelope at me. Shoving back my rumpled quilt, I grabbed my glasses and pushed them on my face as I sat up.

Mama's forehead wrinkled. "You're not secretly writing letters to anyone, are you?"

"Of course not, Mama."

"You better not have told anyone about this mess you're in, Laura."

"I haven't told anyone," I snapped back.

Mama stood there, arms crossed, eyes watching my every move. "Well, open it."

Working the sheet of paper out of the envelope, I unfolded it carefully. Pieces of brightly colored paper squares had been glued on blue-lined notebook paper. Each square was precisely cut around an individual letter. The jumble of different colors and assorted sizes was off-putting. Was this a joke? I stared at it and began sorting out individual words. A chill ran through me as my eyes darted to a small photo of a baby glued to the bottom of the page, the edges ragged and uneven, as if it had been ripped from a magazine. The baby was crying.

1

Someone had meticulously cut out each letter and pasted them on this sinister sheet.

I shuddered as I read the words "I know what you did. You disgusting whore."

Dropping the paper as if it had scorched my hand, bile filled my throat and my eyes welled up as Mama grabbed the mysterious sheet and silently puzzled over it.

She crumpled the paper as if it were poison and folded into herself, sliding down onto the messy bed, tears of fury in her eyes. "How dare they?"

"Mama, who are they? Who would do this?"

I stared at the paper ball between us and carefully picked up the envelope. The typed address was faint, as if the used typewriter ribbon was well past needing replacement. The postmark was from Biloxi, the day before. No return address. We both sat speechless. It could have been from anyone.

Silence ate at the space between us. Mama looked as lost as I felt. I reached out, trying to comfort her, but she didn't budge. Fear replaced shock, and I shivered watching endless rain sluicing down the windowpanes.

For once, the prison of my bedroom walls felt like a safe haven, not a jail sentence.

"Well, somebody knows." Mama snatched the envelope out of my hand, reaching for the discarded wad of paper. "And whoever sent this wants you to know that they know." Heading out the door, she glanced back at me. "I hope you're happy. Look what you've done."

My face burned with shame as dread pounded furiously throughout my body with each beat of my heart.

How do they know? I shuddered, the feel of that piece of paper still blistering my fingers.

I'm not a whore. Am I?

Chapter 1
March 1967

"Well, this is the place." Daddy lowered his head, squinting out the car window.

"I don't think this is it." Mama peered out the front passenger-side window.

From the back seat, I looked long and hard at the scene in front of me. My hands felt clammy despite the stagnant warmth of the closed car, goose bumps skidded up my arms.

They won't leave me here.

"Yes, this is the place, Ann. Come on, y'all. They're waiting for us." Daddy turned around and glanced at me. Conversation had been sparse during the two-hour trip to New Orleans from our home on the Mississippi gulf coast.

I remember my feet hitting the ground when I stepped out of the back seat of my daddy's white '65 Chevy. There was a slight chill in the air and bloated clouds fluffed across a sapphire sky. The day was fresh, clear, and picture perfect.

Stretching my legs, I surveyed my surroundings, hoping to appear nonchalant, but my head was fuzzy and my grits-and-eggs breakfast threatened to move up into my throat. I glanced down at the front of the peach-colored gingham shift that Grammy had sewn, trusting that the empire-style dress disguised my thickening waistline.

3

As I carefully sidestepped a massive root shooting up through the cracked sidewalk, my heels sank into damp black soil. I took a deep breath, and rotting vegetation, along with car exhaust, assaulted my senses. Combined with that toxic odor was the faint scent of fresh bread and sizzling sausage.

It's Monday. Someone's baking biscuits and cooking sausage for a batch of red beans and rice.

Everyone born and raised in New Orleans and all along the gulf coast knew that Monday was the day your mama made red beans and rice, just like they knew Fridays were fish days.

God, what's wrong with me? How can I think about food at a time like this?

We had parked in a shaded spot in front of a nondescript two-story structure. The red brick was dreary and dark. Scruffy grass and dandelion weeds peppered the exterior grounds. Grey venetian blinds covered the dusty windows. Plain and generic, this place could have been any ordinary office building. It revealed nothing of the business that went on behind those walls.

All was quiet and peaceful on the outside as a damp breeze rustled the leaves on the old street, lined with an array of beautiful, ancient oak trees. Their emerald limbs canopied across the residential city street, creating a beauty common in old Southern neighborhoods.

But that beauty was lost on me. Nothing mattered except the fact that my knees felt weak and my heart banged frantically in my chest. The buzzing noise in my head was deafening, and I blinked, willing myself not to cry.

Am I dying? Can a heart pound this fast without killing you? God, let me die, or at least let me disappear. That would be the perfect ending to this whole sorry story.

I visualized myself slumping to my knees, prettily folding onto my side, face white, lips pale blue, hair spread out like a shiny brown halo beneath my head. Dead. Everyone would be devastated. They would be sorry they had been hateful toward me. All my family worried about was "what people would say." I wanted them to pay.

No such luck. I kept breathing.

Daddy grimaced. He appeared lost; his shoulders caved inward, and his movements were stiff. I couldn't look him in the eye.

In his forties and of average height, Daddy had a thin, wiry frame. Women had always fawned over him, pushed food at him, since my earliest memories. They fussed over him at every church meeting and family gathering.

"Here, Billy, have some of this here blackberry cobbler."

"Billy, let me butter you one of my biscuits to go with that coffee, honey."

He would smile shyly and politely take the offered food but seldom finish it.

His quiet aura and gentle nature defined this handsome man with light brown hair threaded with an abundance of silver. Glasses covered his intelligent hazel eyes. I loved inhaling his smell, a mixture of clean cotton, strong coffee, and Old Spice aftershave. Self-educated and well read, my daddy was the smartest man I knew.

I glanced at Mama, feeling a hot flush crawl across my cheeks. She had stepped out of the car and was staring up at the redbrick building. She had always been prone to emotional outbursts, and this past month she had been fluctuating between rage and humiliated crying jags. My brothers and I never knew what to expect from Mama. It seemed not a day had gone by that she had not reminded me that I was the reason for her anguish.

Please don't cause a scene, Mama. Can't you get ahold of yourself? Don't embarrass me again. I immediately felt ashamed thinking those hateful thoughts. This was my own fault, after all. She was right about that.

I hurried to her side. "Mama, here, let me help you."

She pulled her arm away as I reached for her.

"Just get your things," she mumbled, holding a soft embroidered handkerchief against her cheek, scanning the street.

"I'm sorry, Mama."

"What's done is done." We locked eyes, hers defiant and swollen.

Mama was a tiny woman, barely five feet tall. She appeared vulnerable, simple, and charming, but a complex woman resided in that petite frame. A beauty in her youth, she had been blessed with clear, pale skin; shiny, dark hair; and flashing eyes. Her only nod to makeup, Revlon's bright red Queen of Diamonds lipstick, dramatically set off that soft white complexion and those black-coffee eyes.

Most photographs from her youth showed a serious, pensive face. I studied them often, looking for the Mama I knew. In some, a young, pretty woman wore a joyful smile, mouth open wide, laughing out loud. I often wondered what had happened to that girl.

My mama's mood changes could be lightning quick, jumping from sugary words to biting mockery, then on to joyful singing. With her lovely voice, she'd belt out showtunes. Her laughter was magical, and her smile lit up her entire face. The problem was that she rarely smiled. A grim frown or unexplained sadness often marred her beauty.

I prayed for good days.

She would hug me tight. "I love you, hon."

"I love you too, Mama." I'd snuggle into her soft embrace, inhaling her Mama smell of Ivory soap and her own unique spiciness.

Trying to prolong the moment, I'd race into telling her a story about my day or the worries on my mind, but too soon she'd tire of me and would roughly push me aside, saying, "That's enough. I'm exhausted. I cannot bear to listen to you. Leave me. Give me some peace."

Many a day walking home from school I'd pray my friends wouldn't ask to come inside our messy and chaotic house. Who knew which Mama would greet us? The smiling one baking a fresh banana pudding, vanilla wafers marching along the sides of the serving dish, topped with perfect meringue, or the Mama suffering a crying jag, refusing to get out of bed for the entire week?

Since toddlerhood, I had walked on eggshells with my mama, and had learned early on to glory in her good days and not mention the bad days. I had been raised to keep secret her outbursts of anger and the days, sometimes weeks, of depression.

Now we had another secret, thanks to me. After learning of my shameful condition, she had worsened, her depression sinking to new depths. She stayed in her bedroom crying for weeks, coming out only when she absolutely had to, glaring at me if I tried to make conversation. God forbid I smiled or laughed out loud. Any questions I asked went unanswered. Fresh guilt bit at me daily because Mama's sadness broke my heart.

Look what I had laid on their plates, these parents who loved me and had worked hard to "raise me right." Look what had I done to myself. My life was over, and I was only seventeen years old. This nightmare was not something any of us had ever imagined as we stood in front of an unwed mothers' maternity home in a run-down, dubious neighborhood of New Orleans, Louisiana.

Chapter 2

Two teenage Black boys ambled past us on the sidewalk, heads down, faces turned away. I averted my face too, embarrassed because I knew they were aware of what this place was.

I knew Mama was worried about the neighborhood. As a girl raised in the Deep South in the 1950s and '60s, I had little contact with Black people except for my aunt's maid, Gladys, who ironed for us some days. Black people stayed on their side of town, and white people stayed on the white side. Signs above all public restrooms and public water fountains read WHITE ONLY or COLORED ONLY. Federal law required Mississippi public schools to be desegregated in the '60s, but only a handful of Black students had bravely attempted to register at our high school.

Civil rights, riots, and sit-ins played out on television news nightly. My parents and Grammy sat silent, shaking their heads, their lips set firmly each evening, watching Walter Cronkite. They were shocked by the black-and-white news photos of the sit-ins, students protesting the war in Vietnam, and long-haired young white and Black people demanding equal rights. Uncertainty and anger seemed to be the theme of our country, and it was rocking even our quiet little backwater world.

There had been a riot on our public beach four years earlier, in 1963. The Black community dubbed it a wade-in, commemorating the recent death of Medgar Evers. Two thousand white people had counterprotested, and violence had erupted. Guns were fired and Black protestors beaten, some with chains. Black flags, along with blood, peppered the beach. That protest ended with seventy-one arrests in our sleepy beach town, sixty-eight of them Black people.

The wade-in made national news. According to the locals, it wouldn't have happened if those Blacks had not had the audacity to think they could congregate on the white-only beach. Nobody wanted to acknowledge that the beach was supposed to be public to all tax-paying citizens.

"This is horrible. I think those police made it worse," Mama commented, as she sat reading the newspaper. My parents never blatantly said or condoned anything hateful happening to Black people, even though they had never taken up for them either. I sat silent, secretly glad Mama had firmly stated that the police and whites were all criminals and trash themselves.

I squirmed when Daddy and Grammy agreed with each other. "What were the police supposed to do? Those Negroes shoulda stayed on their own beach."

That statement ate at me, but I held my tongue, knowing there was no changing their minds. Still, it scared me to think of anyone fighting with chains and baseball bats on the beach, Black or white. I knew what had happened on the beach was wrong, but I was not brave enough to voice it out loud.

As flawed as segregation was, it was a product of the South I grew up in seventy years ago. As unjust as it was, I knew this diverse and dilapidated neighborhood in New Orleans was not the neighborhood that Mama had thought she would be leaving me in. Her worried face frightened me. Would I be safe? I knew Grammy wouldn't approve of this area as I watched the Black boys push at each other playfully while they hurried on down the sidewalk.

They will not leave me here.

Once again, Mama asked, "Billy, are you sure this is the right address?"

"Stop asking that question, Ann," Daddy grumbled. He walked around the car and opened the trunk to retrieve the almost new pale blue suitcase we had borrowed from Grammy.

I was watching the first love of my life age right before my eyes. The fact that I was responsible for his pain hurt more than any shame I felt for myself. Looking down at the cracked sidewalk, I blinked at guilty tears and hurried to his side, grabbing for the handle.

"Daddy, I'll help you."

"No, Laura, I got it," he muttered, not making eye contact. "You got everything else you need?"

"Um, I guess."

"Well, this is it. Come on." He hefted the suitcase out of the trunk, shutting it with a loud, final *clunk*.

We turned toward the entry of the building, but Mama slipped back into the car. We both turned when we heard her door shut. Cranking down the window, she peered out and motioned toward me.

"Laura, come here." Still clutching the crumpled handkerchief in her small fist, she had that look on her face that I had come to dread.

"I can't go in there." She sniffed and glanced at me, folding into herself, breaking down once more, wiping her face. "You just go ahead. Go inside with Daddy."

What? She wasn't going to help me get through this? She had to. She was my mother, for God's sake.

She was doing it again. Mama, the queen of last-minute exits. So many times, always at the eleventh hour, she consistently backed out of everything, missing school and church events. Even planned holidays and family outings were not exempt from her moods.

How many times had I found myself pleading with her to please go with us? Her excuses were often flippant: "I changed my mind" or "You kids don't give me a chance. I don't feel like going." Often my begging her to come with us ended with her ultimately demanding that we leave her alone.

Not now, not when I need her more than I ever have.

My mind went back to my seven-year-old self, begging Mama to get out of bed after she had spent all day in her darkened bedroom. My brothers and I did not understand. Was it our fault? Distraught, I would try to think of a way to convince her we needed her.

"Mama, why are you crying?"

"Go away."

"Mama, please get up."

"Go on. I can stay in here all day if I want to. You kids get outside and give me some peace and quiet. Y'all make me a nervous wreck."

"Mama, we're hungry."

"Make sandwiches for your brothers. You're such a selfish child, Laura. Now go."

"Grammy's asking about you."

Furious, she'd sit up and scream at me, "Go on and tell your grammy it's none of her goddamn business what I do, the old biddy. Now, bring me a wet washcloth for my forehead. My head's killing me in this heat."

I would race next door to my grammy's house and make up an excuse for Mama, and I would never tell her what Mama had said about her. After all, it would only cause more problems.

∾

Here we were again, same old story.

My chest hurt. I wanted to beg her to come inside, but pride and resentment stopped me.

Fine, if she won't go inside that building, neither will I. We can stop all this and go home and forget this ever happened.

Even at the eleventh hour, I refused to believe my parents would leave me alone in this strange place. I'd never lived away from home. It seemed as if I had been living a nightmare for months, stubbornly holding on to the belief that it would simply go away. This was not supposed to be happening to all of us.

I was their only daughter. They had taught me everything I knew about being a family and how important it was for us to stick together. Ever since I could remember, each summer Grammy and I traveled on a Greyhound bus to visit her family in the small towns outside Mobile, Alabama. I was happy to sit in a corner for hours while my five great-aunts quilted, listening to the stories of their lives. I would bask in their laughter and in the love these simple farm women felt for each other. I had grown up with the unbreakable assurance that I was one of them.

"Blood's thicker than water, and all you've got is family," Grammy repeated often.

Whenever Mama's sisters visited, I felt loved and cared for by them. My three aunts were different as night and day, but they held on to each other and tolerated Mama's moodiness, forgiving her often. They would laugh and gossip for hours, their sisterhood a shining example that family stayed connected no matter what.

Now, here we were, Mama and Daddy set on dropping me off at this institution, this unknown place. I was their daughter. This baby would be their first grandchild. Weren't we family? Wasn't this unborn baby family?

ᘐ

My life had fallen apart in the past two months. As soon as Mama learned about my pregnancy, I had been forced to drop out of high school. My heartbroken daddy dutifully went to my school, fabricating a tale that I was leaving to go live in Louisiana with Mama's mother, Grandma Effie. If anyone had found out I was expecting, I would have been automatically expelled from school. Even if they were married, pregnant girls were not allowed to attend high school. It was also unseemly for expecting teachers to teach in that condition, and they didn't. I couldn't imagine a teacher wearing a maternity smock in front of a classroom full of students.

Did the school believe Daddy's excuse for me leaving midway through my senior year? I doubted it. I was a good student, involved in school activities. While lying in bed, chewing my nails raw, I had thought up my own lie just in case anyone asked.

"I want to live with my Grandma Effie because there's an art school in her town that I can attend. After all, I love art." It sounded lame even to me. I enjoyed drawing and doodling in my sketchbook, because it seemed cool, but I had never taken an art class in my life.

Daddy ordered the correspondence classes required for me to work toward a high school diploma, and since the day Mama had asked about my pregnancy, I had been made to stay home, hidden from prying eyes, in case someone guessed I was a fallen woman. Attending school, church, shopping, or even going outside in our yard was out of the question. Petrified someone would see me and guess I was expecting, I had complied with the restriction. I was a girl "in trouble," the scandal and shame of it agonizing.

Mama hauled me to our family doctor, who, after my frightening and humiliating, first-ever pelvic exam, assured Mama, "Yes, Laura is pregnant" as we sat in his office. Mama sat ramrod stiff, taking in the news. I squirmed in my seat next to her, unable to hold his gaze, scrutinizing my lap.

The doctor could not decide on an exact due date. His eyebrow cocked upward as he blamed that on me because I had not kept track of my monthly cycle. He said so in a condescending voice as he observed me fidgeting across the desk from him.

In the privacy of our car afterward, Mama fell apart. Between wailing and threatening, she screamed that she had never been so disappointed and humiliated in her life. Sinking further into my own world, I stared blankly out the car window, knowing nothing could hurt her more than I had.

Spending weeks hidden in my room, I wasn't allowed to call friends, which served to make me feel even more like a criminal. I read constantly. I would finish a book, sigh, and, without a break, pick up another one from the stack of "to reads" next to my bed. I pretended to work on my dreaded correspondence courses as I worried and measured my expanding waistline daily. Each day I waited for my brothers to leave for school and Daddy to go to work, before tiptoeing out of my room.

I tried to eat as little as possible, relishing hunger pains. After all, I should suffer, shouldn't I? When hunger finally won out, many a day found me standing in the kitchen over the sink, staring blankly out the window at the old oak and pecan trees in our backyard, shoving sandwiches made of spongy white bread, bologna, and mayonnaise in my mouth. They were easy to make and the only food I felt like swallowing.

Mama stayed in her side of the house, her tiny Boston terrier, Teddy, curled up in bed with her, speaking to me only when necessary. When her best friend, Lena Mae, came to visit, they sat outside on the porch swing, their heads together, for hours. I peeked out the window, hoping Mama wasn't telling her friend what I had done. It hurt to imagine Miss Lena Mae thinking less of me.

When he was home, Daddy avoided me.

Terrified her friends or the neighbors would see me, Grammy warned me not to sit and read on the front porch swing. She also told me to wait until evening to walk the twenty feet to her back porch, as if my body had already expanded to huge proportions. She worried her church friends might make an unannounced visit any day and notice something odd about my being home from school.

"Come over in the evening, honey. I don't want nosy old Miss Quince asking questions," Grammy warned me, wringing her hands. I doubted Miss Quince, an ancient spinster who lived across the road and wore half-inch-thick lenses in her glasses, could see farther than ten feet in front of her.

How could I survive this? Clay, the father of my child, had turned away from me. I had no shoulder to cry on, nowhere to turn. Eventually, after I begged and cried, Mama seemed to either give up or take pity on the lonely, sad girl I had become. She allowed me to call one person, Nancy, my best friend since third grade.

Tall, majestic Nancy. She was stunning, with creamy white skin, a sprinkling of freckles across her button nose, shoulder-length red hair, and vivid hazel-green eyes. We had shared so much of life growing up, though we were opposites in many ways—she, tall and rail thin; I, short and curvy. She, the adored, spoiled only daughter of older parents; I, made accountable as the oldest child and only daughter of much younger parents.

Nancy and I treasured each other with a fierce love.

Now, life as I knew it had screeched to a halt. Everything had become a secret and a lie. It was as if I were living one of those terrifying nightmares that goes around and around in a continuous loop all night long and you cannot wake up from it.

❧

"Come on, Laura. They're expecting you."

"But if Mama isn't going in . . ." I looked from him to her.

"We're still going in. Tell your mama goodbye." Daddy scowled, turning toward the building.

"Daddy?"

I watched him continue toward the door, his back rigid.

"Bye, Mama. I'm sorry." Clinging to the car door, she was unable to speak, just sat shaking her head.

"I'll write to you, Mama."

She nodded silently.

Bending down and reaching to touch her shoulder through the open window, I hoped to comfort her, but she sat unyielding, stricken. As I turned away, I knew I must be the worst daughter in the world.

The neighborhood had fallen silent but for a few children playing dodgeball on the other side of the street. I hurried to catch up with Daddy, the echo of my beige pumps tapping across the cracked sidewalk. A lone man sweeping the entry of a decrepit grocery store on the corner stood watching us. My eyes locked with his for a second, before I quickly looked away. Dirty white paint peeled off the front of the building. Battered Coca-Cola signs and Barq's root beer signs were plastered across the smudged glass windows, along with garishly hand painted ones that screamed, EGGS: 23 CENTS A DOZ! MILK: 50 CENTS! LITTLE MISS SUNBEAM BREAD: 28 CENTS!

I could not have felt more fear if I had been dropped off in a foreign country. This big-city neighborhood was light-years away from the small-town community I had lived in my whole life.

Chapter 3

My rubbery legs continued forward as Daddy pulled open a heavy door leading into a musty lobby and waited to usher me inside. The tile floor was worn, the blank walls stark.

A maternity home? Home? It looks like an institution.

As we entered, a slender older lady greeted us, extending her limp, pale hand, offering it to Daddy as any proper Southern lady would have done. She welcomed us, introducing herself as Miss Felton. She would be admitting me today, she explained.

I extended my hand and forced a smile as she stiffly touched it. I barely caught her words because my mind was distracted, worried for Mama, sitting in the car out front, her handkerchief pressed to her face, frightened of this neighborhood.

Having been raised in the South, I had been taught to always show respect. Not cause waves. I knew it was proper that I appear gracious and courteous, regardless of what I was thinking. Looking at this scene from the outside, anyone would have thought this was simply a social meeting and that we were politely making introductions, preparing to sit down to afternoon tea.

My knees weak, perspiring and anxious, I glanced toward Daddy, feeling a pang of pity for him. He stood with the suitcase hanging at his side, his face and neck flushed red. He cleared his throat several times as Miss Felton ushered us into a stark private office.

"Please, have a seat." She motioned toward two chairs across from her desk. I studied her face. A network of fine lines circled her eyes and puckered around her mouth. Dressed in a dark skirt and white blouse, with a navy-blue cardigan clasped tight with a shiny gold pin, she was all business. Her medium-length, blondish-gray hair was pinned back in a neat helmet with black bobby pins. Heavy, dark shoes with thick old-lady heels completed her outfit.

As we sat in our chairs, I smoothed my skirt, straightened my glasses, and demurely crossed my legs at the ankles. A skinny run wormed its way down my nylons. It was as if I were floating above the room, watching myself. Setting my face in an earnest expression, I prepared to listen intently or at least pretend to listen as Miss Felton began her obviously well-practiced speech.

"This maternity home was started in 1886 as an institute of mercy. We are not only a home for unmarried young women but a child-caring institution as well, and, of course, an adoption agency." She smiled stiffly across the desk.

I recrossed my ankles. Daddy did not move an inch.

"You'll be happy to know we have a large staff of well-trained Christian workers and more than twenty doctors and interns whom we call upon to service us. Many are certified."

Daddy nodded his head. I stared straight ahead.

"At all times, we have a graduate nurse on duty. As you can see, your daughter, Laura, is in good hands." Her smile was warm, sticky sweet as honey.

She assured us of the fine service the Home provided for the hundreds of infants the unwed mothers so unselfishly gave up for adoption each year, and she rambled on about how this was the best place to restore and mend the young women.

"We have an excellent success rate rehabilitating the girls. They leave here with renewed faith and many pledges to change their ways.

Of course, hmm, once they leave, total redemption is up to them." Miss Felton stopped and looked straight at me.

I stiffened. Daddy shifted in his chair.

Rehabilitating?

She didn't skip a beat and continued to explain how the adoptive parents were carefully screened to assure they were "intelligent, responsible Christian people and preferably Methodist." As she spoke in her monotone drawl, she handed a brochure to Daddy.

I blinked as I read the words at the bottom of the brochure: "Go Forth and Sin No More." Between "rehabilitating" and "sin no more," I felt my cheeks burning and I zoned out, numb from the emotions of the morning, staring at the empty white wall behind her, as she blathered on in a flat, weary voice. My bad habit of daydreaming kicked in, and my mind wandered, taking me back to the previous Christmas.

∾

I remembered how terrified I had been that my parents or anyone would find out my secret. The family had been sitting in Grammy's dining room, the table laden with turkey, ham, cornbread-oyster dressing, and greens drowning in glistening pot liquor. As I reached toward the bowl of dressing for a second helping, my aunt Berti Lee playfully poked my swollen belly and innocently chuckled. "Are you getting fat, Laurie Lou? Too many biscuits?" She smiled, salty-sweet, and everyone laughed.

Mama frowned at me. She constantly warned me that I ate too much.

Grammy gently chastised her youngest sister: "Laura is not fat. Now, Berti Lee, you take that back." She gave me a sweet smile.

It took everything in my power not to bolt. Sweat beaded on my hot face as a chill ran through my body. I laughed along with everyone, but inside I wished I could disappear.

Does Aunt Berti Lee know? Can she tell?

Pushing food around on my plate, I couldn't swallow another bite. My plaid A-line skirt grew tighter every second as the waistband cut painfully into my flesh, but I sat through the rest of that dinner, a stupid smile plastered on my face, dying inside.

⌀

I pulled myself out of the daydream just in time to hear Miss Felton say, "The prospective parents are qualified to provide the best possible homes for the babies. We here at the home are extremely proud of our record."

She nodded, that tight smile on her face. "Hmm, Laura, you're doing a wonderful thing here surrendering your child so he or she can be raised by sober, hardworking Christians. We pride ourselves on matching the perfect baby with the perfect parents."

She hesitated, swallowed loudly, and looked down at her notes, then opened her mouth to continue.

My eyes opened wide. *Wait. What? I'm here only to hide away from the world, to protect my family from the embarrassment of having me marching around town with a huge belly. I'm here to avoid the humiliation of giving birth to a baby with no ring on my finger, not to leave the baby.*

That was what I had agreed to when we'd headed to New Orleans. I had believed that after I had the baby, I would take it back home with me. Mama had said she would raise the baby, that it would be like a little brother or sister to me. In my daydreams, I always imagined us going back home with my baby. I could almost see that tiny bundle wrapped tightly in a crocheted blanket. The baby always resembled my old Tiny Tears doll.

Grammy and Mama had made it clear: I had to go somewhere else to deliver this baby. Staying in our town and giving birth there would ruin my reputation.

I agreed because Mama had whispered, "After you have it, you can bring the baby home and I will be its mama."

"But what about Daddy and Grammy?" I had asked. I knew Grammy wouldn't agree. She disapproved of Mama's child-rearing.

My stomach churned. Could I trust Mama?

"Don't worry," Mama had assured me.

Once, when I was six years old, my uncle Al found out the hard way at the dinner table that you shouldn't mess with Mama or her kids. We were all gathered outside, eating under the trees, and he watched for a while as I played with a neighbor's dog, teasing it with scraps and laughing as it lunged at me.

"Laura, honey, be careful. If you tease the dog, he might bite you," he warned. I giggled and continued to torment the animal.

He cautioned me again, and again I ignored him as the dog growled at me.

Uncle Al became more agitated and looked for help from Mama. "Ann, get ahold of your daughter and don't let her pester that dog. I tell ya, it's gonna bite her."

Instead of correcting me, Mama jumped up, all five feet of her, flew across the table, and sank her teeth into Uncle Al's arm.

All hell broke loose, and Mama and Uncle Al's cold war froze over, never to warm up for the rest of their lives.

"That was wrong. Your mama acted crazy," Grammy whispered to me later that night.

"I know," I whispered back.

∾

Once I was back home, my baby would be with me and I would love it just like I loved my little brothers: Billy, Tommy, and Michael. Or maybe it would be a sister. Maybe by the time I had the baby, everyone would forget all this. Now, I visualized an infant wrapped in blankets, this time held tightly in Mama's arms. We would proudly show off the precious bundle as her new child, and life would go back to normal.

While Mama raised my baby, I would go to college or get a job. Who knew—maybe Clay would come back from the army and back into my life and we would take our baby and move away.

Had Mama already told Daddy her plan? Daddy, never a man of many words, was silent, so I figured he must be going along with it.

Chapter 4

As I sat watching Miss Felton's lips move, my thoughts meandered back to the day all hell had broken loose.

It was a Saturday morning in late January. Mama was doing wash out in the backyard shed. I was on the phone in my bedroom, talking to Nancy, and I thought nothing of it when Mama called to me from the back screen door.

"Laura, I need help hanging all these clothes."

"Oh, man, I gotta go," I told Nancy. "Mama's calling me to help her."

Nancy assured me she would check in with me later, reminding me to try using VO5 hair spray next time I rolled my hair. "It'll stay stiff longer." I smiled as I hung up the phone, visualizing my hair in a fantastic bouffant French twist.

The day was cool and crisp. White sheets snapped in the breeze; the scent of Ivory soap, bleach, and damp, clean linen floated in the air. Yellow sunlight sparkled on the shed's window, creating glowing prisms. Feeling lighthearted for the first time in weeks, I had almost forgotten how worried I'd been that I might be pregnant.

I hummed Clay's and my song, "I Got You Babe," as I hurried into the shed to grab a basket and clothespins.

"I'm here." I grinned at Mama.

Mama jerked her head around, her hands on her hips. She'd been crying—her eyes were red rimmed and angry. "Laura, are you pregnant?" she demanded.

The force of her fury slammed me; the word "pregnant" itself stopped me in my tracks, and I jumped back, feeling trapped in the small space. Her eyes stared into mine, daring me to answer.

For months I had hoped I was wrong. I prayed every morning for a drop of blood on my underwear, making silent deals with God. *Just give me a sign that I'm not in trouble, and I will do anything. I will never risk it again. I will go to church every Sunday, no matter what, and I will never have sex again until I'm married. Please, God.*

I'd waited for God to do his magic and had put off telling Mama as the weeks ticked by. She must have been working up the courage to ask me that question, and now, in the privacy of the wash shed, she unleashed her anger and fear on me with a vengeance.

"I think so," I whispered. "Maybe?"

"What? You think so?" She frowned, her face bright red.

I nodded.

"I knew it!" she screamed in my face. "How could you let this happen? Why didn't you tell me? Did you think this would just go away? You stupid, stupid girl."

I hung my head, shaking inside with self-loathing. This was worse than I had dreamed. "When was your last period?" She glared at me.

"I'm not sure. I never keep track. September or August, maybe?"

"Oh, Laura. You don't even know? It's Clay's, right?"

Words flew out of her mouth as Mama became more frantic by the minute. Her normally pale face was close to purple. "Why didn't you tell me?"

"Mama, I didn't know how to tell you. I'm not even sure, because I feel good. I'm not sick, so maybe I'm not, you know, um"—I choked on the word—"pregnant. Don't you get sick and throw up if you're gonna have a baby?" My voice squeaked so badly I didn't recognize it. Humiliation fell over me like a shroud; tears filled my eyes.

I whispered, "But I think I am."

"Did you tell Clay?" She spat out the words.

I hung my head.

"You better answer me," she ordered.

"I did. He doesn't want anything to do with me."

"What? Well, that is just great. I never liked him," she fumed. "We'll see about that. I don't give a damn what he wants, the weasel."

"I'm so sorry, Mama."

"Your poor daddy. He'll be sick over this. His only daughter."

My head snapped to attention, and I reached out to her, pleading, "Please, Mama, please don't tell him. Please. Not yet."

"You've done this, and now you have to live with it. You should be ashamed."

She turned her back on me and stomped back into the house, into her bedroom, and slammed the door. She didn't come out until it was time to cook supper. I wiped at my face as I hung the wet clothes, whimpering quietly. Snapping the clothespins on the line, watching my little brothers playing across our property, next to the bayou, I wondered how this could get any worse. The sun was shining, but my day had turned gray in a heartbeat.

Later that afternoon, Mama refused to look at me or speak to me. I slunk to my room and called Nancy, my confidant these past couple of months, to commiserate and cry over this predicament I had gotten myself into.

Nancy picked up on the first ring.

"Hey. It's me."

"You okay? What's wrong?"

"Nancy, Mama knows. She asked me, and I had to tell her. She hates me." I broke down sobbing. "This will kill her."

"I'm coming over."

I lay across my bed, staring at the ceiling, numbly waiting for her to make the ten-minute drive to my house.

When she got there, Nancy came straight to my room, sitting down across from me at my desk. Long strawberry-blond bangs concealed her eyes; she looked down at her lap, knowing there was little she could say to make this situation better.

I cringed, repeating, "Nancy, this is gonna kill my mama. She's so upset. She screamed the word 'pregnant' at me. I've broken her heart."

Nancy looked up, her forehead creased in a frown. "Um, I don't think it will. It would take a lot more than this to kill your mama, Laura. She's stronger than you think—and meaner."

Ever since the day Nancy and I had met, walking home from elementary school, little girls with Toni perms, we had relied on each other. Now we were bored teenagers with long, straight bangs, brushing our heavily mascaraed black eyelashes. We had always had each other's backs over the years as we'd grown from little girls innocently reading Sunday-school books together into smart-aleck teens, secretly reading passages of the formally banned book *Lady Chatterley's Lover* out loud to each other.

Nancy had witnessed Mama's tirades and knew what Mama was capable of. She had heard the cruel insults Mama hurled at me. She knew like nobody else what I was up against. Nancy and I had no secrets.

As she always had, Nancy calmed me. "At least it's out in the open now. This'll all work out. I know it will. Maybe they can talk some sense into Clay." She seemed so wise.

As awful as it was, she was right. At least now it was real. The secret was out. I was not on my own anymore. My family would help me. I just knew it.

ॐ

The next morning, Mama stood at my bedroom door, glaring at me rolled in my quilt, a book in my face.

"Your poor daddy is heartbroken. This about killed him. I hope you're proud of yourself. He cried all night." She slammed my door shut.

Immediately, I crumbled. I was the apple of Daddy's eye. He had always been proud of me. I had let him down in the worst way. I had seen him cry only once. Although I had been only four years old when PaPa died, I remembered Daddy's tears after seeing his own father dead of a heart attack. It crushed me to think I had inflicted such pain on my beloved father that now he was crying again. My daddy, my Achilles' heel.

It soon became evident that although my parents now knew this awful secret, they were not going to talk about it. Daddy wouldn't even look in my direction. Would he ever love me again?

∾

Sunday afternoon, bored and irritated, I plundered my closet, trying to decide what to wear to school the next day. Thank God I owned a couple of mod baby-doll dresses. They were all the rage, empire style or loose waisted, and forgiving of a growing waistline. I also had a girdle tucked away in my dresser that I had talked Grammy into buying for me a while back at Penney's department store. I had whittled away at her, whining, "Grammy, all the girls wear them. Please, please." After wearing it once, I realized it was absurdly uncomfortable and swore never to put on the awful thing again. Now, I was so grateful for that girdle and would put it to good use.

As I stood peering into my closet, the door opened behind me.

"Don't come in here. Stay out," I ordered in my big-sister voice, without turning toward the door.

"It's me." I turned to see Mama walking into my room and sitting down on my bed.

"I can still fit into this skirt." I held it up to show Mama, hoping to inject some normalcy into this disaster.

"You know you're not going back to school, don't you?" She sighed.

"What? Why?" I was stunned. Nobody at school suspected anything.

"Really, Laura? You have to ask me?" She shook her head.

"No one knows."

"Well, they will soon enough. You're already showing," she said through gritted teeth.

I peered down at my stomach. It didn't look that different. Did it?

"I can wear my girdle or a baggy sweater," I wailed. "I have to go to school, at least for now. I can't quit. Mama, please."

"Keep your voice down," she seethed.

"I can't miss school. It's all I've got now. I need it."

"Humph. You should have thought about that before you started sleeping around."

"Mama, I didn't 'sleep around.' I was just . . . Never mind. I know it's wrong, but . . ."

"You'll never graduate now."

"Yes, I will." I was instantly furious.

"You've messed it all up. You won't graduate."

"I'm going to school!" I screeched at her, not caring who heard me.

Her hand flew at me, slapping me hard across the cheek. Her eyes opened wide, and she gasped but continued screaming, "Don't you dare yell at me! And no, you're not going to school."

With those final words, she stomped out of my room without looking at me again. I stared at her back as she left. More shocked than physically hurt, I was stunned silent for a second, but I quickly recovered as humiliation and anger overcame me.

"I hate you! I hate you!" I screamed at the closed door. "I'm going to school. Watch me. You can't stop me!" I grabbed my hairbrush from my dresser and threw it against the wall. It bounced back, missing my face by an inch. Startled, I screamed again. "I. Hate. You!"

Choking on my words, I slumped to the floor and leaned against my desk, sobbing.

I must go to school. What about my friends? What will they think? I won't quit school. I want my life back.

This was all Clay's fault. All those nights he had promised he loved me. He had been so gentle and sweet. Sure, we had had breakups, but we always made up. I thought he respected me. We had made plans. He'd always said, "One day we'll get married, and we won't be like those boring old married couples, 'cause it'll be just us—no kids. We'll move away, wherever you want to go, and we'll be exciting and see the world." His exact words.

"I'll always love you," he had promised, holding me in his arms. I remembered us walking on the sand at the beach, at parties, going to movies, talking for hours. He was always touching me, telling me I was beautiful. Telling me lies.

For hours I cried and stayed alone in my room, watching the sunshine turn to dusk through the window. The bulletin board on my wall seemed to mock me. Crumbling corsages from dances and proms were pinned to it, and dance cards with "Clay" written across the whole thing, claiming me as his for the entire night. There were ticket stubs from events with friends, programs from plays and dance recitals pinned haphazardly across the top of the board. My saved love notes from Clay looked tired. That wall documented the past two years of my life.

My eyes settled on the black-and-white photos of Clay playing his guitar, and others of my friends and me on the beach, grinning like fools at someone's Brownie camera.

Jumping up, I pulled everything off the wall, covering the floor with the mess of my life. Viciously ripping up those lying love notes, I threw them at the trash can and watched the bits of paper floating like confetti, covering the floor.

"I hate all of you," I growled to the empty room. "It's not fair!" I yelled.

Dark shadows grew in my room as the hours crept by. Spent and numb, I lay curled in a ball on top of my nest of quilts. I glanced up as Mama came through the door and sat down at my desk. Her swollen eyes swept across my trashed room. I turned away, my own eyes sore and inflamed, staring at the wall.

I won't look at her. She only cares about what people will think or say. She doesn't love me.

"You have to stop this, Laura. You're scaring your brothers. You've upset everyone in the house, and I'm a nervous wreck." Her shaky voice was quiet and resigned. "Your daddy can't stand you in here, yelling and crying. He's sick over this. Screaming your lungs out won't help. It must stop."

I lay with my back to her, stiff and unyielding.

She cried softly for a while. I told myself I didn't care if she cried. In fact, I was glad she was crying. The tension in the room shifted slowly as she became silent. Torturous minutes passed, and I wanted to turn and see what she was doing, but I was too stubborn, too angry.

Then she surprised me. "I've had time to think. We'll figure it out. You need to get ahold of yourself, hon. You're making yourself sick, and it's not good for you, or the baby." She sighed calmly, and the mattress shifted as she sat down on my bed and wrapped her arms around me. We wept together, as mothers and daughters had done since the beginning of time.

As we shed tears in each other's arms, our bodies softened. The relief of knowing that Mama still loved me flooded like warmth through my veins. She stayed with me until I calmed down. She assured me I would still graduate, just not with my class, and she said we would figure out what to do for me and the baby. Her voice broke when she said the word "baby," and we held on to each other for dear life.

The baby.

She was right. We would get through this.

Chapter 5

The next day, Mama and I were achingly polite to each other, and then she asked calmly, "Does Grammy know?"

She had always resented the closeness I shared with Daddy's mother. Mama addressed Grammy as Mother, but that was where the respect ended for her mother-in-law. Their mutual dislike for each other was blatant, their disagreements epic.

"No, Mama. I only told Clay and Nancy."

Mama looked smug. It was as if she was gloating that she was the one I had told first—although she had conveniently forgotten she had demanded I tell her.

"Well, we need to tell her, don't we?"

I stiffened. "I guess. But do we have to tell her now?"

Not Grammy. She's always had such faith in me. Not yet.

Mama sighed. "I'll go with you. Might as well get it over with."

I felt stronger with her by my side as she and I walked through the backyard to the small white house on the lot next to ours. Sitting in Grammy's sparkling clean kitchen, I felt my knees shaking under the blue flowered tablecloth. Grammy and Mama sipped strong black coffee and casually caught up on our neighbor Miss Edwina's latest drama. I laced my own coffee with heaping spoons of sugar and a double splash of cream. Hot, fresh biscuits sat on a plate in front of us, and I reached for one, nervously slathering it with butter, watching the golden goodness seep into the fluffy white flakes.

Just as I raised that warm biscuit to my lips, Mama looked pointedly across the table. "Laura has something to tell you, Mother."

Setting the biscuit down, I took a long sip of hot coffee. The syrupy sweetness coated my throat as I swallowed loudly. "I can't say it," I mumbled.

Grammy's forehead wrinkled.

"You have to." Mama sat back. "Now."

My shoulders began to heave as my eyes stared at my lap and a fiery flush scrambled up my cheeks.

"Good heavens, what is it, honey?" Grammy reached for my hand.

"I'm so sorry," I began.

In between sobs, I blurted out the story. I told Grammy the unexpected news that her beloved granddaughter was not who she thought she was. Grammy had warned me about being too involved with Clay, so maybe she wasn't surprised to hear what I had done. She had complained repeatedly about my staying out on dates far too late. She had worried I would go astray and had been vocal about it, predicting I would never finish school and would marry young if I ran with the wrong crowd or spent too much time with one boy.

"I only want the best for you," she had cautioned. "You stay out far too late with that boy. What do we know about his people, anyway? They're Yankees."

In her defense, she did not say "I told you so." Instead, she did worse—she crumbled before my eyes. I had never seen Grammy so distraught. Her blue eyes had never looked so lost.

Mama cried. Grammy cried. Fat, hot tears flowed down my cheeks. *Will my family ever love me again or have reason to be proud of me? I must be the worst disappointment ever.*

After what seemed like forever, they pulled themselves together and agreed that the worse possible scenario would be if people found out about me. They began to commiserate on how to keep this awful news a secret. Grammy was adamant that the ladies at the church not find out. They agreed that Grammy's garden-club friends and Mama's bunco friends must never guess what was happening. They warned me that we had to keep this from the rest of the family as well.

"Remember Edith?"

Edith had been a neighborhood girl who had gone wrong and had a child who was being raised by her parents. She had once been a promising girl—smart, pretty. Once she was in trouble, she quit school, fell into the wrong crowd, and tried to drink herself to death. Her family was shamed forever. The rumor was that she was pregnant again, and still no ring.

I knew how society looked at girls who were unwed and pregnant. They were shunned once found out, and their babies were considered bastards, unless the father did the "right thing" and married the mother. If you did have a forced wedding, better known as a shotgun wedding, all was supposedly forgiven. Even so, there remained rumblings and comments when the baby arrived in six months, not nine. That stain followed the mother and child for life. There was not much forgiveness once you were labeled a promiscuous girl who could not wait until after she was married to let a boy have his way with you. Virginity in the mid-'60s was a Southern girl's most coveted badge of honor.

Grammy and Mama pressed me. "Who knows? Name them."

"Only Clay and Nancy." I stuck to my story. I lied.

I had also told my cousin Mark. Practically joined at the hip since we were in diapers, I loved Mark like a brother. He was a year older than me, and we were the first cousins in our generation. I trusted him more than anyone else on Earth. He had been home from college during the holidays when I told him. I had made him swear not to say a word. He had kept his promise.

After the initial shock and tears, he had asked me if he could feel my stomach.

"Why?" I was surprised.

"Just curious, I guess." He grinned, a little embarrassed.

"Well, all right, but only over my clothes."

He gently placed his hand below my navel, across my flat stomach, where if you pushed down you could feel a small, impossibly hard knot smack in the center.

"I think I feel it. It's like a rock," Mark marveled in his gentle way.

I could never tell Mama or Grammy this had happened. They would be angry at my cousin for not telling them and aghast that I had let him feel the knot.

Now, they wrung their hands and lamented. Why hadn't I told them sooner? What was wrong with me?

Discussing what to do about me and my situation seemed to bring the two of them closer together, for once, as they sat side by side, discussing what to do next.

"What did Clay say?" Grammy frowned at me over her glasses.

"He doesn't want to get married," I mumbled, freshly humiliated, tired of the interrogation.

As if they had not heard what I'd said, they agreed I had to marry immediately.

"I never liked that boy," Grammy huffed.

"Me either," Mama agreed.

No matter whether they liked him or not, the consensus was that he had to marry me to make an honest woman of me.

I cried to deaf ears, "But he said he doesn't want to be married to me. He said he wants no part of it." I wrung my hands. "He joined the army. He doesn't care that this is happening."

"We'll see about that." Grammy gritted her teeth.

The biscuit lay on my plate, cold and forgotten.

༺ঌ༻

It was decided: A speedy wedding must take place. Daddy was not above a shotgun wedding. He wanted the father of this baby to be responsible for his actions, to be a man, to "do the right thing." He had called Clay's folks and, after arguing on the phone with Clay's angry mother and father, had slammed the phone down and turned to Mama.

"Fort Benning, in Georgia," he growled.

My heart froze. Without making eye contact, he said, "Laura, I talked to the drill sergeant. I gave him Grammy's phone number because I don't want your brothers hearing you talk to him. Clay will call you tomorrow afternoon. When he calls, tell him we're headed there."

Chapter 6

I was fifteen when I started my sophomore year of high school. Toward the end of summer, my cousin Mark had driven up to our house with a friend in his car. The friend was gorgeous in my fifteen-year-old eyes. Dark blond hair, icy blue eyes, deeply tanned, with a lopsided smile. Mark said his friend Clay was new to the coast and he played the guitar.

A bit shy at first, I did notice that Mark's new friend Clay could not take his eyes off me. He grinned at everything I said and did. It thrilled and emboldened me. Our teenage hormones raced into overdrive, and it was no time before we began an emotional and rocky roller coaster ride that would last two years.

Now, my mind raced over all those months together. I replayed our long walks, holding hands, our adventures together. Clay was my introduction to the forbidden yet inevitable joys and tribulations of young love. We spent long hours making out in secluded spots, learning the slow ache of desire. Listening to him play his guitar and making up silly songs about me was electrifying. Our fights were always petty, trivial, and our makeups always over the top and passion-filled.

That past summer, he had been a lifeguard at a resort on the beach and played in a rock band, snatching random gigs at iffy venues. Nancy and I sometimes got entrance into those honky-tonks with our eager smiles and fake IDs, which Clay had created for us. I would watch him play in those dive bars, jealous of the girls who surrounded him during the band's breaks but confident I was the one he really loved.

He was my first love, the only one I had felt worthy of gifting my oh-so-prized virginity to. He had promised he'd love me forever. Me only. My face burned. I was a fool.

∽

Clay and I went steady off and on in 1965 and 1966. We broke up late in the summer of 1966—his idea. He said we should date other people. He needed a break. I had to admit, our relationship always seemed to involve drama and arguing. Maybe being unattached my senior year would be fun, I said out loud, while a secret part of me continued to yearn for the safety and comfort of our messy situation. If I was honest, I knew I was being dumped, and it ate away at me.

Breaking up did not stop Clay from calling. He'd call for a Sunday drive or just to grab a bite to eat. Those visits often resulted in more than just talking, because I never denied him. I no longer played "hard to get"; I shared his passion and missed the romantic young love we'd shared.

In front of friends, I acted as if I couldn't care less about the rumor that he had dumped me for some college girl he had met over the summer at the resort he worked at. Inside, I secretly burned with humiliation and anger. I wanted him back, so much so that it became an obsession.

We talked a few times after the final breakup, when I thought I was pregnant, and I told him I was scared. That was when Clay told me he had plans in the works already and was doing what his Dad, a World War II vet, thought best: He was joining the army.

"But, Clay, I'm scared. I missed my 'you know what' this month. I might be, uh, you know . . . expecting," I whispered, humiliated to have to say it out loud.

"Pregnant? Damnit, are you kidding me?"

I was equally shocked. "Army? Since when?"

Our last conversation took place at my house. My parents and brothers out for the entire day, I figured this would be the perfect time to invite him over to talk. I called his house, ready to hang up if his mama answered. "Nice girls do not call boys" was a strict rule of that time. His mama had never liked me to begin with, even back when I had been a "nice" girl.

I bathed in scented bubbles for an hour, practicing what I would say to him. I dressed carefully and applied layers of black mascara to my worried eyes, lining them with black liner. Clay loved the English mod look, so I brushed my straight bangs down over my eyebrows and applied pale pink lip gloss.

What I'd give to look like Jean Shrimpton. I peered at the famous model's face smiling from the cover of the *Ingenue* teen magazine on my dresser and tried to mimic her world-famous pout.

Made up, hair perfect, and spritzed with Chanel No. 5, I waited for Clay on our front porch swing, pretending to read a book, pretending it was no big deal if he showed up or not.

He arrived right on time, seeming a bit standoffish as we entered the house, but soon we were lighthearted, laughing, gossiping about music and friends, and playing a few records in my bedroom. I made sure Sonny and Cher's "I Got You Babe" was in the stack of 45s and offered him a Coke. I even had cookies.

Before long, we were reclining across my bed, his arms wrapped around me and my head resting on his chest as I listened to his heartbeat. I inhaled deeply, dizzy with his scent, a mix of clean sweat and English Leather aftershave. I remember lazily thinking he wouldn't be there if he didn't care about me. There was no sense of urgency—no one was due home for hours—and I could tell what was on his mind as he softly kissed my neck and rubbed my back. My plan was working.

"I missed you more than I realized. I'm so glad you called, Babe," he murmured into my hair.

I smiled up at him, loving his crooked, lazy smile. It gave me hope.

I snuggled in closer, and he kissed me long and hard. I kissed him back. As he became more demanding, I matched his pace, unbuttoning the buttons of my blouse, smiling suggestively at him. His kiss was familiar. My moves were calculated. He expertly pulled my blouse open, and I wiggled out of my bell-bottoms as he undid his belt. I was prepared to do whatever it took to win him back.

Later, as I nestled against him, I whispered, "I miss you every day, Clay."

He gave me a satisfied smile as I softly stroked his cheek, and he playfully grabbed my hand, kissing my fingers, gently biting my wrist. Our eyes locked. I knew he loved me.

In the quiet room, time stood still. *It's now or never. Tell him.*

I pressed my body hard against his and began explaining how happy I was that he had come to see me, how it was killing me not to see him. Turning my face away from him, afraid to see his reaction, I blurted it out.

"Clay, remember what I told you last month? Well, now I'm pretty sure I'm expecting."

I felt an immediate shift in the air. "I'm scared," I whispered to the silence.

"Oh, man, here you go again. You don't look pregnant." He poked my ribs. "I think you're just saying that. Trying to get attention."

"I wouldn't 'just say' I'm pregnant. I'm scared. I'm serious. What should we do?"

"What? What should *we* do?" He glared at me. "I don't even know if it's mine."

I jumped up, pushing away from him. "How can you say that? It is. Who else's would it be?" I protested, tears in my voice.

We sat apart silently, not making eye contact. My face flamed so hot, it hurt. Then he said, "Come on—you know you told me you went out a few times with other guys after we broke up. Who are you kidding?"

"How dare you, Clay? You know it has to be your baby."

A flicker of doubt crossed his face.

"I wanted you to be jealous. I wanted you to want me again. I went out, but I didn't do anything wrong. I promise. I never went all the way."

"Right. You made up all the drunk parties on the river. You think I'm stupid. I know you saw other guys." Indifference colored his pale blue eyes as he stood up, ready to leave.

My heart ricocheted in my chest. Was this really happening?

I forced myself to stay calm. "Yes, I went to parties. Yes, maybe I got drunk and made out, but it was just because I was lonely. I hated being without you. I made up a bunch of stuff to make you jealous. Please, Clay. You have to believe me."

He stood up and peered down at me, pulling on his shirt. Was that doubt on his face?

"You always said you loved me, and I still love you," I reminded him, as I reached for my fuzzy pink robe to cover myself, my eyes brimming with tears.

He watched, and suddenly I could read his mind: *Here we go again.* We had broken up and made up so many times in the past six months. Even I was sick of the constant drama of it all.

"Laura, I don't want to talk about this. We broke up. Remember?" He said it in a condescending voice and shook his head as if I were beyond stupid. "It's final this time. I don't want to be together anymore. Understand? I want to see other girls. You're too . . . too demanding. Besides, I told you, I joined the army. I'm leaving soon.

We're over, okay? Now, damnit, I wish you hadn't called me to come here. You completely ruined this time we just had together."

Bile pushed up into my throat as I watched him move toward the door, straightening his clothes and glancing once more at himself in my dresser mirror. He nonchalantly finger-combed his dark blond surfer hair, mumbling that there were ways to take care of this problem and that if I were smarter, I would have figured that out. But it would cost money. About $300, he guessed, and although he didn't have a lot of money, he would get half of it for me before he left town for the army.

"I don't want to hear about this mess you're in again. If you really cared about me, you wouldn't badger me with all this. I have enough to worry about. Like, what if I get shipped to Vietnam?" His tone was angry, disgusted.

I was stunned silent. I knew he was talking about abortion, but I was naive and didn't fully understand how it worked. I knew it meant getting rid of the baby in a secret, horrible way. I had heard rumors that in New Orleans there were places you could go to get rid of a baby, but it sounded so dark, so wrong and dangerous. It was something "bad women" did.

"I'm sorry. I'll die if you have to go to Vietnam, Clay, but you can't m-m-mean," I stuttered, "kill the baby. I could never do that. I won't. Never. Why are you doing this to me?" I wailed.

He stiffened and glared harder at me. "I'm leaving. There's no talking to you. I shouldn't have come here."

"No. Please. We have to talk now." I grabbed his shirtsleeve as my heart broke.

"Look, I'll call you and we can talk about it later. I can't stand the way you're acting."

"You can't leave me." I reached for his hand.

He frowned at me, shaking off my hand.

"Clay, please. Please listen. I'll go to a doctor. I'll find out for sure; then we can talk." I sobbed.

"I'm not getting married, Laura, no matter what you find out. Think about what I said—you can take care of this. Maybe before I leave town, we can meet up again. Maybe."

Something inside me exploded as he reached a hand toward me. I slapped it and screeched, "Get out of here. Don't ever come back. I don't need you." Blood pumped hot and furious throughout my body as I screamed in his face. With both hands, I pushed violently at his chest. "I won't meet you again. I know the only reason you want to meet me. I'm not stupid. I'm not your slut." I looked down at my stomach and whimpered, "I need you. Please."

He stared at me, slowly shook his head, and smirked.

"You know what? I hate you, Clay. I. Hate. You."

He hurried from my room, glad to be rid of me, and as the front door slammed, I ran to the bathroom, dizzy and sobbing, dropping to my knees as vomit emptied into the toilet. The truth hit me like a bulldozer.

∾

That was the last time I had seen Clay. He had become a stranger. Hadn't he promised we would be together forever? I had proof: his old letters, his photos. He really had loved me at one time. Hadn't he?

I washed my swollen face, crawled into bed, and stayed there for three days after that failure of an afternoon with Clay. I thought about dying. It couldn't be as painful as this was.

"What on earth is wrong with you?" Mama asked that evening when she came home.

"I'm sick. I think I have the flu or something."

She looked suspicious and felt my forehead. "You don't feel feverish. Have you been in bed all day?"

"Yes," I lied, but I wasn't lying about feeling sick. "I have a terrible headache. My chest hurts. And I threw up."

"I'll get you a BC powder and some Pepto-Bismol and a wet washrag for your forehead." A wet washcloth across a forehead was Mama's cure-all for everything. She glanced at me, unconcerned. My family had nicknamed me Sarah Bernhardt for a reason.

A lump lodged in my throat. My voice croaked when I tried to speak. Grammy showed up with her inevitable Vicks, her own cure-all, offering to rub it on my chest and back and cover the areas with a warm cloth. Her soft hands patted my back as guilt and shame flooded through me.

"Get some rest, honey." She switched off my lamp and quietly left the room.

Silent tears flowed down my checks. Vicks ointment couldn't help with what was wrong with me. Rolling myself into my quilt, willing myself to sleep, I tossed about and prayed once again, bargaining with God. I had never been this frightened in my life.

∾

For three days, I faked it. Mama was becoming suspicious, so I pulled myself together and went back to school as if nothing had happened. The strong draw of friends and schoolwork yanked me back into the vortex of being a normal teenager. Almost.

I pushed down my worries of being pregnant. I felt healthy and strong; never once had I been nauseated, except during the meltdown with Clay. Maybe it would all just go away. I tried to be the best big sister and perfect daughter, and I studied with a vengeance. I focused on my grades and went with friends to school activities. I worked on the school newspaper and enjoyed journalism club. If I kept busy, there was no idle time to "think" about what might be happening inside my body.

Maybe I would bleed this month.

I looked normal. Boys asked me out on dates. It made me feel desirable. I drank beer at parties and slowly began hanging out with a rougher crowd. I didn't feel worthy of my good friends and distanced myself from them.

There was a group of boys always up to no good, whom I migrated toward at a few of the parties. Three of them—Wayne, Joey, and Gavin—were older high school dropouts, rough around the edges and full of slick flattery. Wayne and Gavin had already served time in the army. They flirted with me, telling me I was a looker and fun, and even though they made me edgy, I kept seeing them after parties. I woke up mornings afterward hungover, miserable, hating myself.

The good girl I had been knew I shouldn't hang with them. Was I already feeling like I was damaged goods and didn't deserve better? I could have won an Academy Award, because to the outside world, I appeared not to have a care.

Chapter 7

"What is it, Laura? I can't believe your dad called here. My sergeant's fit to be tied. I'm in deep shit now. Thanks a lot."

Clay was livid. I sat speechless. "Well?" he growled over the phone line.

I didn't know how Daddy had pulled strings, but his call to Fort Benning had resulted in Clay's calling me at Grammy's house. I was both worried he wouldn't get in touch and simultaneously scared he would.

My conversation with Clay is foggy after all these years. I remember sitting on Grammy's white chenille bedspread, the phone held tight against my face. I feel the warm sun pouring through the sheer drapes. Sunbeams sparkle through the glass windows and bounce off the pale blue walls. My arm wraps around my waist. I whisper into the phone. Grammy and Daddy wait in the dining room, drinking coffee, pretending they're allowing me privacy. I know their ears are stretching to hear every word.

"You know what this call is about," I squeaked.

"Laura, I told my sergeant I don't want to marry you. He said I don't have to. My folks are furious with me. I can't believe you're doing this to me." Clay sounded like he was going to cry. After all, he was at boot camp. I had heard they wore down the recruits to whimpering little boys.

Maybe he's worn down.

"Everyone's mad at me too, Clay. How do you think I feel?" I demanded. My tears caught in my throat, and I knew even then that calling him had been a mistake. "My daddy says we have to get married," I stated flatly.

"My dad says I don't have to. I can't let him down. He finally respects me because I enlisted. Laura, my mom is beside herself. Your dad shouldn't have called her and upset her. They said they don't think your baby has anything to do with me." And, as if as an afterthought, he threw in, "And, you know, I have a new girlfriend, and my folks like her."

I froze.

Again, memory stops and gauzy fog creeps into the crevices of my brain. I have only a memory of snippets of crying, pieces of words, accusations from both of us, but the end of the conversation is vivid and harsh.

"I'm so tired of this, Clay. Just forget it. I can take care of myself." The words tumbled out of my mouth, but in my heart, I held on to hope that he would say, "No, wait. Let's talk."

"I have to go. Don't call again." His voice was flat. Dead.

That was not what I wanted to hear. No regret, no sorrow, just a warning.

The phone clicked. He was gone.

Daddy didn't give a damn what Clay, his parents, or the army said. He raged, and two days later found us on the highway, heading 350 miles to Fort Benning before dawn. As we wound our way through Alabama and Georgia, Daddy's jaw remained clenched. I hunkered down in the back seat, and Mama, tucked in the front passenger seat, stared out her window, still as a statue.

Slumped in the back seat, morose, unsure of what the future held, I was unable to concentrate on the book in my hands. I dozed off, holding on to a fragile thread of hope that Clay would change his mind once he saw the desperate, sad girl I had become. I hoped I would become more important than making his father proud. Maybe it would no longer matter that his mama didn't like me, and just maybe, there wasn't another girl.

Hadn't he told me I was beautiful and smart the last time he'd been with me, before I'd yelled at him, before I'd told him to get out of my house and never come back?

This would be my salvation. Just like in the movies, he would see me, change his mind, and marry me.

I closed my eyes, fantasizing. Soon I visualized Clay and me living on an army base. There I was, my hair in braids, in a small, cozy kitchen, fixing the spaghetti-bake casserole I had learned to make in Miss Kelly's home economics class. I could see myself holding our baby at the front door of a tiny apartment, waving goodbye to my soldier husband as he headed off to war or whatever soldiers did. When I closed my eyes, I could smell the baby powder sprinkled on the baby boy settled on my hip. I just knew my baby was a boy. I imagined a little towhead with sparkling eyes. He looked just like his daddy.

How could Clay deny me?

જી

Meanwhile, that road trip remained crushingly tense. Mama and Daddy stared straight ahead at the highway, rarely saying a word, each in their own hell as the scraggly pine trees of Alabama flew by mile after mile. Shame closed my throat.

So this is what people mean by the term "shotgun wedding," I thought. No gun involved here, just a furious father wanting to protect his wronged daughter's reputation. It all finally made sense to me. But was I wronged? I had been a willing participant with a boy who said he didn't love me.

We parked in front of a dingy motel alongside the huge army

base. The plan was that Daddy would go to the base and speak to the people in charge of Clay. Mama and I would wait in the motel room with two double beds and a dank underlying odor of mildew and old cigarettes. We thought Daddy would come back with Clay. Then we would find a justice of the peace or a Methodist minister to perform a marriage ceremony. Afterward, we would take Clay back to the base. Maybe we could find a nice place for dinner before we dropped him off. My stomach growled at the mere thought of dinner.

"Mama, can I take a quick bath?"

"Go ahead. Most likely this will take a while." Mama's voice was weary, resigned. She sat back against one of the headboards on the tacky brown-and-orange bedspread, a *Ladies' Home Journal* magazine in her lap. The striped drapes were faded and sealed shut. A tiny TV sat on the dresser, rabbit-ear antennas wrapped in aluminum foil poking up toward the ceiling. We never turned that TV on.

"Mama, I'm sorry."

"I don't care how much you say it. You've gotten yourself in a fix. I'm a nervous wreck, and your poor daddy . . ." She shook her head. "Sorry ain't gonna help this time."

"I don't want to be here either, Mama."

She waved me away. "Go take your bath. When Daddy gets back, I can't wait to give Clay a piece of my mind."

I soaked in the dingy tub. Warm water trickled out as steadily as I refilled it, the ancient rubber stopper useless. Ivory Snow soap mingled in the steamy fog with a hint of mold as tears ran silently down my face. I studied my hands, torn nails bitten to the quick. Grammy always said, "You can tell a true lady by her well-manicured nails." These weren't the hands of a lady.

Hours ticked by.

Tying back my hair with a white ribbon, I stared at my reflection. Red-rimmed eyes stared back behind my glasses. I had packed a simple cream-colored dress and a pair of white pumps for the civil ceremony. Certainly not the wedding I had sometimes visualized for myself, but at least I would look fresh and nice when Clay laid eyes on me.

At dusk, Daddy arrived back at the motel room and avoided looking in my direction once again.

Mama stood up, hands on her hips. "Well, what happened?"

"He doesn't want any part of this or any part of Laura. They said he doesn't have to see her. It's nearly impossible even to get in there. I never even saw the son of a bitch."

"What? That's awful," Mama said.

"We're going home," he muttered, not looking in my direction.

"Billy," Mama began, "you should have demanded—"

Daddy roared, "Ann, get your stuff together. He doesn't want her. Hell, he doesn't deserve her. We're leaving. Now."

Veins stood out on his neck. His face flushed so red it frightened me. Mama huffed but began gathering the few things we had taken out of our bags. Wasting no time, we were soon back on the highway. As the night closed in, silence and tension filled the car, thick and palpable. I sat in shock, shaken to the core; my bladder felt it would explode, and my stomach growled, but I dared not say a word.

෴

The next day, eavesdropping at my parents' bedroom door, I heard Daddy talking to Mama. The drill sergeant who talked to Daddy had told him Clay refused to see me. He claimed he had nothing to do with the baby. The army warned Daddy that he would have to retain an attorney and go to court and prove this problem was all Clay's responsibility. This would drag through the courts for who knew how long. And the military men promised they could make his daughter's life hell.

"They will interview every boy she's ever known, and her reputation will be dirt after they finish with her. They believe their recruit."

We couldn't afford a lawyer. I had let them all down in the worst possible way. I was an embarrassment. A girl in trouble. There was nothing more to say, no tears left. It was doubly worse when the father of the baby flat-out refused to entertain the thought of marrying me. I let it sink in: I was branded for life, not to mention this innocent child. A child I could not imagine.

Who knows what else was said all those years ago? I wish I did. Now, decades later, I wish I had had the confidence and strength to demand to see Clay. As a young girl in the 1960s, I had no voice. Men decided what was best for me. I was simply a terrified teenager who was told over and over that she had ruined herself for life.

∽

"I've decided: After you have the baby, I'll raise it. It will be your little brother or sister," Mama told me when we were alone one morning. She stirred her coffee. Her eyes seemed to challenge me. After all, Mama loved babies. She was only thirty-eight years old and had suffered a miscarriage the year before.

How could I ever forget that awful experience? I had been invited along on a family vacation with Nancy and her parents to Huntsville, Alabama, and had been embarrassed when my daddy called there, disrupting our trip. I was doubly scared when he told me Nancy's parents were turning around and bringing me back home to help with the boys. Mama was in the hospital.

"Why? What happened?" I cried out.

Daddy stated flatly, "Your mama lost a baby. Miscarriage."

Mama was pregnant? Nancy and I were aghast at the knowledge that old people like my parents had sex, and I was horrified by the mere thought that here I was, a high school girl who would have had an "expecting" mother. How embarrassing. It pained me to be honest and admit I felt nothing but relief when I learned she had miscarried. Such a selfish thought, but it was the truth.

Maybe it would make her happier to have a baby in the house. This baby could replace the baby she lost. Mama didn't talk to me about that baby, but maybe this was another reason why she was sadder than ever lately. This seemed like a simple solution.

Still, the problem of where I would give birth to this baby loomed before us.

"Maybe you could go live on Uncle George's farm in Alabama for now?" Grammy offered, as we sat in front of cups of untouched tea.

Is she serious? They have an outhouse. I shuddered. *But it might serve me right to have to use an outhouse now.*

"Aunt Berti Lee would take Laura in if we asked," Grammy suggested, wringing her hands, her blue eyes rimmed red.

"My mama is a better choice," Mama stated.

I hardly knew Grandma Effie. She barely spoke to me when she visited us.

Grammy bristled. "She'd be close to a hospital in Mobile if she went to Aunt Berti Lee's."

"Well, Mother"—Mama glared at her nemesis—"Laura would be closer to a hospital in Mandeville if she was with my mama. For God's sake, Louisiana is better than Alabama."

"Ann, I was born and raised in Alabama," Grammy reminded Mama, with a glare.

They silently began clearing the table together, their faces set.

Here they go. Another standoff. The writing was on the wall. These two would never agree on anything.

Unknown to me, other plans were in the works as well. Daddy had paid a visit to our minister, with whom the plan for the maternity home in New Orleans had been formulated. Nobody asked me how I felt. Everything was arranged by the adults in my life, who left me with no choice. No voice. Everyone simply assumed I would do what my parents decided was best.

Without a high school diploma, a job, any means of support, or, most important, no husband, I was at the mercy of my parents, my church, and society. A society that had little sympathy for my predicament, along with offering no education or support for young women faced with the unplanned birth of a child. A society that allowed the fathers of those illegitimate children to skate free.

Chapter 8

Now, here I sat with Daddy, across from this fussy woman telling me that I would leave my baby at this place. Was this really happening?

The biggest worry I had ever had was what dress to wear to the next dance. Now, I frantically realized I must change the way this conversation was going. The walls were closing in on me, and listening to the words this old crone was saying shook me to my core.

"What? Please, wait," I stammered. Sitting up straighter, I pulled my shoulders back. "Wait, there's a mistake here."

"Excuse me?" Miss Felton's eye twitched, and she frowned.

"I'm sorry, ma'am, there's a misunderstanding." Heat radiated from my cheeks.

I never interrupted authoritarian adults while they were speaking. I was not that bold or that rude. For me to challenge this official woman in the middle of her rehearsed spiel about the Home surprised both her and Daddy, but it surprised me more.

Trembling with fear, I cleared my throat. "You see, there's a mistake. I'm going to have the baby here, but I'm not leaving it here. I'm taking it home to my mama. She says she'll raise it. She'll explain. She's out front, waiting in the car."

Daddy and Miss Felton exchanged a look. She turned to me, her lips thin, tight. She pulled out her notepad and wrote something. I imagined her scribbling "troublemaker" next to my name.

She turned back to Daddy. "I'll leave you two to discuss this further. Please take your time," she murmured, with a nod of her head. Shoulders hunched, she minced across the room.

As the door clicked shut, Daddy turned and looked me square in the face. "Laura, you cannot keep this baby."

"Why?"

"It's best for this child if you give it up for adoption. It's best for you too. And for the family."

"But, Daddy, Mama says I can have the baby here and then I'll bring it home. She says she'll be its mama and I can be the big sister, and, um, Daddy . . ." Fury began to replace fear, and I started to sob, hating myself, hating this whole situation. How could this be happening?

"I'll go to the car and get Mama." I sprang out of my chair, heading toward the door. *If anyone can change Daddy's mind, she can.*

Daddy stood and grabbed my arm. "No, Laura. Sit back down. Now, listen here. You don't want your mama raising this child. Believe me. You can't pretend like you're a sister to your own child. That never works out. You need to think about this. You can't take care of this baby, and neither can your mama. That's the way it is."

My legs collapsed, and I folded back into the stiff chair. A roaring noise filled my head.

"Daddy. Please." I reached out to him. "I can do it. Please."

"No. You're not thinking straight. You can't make this decision."

"Daddy, Mama said so. I'm getting her." I rose again to leave the room.

"Sit down." He gently pushed me back down. "If you care about this baby, you must give it up for adoption. You can start living your life again when you come back home. Good people will adopt this baby and give your child a better life."

"Daddy, *we're* good people," I whimpered.

"It just won't work, hon." He released my arm.

Daddy said all of this in his quiet way, never in anger, but with the firmest voice I had ever heard him use. His mind was made up. He was finally telling me what he thought best. He did not say he would disown me, or threaten me, but I knew my father was insisting this was the only way.

"Daddy, I'm sorry. Don't leave me here. Please. I'll help Mama. I'll help with everything around the house and I'll take care of the baby for her. I'll make it up to both of you."

"No. It wouldn't work out. You know your mama. She's not up to it. Besides, you would never let her take over raising your child. Y'all would fight over that baby. You know that. It would be too hard on everyone."

"No, you're wrong. I won't fight with Mama. I'll let her take over. Please?"

He sat quietly for a while, staring at the wall in front us. Then he turned to me. "Hon, no. It won't work. You'll understand one day. This is best."

Misery crushed me, yet the relief that my daddy was finally talking to me, advising me, and reaching out to touch me filled my heart as well. I had been starving for his attention, his counseling. Hot tears streamed down my cheeks.

He never reached out for my hand again or hugged me, just slowly repeated these words. "If you care about this child, you need to let it go. A good family will raise the child and give it what you cannot give. You're just a kid yourself. You can't raise a baby, and, Laura, believe me, you don't want your mama raising this baby."

He looked straight into my eyes again, his hazel eyes sadder than I had ever seen them. *Did I really believe Mama's plan would work? It's heartless and wrong to leave a helpless baby here, but he says it's the right thing to do.*

His eyes brimmed with unshed tears. My very soul felt ripped in half, but I knew this was a chance to make my father love me again. My heart thudding, I whispered, "All right, Daddy."

And that is how easily I gave up my child. Those three words would haunt me for the rest of my life.

ॐ

From that day forward, I held a kernel of hate in my heart for my father, which took hold and refused to budge for decades. In my mind, Mama had abandoned me when she was not there to argue that she would raise the baby. I couldn't understand my parents' point of view, or my own mixed-up emotions. I wasn't sure what I wanted, but this change of plans hit me hard, with a force that would leave me broken in many ways for the rest of my life.

ॐ

When I remember that time, my mind goes cloudy after that conversation with my father. I have strained my brain for years, trying to remember exactly what was said or done after I agreed to do what seemed wrong in all ways, but my memory simply shuts down.

The next thing I do remember is Miss Felton asking questions about our family, and then the baby's absent father and his family. As she jotted down my answers, I squirmed in my chair, worried about whether I was answering them correctly. Daddy sat stiffly next to me and after the list of questions, Miss Felton began chattering about how much the Home did for the unwed mothers and how we young women had a second chance now. She reiterated that after the women left the Home, they could forget this time and move forward into a better Christian life.

With a smug, oily smile, she casually asked, "Laura, have you thought about what name you would like to use during your stay?"

My cheeks burned. "Excuse me? I don't understand."

"It's for your protection. Most of the girls change their names because it's best not to divulge their identity, to protect their reputation now and in the future."

Change my name? This was another surprise I had not planned on.

"No, thank you. I want to keep my name." My knees shook, but I held firm.

Daddy's face turned red. He turned to me, exasperated. "Laura, do as Miss Felton says. It's the rule."

Miss Felton huffed, "Well, it is highly encouraged. It's not mandatory, but it's certainly the 'smart' thing to do." Her voice rose comically as she emphasized the word "smart," looking pointedly at Daddy, her lips pursed, eyebrows perfect black half circles reaching toward her thread-like hairline.

Does she think I'm not smart?

"I'm not changing my name." I didn't flinch as her eyes met mine.

Daddy squirmed in his seat, always one to avoid confrontation with strangers. I didn't budge. I straightened my back, looking stronger than I felt.

"Hmm, are you sure? You may regret this decision, but it's your choice." Miss Felton shrugged and began scribbling across the papers in the folder.

If I kept my legal name, I figured it would be easier for my child to find me. As I stared at the wall behind Miss Felton, a vivid scene filled my mind. A car drove up to my home in Mississippi. A young blond man walked up to the front door, and Mama opened it. He asked for me by my first and last name. In that instant, I knew in my heart that my baby was a boy. I could see him as a grown man. Oh, it was a daydream, a fantasy, but I had to believe it with my whole heart and soul.

We finished the registration process, and Miss Felton asked Daddy how much he could afford to pay at this time. She made a point of reminding us that churches contributed a portion for each sponsored guest as well, and how lucky I was to have my church sponsor me.

Daddy nodded and fumbled his checkbook out of his top pocket. Miss Felton's thin lips stretched into a smile as she turned toward me. The only sound in the room was the scratching of Daddy's pen as he wrote out the check.

Knowing my parents had to pay to leave me here added more humiliation to the hurt. Mama complained all the time that money was tight, and here I was, causing another hardship. Daddy pushed the check across the desk to Miss Felton, then turned toward me with a small nod and half smile, as if to reassure me.

"Thank you, sir. We'll take care of Laura from here. No need for you to worry. She's in very good hands, and I'm sure she will fit in well. Remember, you're welcome to visit her, and she's allowed to call home and, of course, write letters."

Daddy thanked Miss Felton and turned back to me. "Okay, hon, well, I'll be going now." His voice was gentle as he stood up.

The lump in my throat swelled. Taking my lead from Daddy, I stood and inched away from him. Stone-faced, I croaked, "Okay, bye, Daddy. I'll write."

I will not cry. I will not cry. Inside, I broke in half.

Chapter 9

"Let's take your suitcase to the holding room, Laura. You'll stay there tonight. We're not quite ready for you in the dormitory." Miss Felton was all business.

I nodded, squeaking, "Thank you, ma'am."

"Laura, you'll do fine here if you follow the rules. This is the best place for you, and I think you'll agree once you settle in. You'll return home before you know it."

She marched down a long corridor while I followed, struggling with my suitcase. A window ran along one whole side of the hallway. The window looked into a room with about a dozen shining metal bassinets placed around the space, filled with tiny babies wrapped in blankets. I peered in, startled at the sight of the small pastel cocoons.

I had seen a hospital nursery only once. Mama had given birth to my baby brother, Michael, nine years before. And because children were not allowed to visit, Daddy had snuck us kids up the back stairs to the second floor for a peek at our brand-new sibling through the nursery window.

Miss Felton paused. "This is where we keep all of our babies. This nursery is fully equipped. The babies are safe and sound here and well taken care of until they are adopted by their new parents." She turned to me, her head cocked, smiling.

A thin nurse looked up from one of the bassinets she stood over and smiled at Miss Felton and then at me. Her smile lit up her entire face, and I felt an immediate warmth from this woman. I caught myself smiling back at her. Miss Felton lifted her hand, waved quickly, and galloped on.

My heart hurt when I looked at those babies. It was hard to pull my eyes away from them. They were so new. So innocent. Masses of black hair sprouted from a few small round heads; others were shiny and bald. I had never imagined a roomful of babies being part of the Maternity Home.

Miss Felton continued down the hall, so I pulled away from the window, Grammy's blue vinyl suitcase banging continuously against my calf. We passed a corner, and I spotted a phone attached to a wall.

Miss Felton pointed to it and chirped, "This is where you can make phone calls to your family," and then she quoted the telephone rules:

No loitering in the hallway.

Please respect each other's privacy.

Only collect calls.

Do not abuse the privilege of being allowed to make a phone call.

Coming to an abrupt stop, she bent to unlock a door at the end of the hall. Darkness and cold air met us, along with the heavy scent of bleach, as we stepped into the room. Goose bumps inched up my arms.

The room contained a single bed and a small bathroom. Pristine white starched sheets and a snowy blanket covered the bed. The unadorned walls seemed to glow. When Miss Felton flipped on the light in the bathroom, the white tiles sparkled. The entire space was immaculate, silent, and eerily soothing.

Almost immediately, the quiet room calmed my frayed nerves, a peaceful contrast from my chaotic and messy home life back in Mississippi.

Maybe I can hide here forever. That would work for me.

"Now, leave your pocketbook and belongings here, and we'll take a quick tour of the Home, Laura."

I nodded, placing my handbag on the bed and pushing my suitcase into a corner. Miss Felton was already out the door.

The very last thing I wanted was to walk around this place. I had never felt so alone and lost; plus, my head continued to buzz with a deafening drone.

I don't think I can do this. I wished I were brave enough to refuse to go on, but I hurried after Miss Felton, glad to be free of the suitcase, my feet aching in my pumps with every step.

Down the hall she pointed out the clinic, an examining room, a delivery room, and a recovery room for the mothers. She explained that some of the mothers gave birth right here at the Home, others at area hospitals.

"We are prepared for just about anything." She laughed.

I wondered what "anything" amounted to.

The only birth I had witnessed had been when our cat had a slew of kittens. I had watched for a minute but quickly looked away from her birthing box the minute the first kitten had been born. It had been messy and frightening.

Family life and hygiene classes in junior high had essentially been brief and embarrassing. Basic drawings of a vagina, a uterus, and fallopian tubes, along with a penis, a scrotum, and testicles were projected on a screen. We thirteen-year-old girls had squirmed and stifled our giggles as a cartoon character explained how the sperm swam like fish, squiggling toward the egg.

After the class, the girls had to line up in the hallway and the vice principal, Mr. Paul, along with the home economics teacher, Miss Kelly, made all of us kneel on the floor so they could check that the hems of our skirts touched the floor. Anyone whose skirt they deemed too short was sent home to get a longer skirt. They must have figured our knees were driving those adolescent boys to distraction.

They also handed out Kotex information showing how to use a sanitary belt and lumpy white cotton pads. We each received a pink brochure, "Becoming a Woman," that listed all the glories of menstruation. We girls scoffed and hid our chuckles behind our fists, some of us having started our monthlies long before that class was presented.

Not a word about preventing pregnancy was mentioned in the class, but in the hallways at school there were always whispers about the girls with bad reputations who "put out" for boys, and insinuations about birth control. Sex, much less birth control, remained for the most part a huge secret thing but something we were all interested in. We dared not act too interested, though—after all, if we were interested in preventing pregnancy, we risked appearing like one of those bad girls.

"There's a new pill you can take so you won't get knocked up. But you have to be married and over eighteen to get it," the streetwise girls would whisper.

"I heard it's dangerous and deforms the baby," another would add.

The slick girls who often wore too much pancake makeup, ratted their bleached hair, and smelled of a mix of musk and Evening in Paris perfume would offer their advice as they snuck cigarettes in the girl's restrooms.

"The only thing that really works is if your boyfriend pulls out or can get someone to buy him rubbers. You gotta be eighteen to get them, so an older guy has to buy 'em for your boyfriend if he's not eighteen."

Inevitably some girl would warn, "Hmm, sometimes those rubbers bust open, and guess who ends up with a bun in the oven?"

Even if you wanted to know about birth control, what kind of lowclass harlot would you risk looking like if you asked about preventing pregnancy? None of my friends had ever discussed birth control, labor, or birth in front of me. It was far too indelicate a subject to bring up.

∾

Sweat trickled down between my breasts and my legs felt weak as I trudged down the hall, following Miss Felton marching ahead of me.

I could hear the muffled cries of infants, and I peeked in the nursery window again as we hurried by. A young girl wrapped in a white smock, wearing a hairnet, was sitting in a rocker at the back of the nursery. She held a bottle, feeding an infant. Across from her, the same nurse I had seen earlier, her back to us, tended one of the babies.

Is this really happening?

Unsettled and silent, I hurried on with Miss Felton, who seemed oblivious to the nursery and walked at an even faster pace now. The building was in a shape of a U; we walked back past the front and started up the opposite corridor.

"This is our lounge for the girls." Miss Felton and I found ourselves in a room with sofas and chairs. Books lined the dark wooden shelves. The room was empty, but the television in the corner was on and a commercial was advertising Frosted Flakes. Tony the Tiger looked fuzzy and bright orange with a green-tinged overlay.

A color TV?

"You may watch television or read in here. Some girls knit." Miss Felton glanced my way. "Oh, and there's a sewing room. Do you sew?"

"No, ma'am, but I read a lot."

Pushing open double doors and ushering me in, she announced, with a flourish of her hand, "Our dining room and kitchen area."

The aroma of simmering tomato sauce greeted us as we stood in the middle of the large dining room. Three girls in various stages of their pregnancies were setting up trays of food on a counter for a buffet-style lunch. The room was boisterous; girls laughed and beckoned friends to come sit at their tables.

"Hello, Miss Felton," one of the girls called cheerfully, waving from across the room.

We both turned around at the sound of the door behind us swinging wide open.

There in the doorway, balancing a large, heavy tray covered with tall glasses of orange juice, stood a tiny black-haired teenager. Her eyes opened wide when they met mine.

I blinked. An electric shock rippled through my body. Was I seeing things? *What? How can this be? Pepper? Can it really be her?*

I squealed as I hurried over to her, "Pepper. Oh, Pepper!"

∾

We had been best friends in junior high before the military shipped her parents to another state. Joined at the hip as twelve- and thirteen-year-old girls, Pepper and I had together navigated the experiences of leaving childhood and entering the world of teenagers. Marveling at our budding breasts, applying gloss to our virgin lips, and sharing our manic love for the Beatles had bound us to each other forever. We had found boys newly irresistible at the same time and spent countless hours of sleepovers planning our futures.

My friend is here! How could I be so lucky? I could not get the silly grin off my face. The noise of the room receded in my head, and Miss Felton, along with everyone else, seemed to evaporate. Suddenly, we were the only two in this room.

Small-boned, like a baby bird, Pepper wasn't much taller than when we had last seen each other, years before. Black curls cascaded down her shoulders. Her bright brown eyes opened wide behind blue cat-eye glasses. I would have known her anywhere but never could have dreamed I would see her in this place.

Automatically I reached out, aching to wrap myself around her and hug her for all she was worth, but the heavy tray balanced atop her round middle created a barrier between us. Her belly dwarfed her. I looked up at her face as a deep frown line creased her smooth forehead.

"Pepper." I shook my head, laughing. Girls were turning toward us as I practically danced a happy dance.

"Tina," Pepper said in her soft drawl.

I didn't understand. "Sorry?"

"I'm Tina," she stated firmly, locking her eyes with mine.

"Tina?" My voice dropped to a whisper, and she nodded.

Slowly it began to sink in. Never one to rock the boat, always a good girl, when told by Miss Felton she needed to choose a new name, Pepper must have complied.

"Goodness. You know each other?" Miss Felton peered at us, her head cocked to the side. I didn't trust prissy Miss Felton, but I wanted her to like me, so I quickly lied through my teeth. "Kind of. We attended the same school a long time ago."

"I just got here today," I explained to Pepper.

Pepper continued to look into my eyes, her face expressionless, silent.

"Best get back to your job, Tina," Miss Felton chirped.

Pepper nodded politely and hurried past us. I stood, mouth open, as my friend marched away, all that orange juice weighing down her thin white arms. Watching her small, straight back filled me with dread. Did Pepper not remember me? Was she ashamed and embarrassed? Why was she working as a waitress?

As if reading my mind, Miss Felton continued, "Each girl is assigned a job, Laura."

A job?

"Working teaches responsibility, and you'll learn a new skill as well. Keeping busy helps pass the time, and, as everyone knows, a busy girl is a happy girl. Having a purpose and something to do each day is an important lesson for all of us. Don't you agree?"

I nodded, biting my lip.

"We've assigned you to the laundry, Laura. You'll start tomorrow morning."

Laundry? When would I have time for my correspondence courses? No one had said anything about a job.

☙

Once I was told I was going away to this place, I had imagined myself languishing about, reflecting on life, reading best sellers, and writing letters as I waited for the baby to miraculously appear. I had not known what to expect, but washing other people's clothes was the last thing I had imagined.

I fixed a false smile on my face and followed Miss Felton while she continued her tour. Warm air bathed our faces as we stepped out of the comfortable, air-conditioned cafeteria into a courtyard. The combined smell of rotting, swampy vegetation and acrid cigarette smoke greeted us, and my queasy stomach lurched. Miss Felton continued her babbling, quick to point out that many of the girls enjoyed congregating outside around the patio.

The Beatles' hit "Penny Lane" floated through the air, staticky and loud, from a battered transistor radio, and I took in several girls slouched on a variety of wooden and metal lawn chairs. Except for the fact they had round, protruding bellies, they looked like any other group of teenage girls. Soft giggling filled the yard as they talked over each other. One girl's legs stretched across the legs of another, who rubbed baby oil on her friend's puffy feet. A sooty cloud of smoke hung suspended in the air.

In the center of the group, a tall, very round red-haired girl sat excitedly regaling everyone with a story. It must have been hilarious because everyone laughed and hooted, hardly acknowledging us as we entered their circle.

How can they be so carefree? Aren't they the least bit humiliated to be here in this place?

Miss Felton cleared her throat. The chatter stopped, but the Beatles song played merrily on.

"Girls, we have a new girl, Laura. Please make her feel welcome."

They nodded with hooded eyes that screamed "uninterested," and a couple of weak "welcomes" floated in the air.

"Almost time for lunch, girls." Miss Felton smiled, having decided not to interrupt the red-haired girl's storytelling. "Do carry on," she twittered, as she guided me along with an outstretched hand back to the building.

Who would ever have thought this world existed?

As I opened the dining room door, the delicious smells of cooking greeted us and my stomach grumbled. Girls had started filing in for their midday meal. Miss Felton introduced me to a handful of them, quickly seating me at a table with a promise to come "fetch" me after the meal.

Around the table, girls patted their lips with their napkins and politely began to ask me questions.

"How old are you?"

"How far along are you?"

"When is your due date?"

As my condition had been a secret for months, I felt odd having these questions tossed out willy-nilly. I gulped and tried my best to answer.

"I'm seventeen. The doctor, well, he's not sure."

Should I tell them how I wasn't even sure when my last period was?

They stared at me, eyebrows lifting, and I watched as the curtains closed behind their eyes.

I quickly added, "My mama says four months."

As time went on, I would learn that these were the prerequisite questions every newbie was asked upon arrival. At that time, I honestly thought they were interested in me, until they turned away and began talking among themselves. I sat rolling spaghetti noodles around my fork tines, trying not to splatter the tomato sauce on my pale peach dress.

Never one for strained silence, I desperately tried to think of something clever to say. I glanced over at the pretty blond sitting next to me, noticing the delicate gold watch on her dainty wrist.

"Wow, nice watch," I said.

Flat, expressionless eyes met mine. "It's a watch. Big deal." She continued eating, eyes rolling.

Looking across the room, she commented to the group, "Heavens. Look at Becky Ann. There she goes, stuffing herself again." Then she made a loud oinking sound. "Such a piggy. No manners at all."

My cheeks burned. Did Becky Ann hear her?

I glanced at the unkempt, heavy girl sitting alone. She wore a faded, wrinkled dress; her hair was pulled tight into a lank ponytail. She shoved food in her mouth, head down, oblivious to the laughter that rang from our table as she reached for another roll, dragging it through the bright red sauce on her plate. She popped the entire roll into her sauce-covered mouth, and the girls at my table groaned.

"Seriously, I cannot eat now after watching her." A prissy, plain-faced girl pushed her plate away and pretended to gag. My face burned hotter. *Are all the girls like this? One day it could be me they laugh at.*

The girls mumbled complaints about the food and living conditions. The prettier girl, who was nasty about Becky Ann, warned me to watch out for certain people, and they all laughed at their private joke. Squirming in my seat, I wished I could simply disappear and never have to eat in this dining room again.

"Did you notice the eyes on that doctor yesterday in clinic?" the pretty girl asked, lowering her head, a mischievous leer on her face.

"Ugh. I didn't look at that doctor's eyes. I hated him putting his hands on me." Another girl frowned.

"Oh, yeah, I noticed Dr. Dreamboat's eyes. Better than that nasty old doctor last week." A plump brunette laughed, wiggling her eyebrows.

"Honestly, I've been so damn constipated, it's a sin." A petite blond changed the subject, her mouth full of food while she talked.

"God, me too." The pretty one laughed. "Get a stool softener from the nurse. It helped me."

"Those softeners gave me the worst gas, and I was so damn bloated when I tried them. Ugh, I'd rather be stopped up," the constipated blond complained loudly. They all cackled along with her.

How can they talk like this? No manners.

Thankfully, the plain girl changed the subject. "I love that new look in *Seventeen* magazine. Did y'all see the way the models line their eyes? I'm gonna try that." She opened her eyes wide, batting her lashes.

"Edith told me her mucus plug is leaking," one girl whispered excitedly.

I tried to appear nonchalant, but inside I cringed. All the while, they continued eating with gusto. My appetite had left, and as the noodles and red sauce congealed on my plate, I quietly pushed the mess away. Folding my hands across my lap, I plastered a mindless smile on my face while my thoughts raced.

Mucus plug? What on earth? All I knew was that it sounded hideous.

The more they excluded me, the more it became clear that I had dues to pay before I would fit in. Sitting there unable to move, isolated and miserable, I was desperate to work up the courage to excuse myself.

True to her word, Miss Felton appeared minutes later, saving me.

"Did you enjoy lunch?"

"Oh, yes, ma'am," I lied.

She pointed to the stairs as we turned, heading to the second floor.

Knocking on a door, Miss Felton explained that each suite contained two separate bedrooms connected by a joint bathroom. Each bedroom had two single beds and two dressers. Some rooms had desks as well. All four suitemates greeted us and seemed happy to show me their home away from home, as one girl described it.

I stole glances at each of them, still thrown off a bit by the round bellies they all possessed. One girl was reading at the desk, one straightening up her closet, and another was spread across her bed with textbooks. The fourth girl, clearly Miss Hospitality, seemed older. She had lacquered black hair done up in a fancy French twist. Her makeup was subtle and ladylike, her Southern accent thick and honeyed. With gushing enthusiasm, she pointed out how they all worked together to keep their suite and bathroom neat and clean.

"We're so very lucky to have such nice rooms," she bubbled on.

Miss Felton beamed.

Teacher's pet.

I stretched my fake smile and pretended it was peachy keen to be part of this. We said our goodbyes, and Miss Hospitality, who looked about ready to burst, smiled back and said, "Laura, you are certainly welcome to sit with us anytime in the dining room."

"Oh, thank you!" *God, why do I sound so needy?*

Our next stop was a room with pews and a podium, obviously a place of worship. "This is our chapel. Please plan to attend chapel on Sundays, Laura," Miss Felton said.

"Yes, ma'am."

"I think you will learn many lessons here during your stay."

"Yes, ma'am."

I couldn't have cared less about her chapel or lessons. All I could think about was finding Pepper and asking what had happened to her and how had she ended up here in New Orleans.

"Miss Felton, may I please go to my room?"

"We're headed there now, or, if you like, you can go out to the patio, perhaps get to know some of the young ladies out there."

"If you think I should go outside to the patio, I will." I tried not to grimace.

She glanced at me, offering me that tight-lipped smile. "Perhaps a nap is in order. You're starting to droop. You've had a big day."

Relief flooded through me as we headed to the holding room. Once inside, I pried off my stiff beige pumps and fell onto the bed, fully clothed, with a groan. The smooth starched sheets were blissful, the silence golden. In minutes, I was carried off to a deep, dreamless sleep.

༄

Disoriented and stiff, I pulled myself awake. My mind was muddled, but soon everything came flying back at me. The Home and its rules. Mama and Daddy leaving me here alone. Those girls. This holding tank, or whatever it was.

My stomach rumbled. I was miserable, hungry, and alone.

How could they have left me here?

The pressure of my bladder forced me up, and in the bathroom mirror, a sad, frightened girl stared back at me through her smeared glasses.

Washing my face and freshening up a bit made me feel stronger, so I heaved the suitcase onto the bed. Opening it, I rummaged through neat piles of clothes Grammy had packed. I pulled out a loose shirt, along with some cotton culottes and new white sneakers. There was no reason to dress in one of the maternity dresses Grammy had sewn for me. None of the other girls were dressed fancily, and a few even wore a severe, unattractive white uniform. I would learn later that the Home supplied that garb.

As I plundered the suitcase, the beautifully sewn tops and dresses made my chest hurt. My grammy worked magic with her timeworn Singer sewing machine. Born poor and raised on a sharecropper's farm in rural Alabama, she had learned to sew out of necessity at a young age. As a girl, she had been responsible for most of her large family's clothing needs and had eventually become an accomplished seamstress.

Grammy, always concerned that her beloved granddaughter should have nice clothes and look her best, had striven to give me the advantages she had never had herself. Better yet, she had believed in me and had always been my biggest supporter. Even in this difficult time, after getting over the shock and disappointment of my pregnancy, she had set to work sewing. Neatly layered in the suitcase, maternity tops and shorts, along with dresses in beautiful lightweight fabrics for the warm spring and summer days ahead, were the results of her act of love.

I thought back to the week before, as Grammy helped me decide what to pack.

"Laura, honey, look at this pretty pink top. I got this fabric for next to nothin'. I always love you in pink. I made a simple yellow-and-white gingham maternity dress for you too, honey. Look at this blue dotted swiss."

My chest hurt as I remembered her words and realized how much pain this must have caused her, secretly sewing maternity clothes for her beloved unwed granddaughter long into the night, instead of plaid A-line skirts for school or fancy dresses for dances.

Closing the suitcase, I left the room nervously. This was my new life, here at the Home, whether I liked it or not. Finding my way through the hallways, I arrived at the dining area, only to find it empty of girls and remnants of supper.

A round-faced girl with stick-straight blondish hair pushed through the swinging kitchen door.

"Hi, I'm Abby. You the new girl?" Her voice was deep and back woodsy. Freckles covered her bright pink cheeks. She was solid and big boned, feisty and confident. I liked her immediately.

"Hey, I'm Laura. I think I missed supper."

"You did, darlin', but wait and I'll sneak you a plate." Her blue eyes sparkled.

Abby brought out a plate of grayish string beans and what appeared to be chicken and dumplings, along with a gigantic glass of milk. My mouth watering, I sat down to eat, trying hard not to wolf it down like Becky Ann.

Grammy's lectures came back to me. "Laura, slow down, dear. Please don't gobble your food. What will folks say? Honey, always try to eat like a lady."

"Thanks," I mumbled between bites. "Sorry I got here late. I fell asleep."

Abby winked and headed back to the kitchen before I could ask her any questions. Where had Pepper run off to?

Shoveling in the last chunk of a dumpling, I sat back, watching as Abby appeared, as if by magic, picked up my empty plate and glass, and sailed back to the kitchen, from which an array of sounds burst forth. Women's laughter, a grinding commercial dishwasher, and clanging pots and pans rang through the air. Each time that swinging door opened, the noise level pitched higher. A loud, giggly squeal shrieked as the door opened.

"Let's go have a smoke, you and me." Abby grinned as she sauntered back to the table.

"Uh, okay, but I don't smoke."

She laughed. "You will after a while in this boring-ass hellhole."

"Do you know Tina?"

"Not really, but I know who she is. She keeps to herself." Abby steered me to the door.

Heading outside into the muggy evening air, I noticed the same group of girls, smoking and laughing. Once again, a staticky transistor radio was playing the top ten hits. The band, Herman's Hermits, softly crooned their latest song, "There's a Kind of Hush (All Over the World)."

"I love Herman's Hermits. My friend Nancy and I met a band on the coast that sings their songs. The band members even look like the Herman's Hermits band," I bragged.

Abby chuckled. "Really?"

All heads turned and watched as we walked across the lawn. The tall red-headed girl waved us over. "Leader of the pack" was written all over her.

"Hey, Taylor." Abby nodded at her and gestured toward me. "This here's Laura."

"I'm sure that's her name." She sounded hateful. They all howled with laughter, as if that was the best joke of the day.

"No, really. My name is Laura." They laughed harder. I gave up and smiled, trying to fit in.

Looking for a place to sit, I noticed that Pepper was not among the girls. Wedging myself into the only chair available, I smiled at the girls on either side of me. One fanned herself with a true-crime magazine. The other one took long drags on her cigarette, expertly blowing smoke rings.

She was a tough-looking girl with harsh, angular edges, a mountain of a belly covering her painfully thin body. Emaciated legs emerged from baggy shorts and splayed in front of her. Lank, oily hair surrounded her face, and her heavy bangs were cropped just above her angry, piercing eyes. I quickly looked away.

"Well, Laaarra," she drawled in a grating voice. "What do you think of this place?"

I opened my mouth to answer, but before I could say a word, she started throwing rapid-fire questions at me.

"When's your due date? What happened to your baby's daddy? What's your story?"

As she sucked a long drag from her cigarette, I held my breath. She blew out the smoke in my direction.

"Huh? Why you here? He won't marry you? Raped you? Ran out on ya? Vietnam? Died?" She cocked her head at me and sneered, "Or is he just another fuckin' asshole?"

Shocked that she had blasted out the f-word, I choked and swallowed hard. The girls laughed loudly.

"Damn straight, Bonnie!" her sidekick yelled. "Ain't they all?"

Maybe this was a test?

They turned and waited for my answer. "He's in the army."

"Oh, I see." Her eyebrow cocked as she stared at me, then belted out, "So, he's just another a-s-s-hole."

Her sidekick roared with laughter, nodding her head enthusiastically.

She inhaled again and looked around the group, smirking. I cringed, feeling my face heat up.

The pack of girls giggled and seemed to think these two were outstanding comedians. They turned their attention away from me. Abby lit her second cigarette, pointedly offering me one. I simply shook my head and fell silent, looking around the courtyard. Dusk was falling; ragged grass with bald dirt patches covered the grounds. Bugs were starting their serenading in the low shrubs that grew around the perimeter of the square space. Vines crept up the ten-foot fence that encircled us.

I was no match for this group. I prided myself on being a good and respectable girl. I had proudly held office as Methodist youth fellowship president at my church. At school, I tried to be everyone's friend. For heaven's sake, I'd been voted Miss Personality in ninth grade. I made good grades and was vice president of the Quill and Scroll Club at my high school. None of my girlfriends used vulgar language.

Taylor continued boasting, telling stories featuring her as a debutante, living in the Mississippi Delta. Everyone was mesmerized by her. I was pulled into her charming ways as well, noting with envy how self-assured this girl seemed. She made jokes about her wealthy family and bragged that she'd be heading right back to college once this was all over, like it had never happened.

With perfect peaches-and-cream skin, a darling nub of a nose, and thick hair pulled up in a messy ponytail, Taylor oozed more confidence than all of us put together as she entertained everyone with funny stories of her sorority life at Ole Miss. She was something to behold in her fuchsia maternity top and bright yellow madras shorts. Her hair needed a shampoo, her legs were peppered with inflamed sores where she had scratched mosquito bites until they bled, but none of that detracted from the fact that "old money" was written all over her.

Invisible, I sat there, the country mouse come to town. They all pointedly ignored me. The Monkees' song "I'm a Believer" blasted cheerfully through the air as someone turned the volume on the radio a notch higher.

I mumbled, "I think I'll go in now."

Nobody acknowledged me as I stood up and began threading my way through their smoky tangle of chairs. As I made my way back to my room, I held back humiliated tears. I glanced into the nursery window. The lights were dim. Not wanting to think about those babies, I looked away and hurried on.

Once safely alone in my room, I showered in the hottest water I could stand as pent-up sobs broke loose from deep inside me, almost bringing me to my knees.

How will I stay here for five months?

I changed into a new stiff cotton nightgown and fell back onto my bed. How blissful to simply lie in between the crisp sheets and pretend none of this was really happening. As I stared at the ceiling, my eyes spotted an almost transparent spiderweb in the corner, and I aimlessly watched a brown spider meander down the wall.

Then it happened, that fleeting flutter that I had felt in the past few days, so vague, but definitely there in my lower stomach. It happened only if I was lying perfectly still. I cupped the hard, grapefruit-size hill between my hipbones and pressed down, hoping to feel it again.

Again, an elusive quiver deep inside me. Warmth shot through my body. A smile spread across my face, and I knew beyond doubt what it was.

As if on cue, it happened again. I pressed down.

This was my baby. It had to be. For the first time, he seemed completely real.

"Is it you?" I whispered to the tiny flutter.

Then nothing. I waited, but nothing happened. Had I imagined it?

The new best-selling book *Valley of the Dolls*, by Jacqueline Susann, could not compete with my exhaustion, and soon I gave in to my tired body, drifting off, my hand resting gently on the small bump.

Chapter 10

I rolled over, disoriented and confused by the white walls and complete silence, until I remembered yesterday. Those mean girls at lunch and that one who talked about a mucus plug leaking. That rude, awful Bonnie girl. Miss Felton. Daddy. Mama.

And Pepper. Did that really happen? Where is she?

And the baby. I felt him. I reached down and touched my stomach.

Turning over and pulling the covers tightly over my head, I groaned. I was afraid of what the new day would hold, but my stomach rumbled and I was more afraid I'd miss breakfast.

After quickly dressing, brushing my teeth, and running a brush through my matted hair, I hurried toward the dining room, past the nursery windows, covered with blinds today. As I got closer to the dining room, the tantalizing aroma of bacon and hot biscuits made my stomach tighten.

"You're almost late again, darlin'." My new friend Abby chuckled as she cleared dishes and marched with authority through the dining room. Looking over her shoulder, she grinned at me. "You'll learn."

I smiled at her, excited to see a friendly face.

The dining room rang with cheerful chatter, and I searched the room to see if I could spot Pepper. I grabbed a plate, filling it with room-temperature scrambled eggs and bacon. For the past month, I seemed to have been hungrier than I ever had been in my life.

"Are you Laura?" A bubbly girl with vivid green eyes was bouncing toward me.

"Yes, that's me."

"Miss Felton sent me. When you're finished, I'm 'sposed to take you to your room. But just take your time, sugar. I ain't in a hurry."

I watched her laughing with one of the girls busing the tables. Her stiff bouffant hairstyle was adorned with a green bow pinned precisely above her long bangs. She laughed easily and fluttered her hands around as she spoke to friends, never rushing me as I finished my meal.

As we walked down the hall, she beamed. "My name's Janice. I've been here two months, and I'm due in two months!" Her wide smile showed off her perfect teeth.

You couldn't look at Janice without smiling, because being in the company of this effervescent girl felt safe and joyful. Janice reminded me of my girlfriends at home. She didn't seem to have a care in the world as her flipped-up hair bounced with each step she took. Suddenly, I felt a bit of hope.

After I gathered my things and we made small talk, we headed up the hall once again with the blue suitcase. Miss Felton joined us, and she and Janice chatted easily. I walked behind them, catching a few disjointed words.

"Yes, ma'am, my parents are coming to visit." Janice looked back at me and smiled.

With a quick knock on one of the doors lining the hall, we entered a dark room and Miss Felton called out, "Ella, I want to introduce you to your new roommate. This is Laura."

Miss Felton marched directly to the window and pulled open the closed window shades, illuminating the sparse room with pale morning light. My new room was at the end of the building, on the second floor. It overlooked the inside court patio and shabby lawn. Two dressers, along with two twin beds, sat against opposite walls.

The bed coverings were dingy and a bit frayed, obviously laundered to death, giving the room a sad and dreary feel.

My new roommate, a matronly older woman, sat on her bed and barely looked up as we entered, though she issued a sarcastic "welcome." I would soon learn that she seldom smiled. Combing her hair must have been too much of an effort, because short, stiff brown locks stuck out oddly from the sides of her head. Despondent dark blue eyes glanced my way and quickly turned away, but not before I noticed that there was no light in them.

A blousy brown maternity top hid her belly and she sank down deeper onto her bed as Miss Felton bustled around, pointing out the bathroom, my small closet, and a desk we could share.

"There you have it. Enjoy getting to know each other." Miss Felton swished out of the room, eager for more conversation with Janice even before the door closed.

Tension permeated the stale air in the room once we were alone. As Ella watched me from under hooded eyes, I heaved my suitcase self-consciously onto the bed opposite hers. She had already claimed the bed by the window. Nothing cluttered her nightstand.

"I bet this room is quiet, since it's near the end of the hall." I smiled in Ella's direction as I began to unpack.

"I guess."

"Have you been here long?"

"Long enough." She grunted.

"So, we have suitemates. What are they like?"

She shrugged. "I don't talk to them."

I continued unpacking. Ella turned away from me, closing the blinds again and darkening the already gloomy space. I quickly hung my clothes in the closet, desperate to get out of that sad room. Why couldn't Janice be my roommate?

"Um, okay, well, I have to head down to the laundry. Miss Felton said I'm to report down there." I twirled around, grinning and oddly proud that I had a job to go to.

"Everyone starts in laundry," Ella stated flatly, with a bit of disdain, but quickly added in a lofty voice, "I work the autoclave these days."

Autoclave? What the heck does that mean?

"Oh, all right, then. I'll see you later, I guess." I couldn't escape quickly enough. Ella made me nervous. I couldn't imagine trying to make conversation with this difficult roommate for another minute, much less for months. I hoped she'd have her baby soon.

The laundry turned out to be a stifling room, vibrating with loud gyrations of commercial washers and dryers. The supervisor, Miss Sally, greeted me cheerfully. Sweat trickled in lines down the sides of her flushed face. Her pale blue uniform strained across an ample bosom, and her forearms were meaty and thick with muscles.

Four or five girls turned my way before going back to work, diligently removing all types of bedding and towels and clothing from the commercial dryers and dumping them on long wooden tables to fold. I had never seen such mountains of laundry in my life. The girls showed me how to fold these items "precisely this way and not that way." An uncomfortable wetness quickly spread under my arms and sweat beaded across my forehead.

At first, I was slightly amused at how serious they all seemed. Soon I understood why. While the job wasn't difficult, it was awfully monotonous, and Miss Sally was critical about being precise with every corner, every seam. Within the first hour, I had to refold a second or third time almost everything I had folded, until it met with Miss Sally's standards. The constantly noisy washer and dryer were irritating, the moist heat uncomfortable. My head and back began to throb.

At long last it was lunchtime. It had already become obvious that our days would revolve around mealtimes. Girls rushed to the dining room, ready to gossip and socialize and fill up on the heavy fare.

My eyes searched the room again for Pepper. *Where can she be? Is she hiding from me?*

Cheerful voices floated through the air. My ears caught smoky Alabama drawls, softer Mississippi accents, and harsh New Orleans accents. As we all gathered to have lunch, I noted choices of desserts and pies and chocolate pudding. My mouth watered.

From a table along the wall, Janice stood up and waved eagerly at me. "Come sit with us," she called across the room. I breathed a sigh of relief and made my way to her table. As I sat down, I was flooded with a heady gratitude at knowing this kind girl was including me.

"Come upstairs to my room when you can, Laurie." Only my best friends called me Laurie. It was music to my ears. I jumped at the voice whispering in my ear and a hand gently grasped my shoulder.

My head swiveled around. "Pepper . . . Uh . . . Tina. Finally. Where have you been?"

She whispered her room number and whisked away.

"I'll come up after lunch," I called to her, but she was already gone, disappearing behind the big double doors back into the kitchen.

Chapter 11

I hurried upstairs, eager to see Pepper after bolting down my lunch. A quick knock, and there she was, calling from behind the closed door in her soft voice, "Come in, Laurie."

Pepper sat on her bed, back against the headboard, notebooks and textbooks scattered about. Her glossy black curls framed her pretty face, which seemed to glow in the single ray of sunshine pulsing through her window. She pushed herself up from the bed as I rushed to her. We hugged and laughed, looking down at her belly between us.

"Oh, Laurie, I couldn't believe my eyes when I first saw you." She held me at arm's length, studying my face.

"Pepper, I almost fainted when I saw you," I squeaked. "Why did you act like you didn't know me?"

"I don't know. I was shocked. I don't want these people to know anything about me."

"I get it." I grinned at her. "I'm so glad you're here. This place is so strange and, well, kind of scary."

"I know, I know. I hate it here."

We sat side by side on her bed, smiling shyly at each other.

Pepper's room was at the front of the building, and her window looked out over the tree-lined street. We could almost forget we were hidden away at a maternity home for unwed girls; it almost felt like the old days, when we had sat swinging on my front porch, laughing and talking about our junior high school dramas.

"Oh, Laurie, how did we both end up here? I know how I did, but you? If this isn't the craziest thing." Pepper shook her head as she gathered her books off the bed, stacking them neatly on her nightstand.

"Pepper, I thought I'd never see you again. Now this."

We continued to marvel at our good luck in having each other to talk to and the bad luck that had brought us together. She told me her family had moved to an army base in Texas. How she had hated the town and her new school there. She and her mother had fought constantly, and her daddy was away most of the time. Lonely, she had kept to herself in her room, reading and studying. This didn't surprise me. Pepper had always been an honor student, never one for socializing.

"What happened, Laurie?" She glanced down at my middle.

I told Pepper my story, about the months of worry, the hiding, the lying, and how Clay had refused to have anything to do with me. How our minister had suggested this place to Daddy and Grammy. I told her how I hated myself for having let this happen.

She shook her head. "I'm here because I was stupid." Pepper's face turned stormy. "I kind of became friends with this boy from church. Jack. He went to an all-boys school. I had a crush on him. One day I drove by his house. I know, I know, it sounds forward, but I had just gotten my driver's license and I guess I was showin' off." She shrugged and continued talking into her lap.

"Jack's folks weren't home, but he had a friend there visiting from out of town. A cute guy, but kind of pushy. You know the type. Full of himself. He looked a little like Dale from junior high. Remember Dale, the class clown?"

"Of course I remember Dale. He and I go to the same high school too. He's dreamy. That black hair and those blue eyes." I quickly added, "But he's even more full of himself now than when you knew him. I don't really like him."

"This guy's name was Dawson."

"What happened?"

"Jack had some bourbon from his daddy's liquor cabinet. They were kind of drunk when I got there. I was a little scared but didn't want to act like a ninny, so when Jack handed me a bourbon and Coke, I took it from him. It smelled like crap and tasted worse, but I drank it down." She shook her head. "I was so dumb."

"Been there," I assured her, remembering all the times I had drunk beer with Clay, hating the taste of it. I had done stupid things just to fit in so many times.

"Jack left. He said he had to pick up a few of his friends and he'd bring them back to party. He said for me to wait there, and he left me alone with Dawson. I saw him give Dawson a look as he left. I knew something was up. I should have left then."

Pepper's bottom lip trembled, and tears flooded her eyes. I grabbed her hand.

"Dawson raped me, Laurie." She broke down sobbing. "He punched me when I screamed. He hurt me bad."

"Oh no, Pepper." Tears filled my eyes as I watched my friend fall apart. I was sickened at the thought of her being violated. Rage surged through me as I realized how helpless I was to do anything about it. I hated that creep Dawson and all boys right then. We held on to each other in our separate sorrows.

In a flat voice, she stated, "I shouldn't have gone over there. I learned my lesson."

"But, Pepper, how could you have known? Did you tell Jack?"

"No, no. No one knows, and they never will." She wiped her eyes. "I hate all of them, and I'm leaving that town as soon as I graduate."

I was stunned when she told me her mama had dropped her here at the Home only a week before I arrived. She had continued going to school even when she knew she was pregnant, wearing a tight girdle and an oversize jacket, even on hot days. All those months, her mother had commented only about how sloppily she dressed.

"You remember my mama. She's far too busy to notice me. I lived in my room when I wasn't at school. I was so afraid to tell her, Laurie."

"I was scared to tell my mama too."

We both sat silently. Then Pepper took off her blue cat-eye glasses, wiped them with the hem of her blouse, and continued with her story.

She was eight months pregnant when an embarrassed male vice principal at the high school called her mother and asked her to come pick Pepper up, telling her that Pepper could not attend school in her condition. Her mother was stunned and furious. She quickly found a place to take Pepper, far away from Texas. That's how she had landed in the Home in New Orleans. No one could ever know the scandal of her secret baby.

Sitting next to her almost nine-months-along round belly, I wondered how she could have stayed at school and been so obviously pregnant. Her baby was due in two or three weeks, and she had been in school the month before. Somebody had to have noticed before eight months.

She's so much braver than I am.

I looked around her room. It seemed even more dreary and darker than mine. I looked at the unmade, messy bed on the other side of her room.

"Who's your roommate?"

"Oh, Lord, you don't want to know." She laughed nervously and pulled an ashtray from beneath her bed, along with a pack of Winston cigarettes. "Her name is Shirley, and she's a head case. Smoke?" She tipped the pack at me. I shook my head no, surprised as I watched her open the window and light up.

Wearily, she told me she was having awful aches and pains and just wanted this over with. I told her how I wanted to keep my baby and how Daddy had said no. She stared at me, her eyes huge.

"Oh, Laurie, you can't keep this baby. How would you take care of it? Aren't you going on to college? Don't you want a life?"

"I guess. I don't know. Well, yes. I want my life back. Maybe Clay will come back."

Pepper frowned. "Why would you want him to, after what he said to you?"

I shrugged.

"It's better for the baby," she added. "And you too."

I looked away so she couldn't see the tears threatening to fill my eyes.

Some way, I'll keep my baby.

"You can't take care of a baby."

"Maybe you're right," I mumbled, and changed the subject.

༄

Pepper and I quickly developed a routine, working at our jobs in the mornings, visiting with each other in the afternoons, ever-present correspondence course books spread across her bed.

We would sit at her bedroom window overlooking the street, watching the world under the ancient oaks going about its business. Scruffy children ran by, and old people shuffled up and down the sidewalk, going in and out of the tiny neighborhood market across the way. We watched romances go bad, young lovers fighting right there on the sidewalk, screaming cuss words for the whole world to hear. We watched in horror as one man slapped his woman around and then they walked off arm in arm. This was a side of life neither of us had been privy to back in our predominantly white middle-class hometowns.

Always curious, we peered down from our window as cars pulled up in front of the Home. We watched a couple of new girls arrive and a few girls leave the Home, no infant son or daughter in their arms.

"I don't ever want to get close to any of the girls in here." Pepper took a long drag on her cigarette, blowing the smoke out the open window one lazy afternoon. She fascinated me with her expert smoking. I thought she looked sophisticated and beautiful with her glossy curls and sultry eyes, and smoking made her look dangerous, cool, and grown-up. Soon I was smoking right alongside her.

"I like most of the girls," I mumbled, and mimicked her by taking a long pull on my Winston cigarette and smugly blowing an identical stream of smoke out the window.

"Look, Laurie. There's that little girl. What's her name?" She pointed down on the street at the youngest girl staying at the Home. She said she was fourteen years old, but she looked closer to twelve, with her frail, childish body, which looked unnaturally heavy and deformed by pregnancy.

"Oh, that's Sadie."

"She's such a sad little thing." Pepper sighed.

I stretched and smashed my cigarette flat in the old ashtray Pepper kept hidden. "Let's go for a walk. Get a root beer. Anything. I need to get out of here."

As we headed out the door, Pepper said, "Hey, Laurie, I hear you can request a friend to stay with you when you're in labor. Will you sit with me when I'm in labor?"

"Of course I will," I answered, without a second thought.

ॐ

Pepper continued to work steadily on her schoolwork, while my own correspondence courses lay dormant in my room. She had always been disciplined. Me, not so much. Her plan was to finish her courses, have the baby, and go back to school to graduate with her class. I, on the other hand, knew that could never happen with me. I would be eight months pregnant when my senior class graduated.

Pepper ignored her roommate, Shirley, who seldom showered and was loud and apt to jump up on the dresser and go-go dance to her transistor radio at any given time. She emitted a strong, nauseating cloud of flowery Avon perfume, along with unwashed body odor. I usually found a reason to leave quickly when Shirley entered a room. She made me nervous, and the overload of Sweet Honesty cologne made me queasy.

ɔ

I often sought out Abby in the courtyard. I offered my paperbacks to her after I read them, and she always shared her old movie-star and detective magazines with me, along with a smoke. I'd accept the cigarette and pore over the lurid photos in the pages. With a cigarette between my fingers, I fit in better.

The days marched on, along with the structured discipline of the Home. My sad roommate, Ella, kept to herself. We seldom talked. I gave up quickly on expecting her to become my friend. At night, with my mind unable to shut down, I lay across the small room, listening to her muffled cries in the dark. Uncontrolled tears of sympathy would well up in my eyes.

Working up my courage one night, I quietly asked, "Ella, can I help?"

She never responded. After a while, I figured she wanted to be alone in her sorrow, so I didn't ask again and never mentioned it in the morning. But during the day, I made an effort to invite her to join the other girls and me.

"Hey, Ella, want to go down to the patio?"

"Hell no. I don't like any of those stupid girls," she growled.

"Ella, a few of us are going for a walk down to Magazine Street. Want to come along?" I'd be in the bathroom, door open, fixing my hair, drawing black eyeliner across my lids and painting my lips bubble-gum pink.

"Hell no."

A social butterfly, I longed to be everyone's friend. I relished long conversations about life—everyone had a story, and I wanted to hear them all. But I soon realized this wasn't going to happen with Ella. Her shell hardened with each of my attempts to befriend her.

"God, another silly girl. Can't y'all take it outside?" Ella grumbled one day when yet another girl knocked on our door.

"They're nice girls. Give them a chance. Besides, it's raining. We can't take it outside."

She glared at me.

I winked at the two girls as I opened the door and stepped out into the hall. "Hey, y'all, let's head back to your room. Ella has a headache."

"What's her problem? How do you stand her?" the girls asked, inclining their heads toward my room.

Chapter 12

Some evenings, as spring weather warmed and stretched out the days, we girls made the quick trip across the street to the tiny market. We would carry our stash of sugary snacks and cigarettes back across the street, hoarding them in our rooms. I felt lucky if I had three dollars in my pocketbook. I doled out my change for Hershey bars, which cost a nickel, and bottles of Coca-Cola, for ten cents. I hated when it was my turn to buy smokes. At thirty cents a pack, they were expensive, and they disappeared quickly.

I seldom found myself inside in the TV room, preferring to sit on the patio and read books and magazines. I particularly relished indulging in my new vice, smoking, and my old vice, gossiping.

∾

Unable to sit outside one rainy afternoon, or to bear another minute with angry Ella, I wandered downstairs to the TV room. Girls sat watching TV, knitting and chatting softly. They glanced my way and smiled a shy welcome as I scooched next to them on a lumpy couch. *Dark Shadows*, the most popular soap opera on television, had just ended.

I didn't understand the fascination so many teens had with the ABC show, which ran every afternoon. High school kids all over the

country raced home from school in time to watch. It featured a vam-
pire, something unheard of in a daytime soap.

"You're Laura, right?" one the girls asked shyly. A pile of soft yellow
yarn nestled in her lap.

"Yes." I settled in, grinning at her.

"I'm Mindy. Do you knit?"

"No, I don't. What are you making?"

She proudly held up her work. "A little blanket. I'll leave it here
when I leave. I hope my baby's new mama takes it home." She smiled
wistfully.

"Oh." I gulped. "Very nice."

"Do you follow the show *Dark Shadows*?" another girl asked, after
she held up blue-and-pink-striped baby booties, showing me her
work.

"Kind of. My best friend loves that show." I laughed, thinking of
Nancy back home.

An advertisement for the movie *Mary Poppins* lit up the screen.

"Oh, my favorite!" a girl cooed. "My folks took us to see it in
Jackson."

A heavily pregnant girl pushed herself up from the sagging couch
and walked across the room to change the channel.

I nodded toward her gratefully. I wasn't in the mood for all
that frenzied singing and dancing with the deliriously happy Julie
Andrews. It made me sad. My life would never be that carefree again.

The national news burst onto the screen, with an announcement
that thousands of young people were flocking to some place in
California called Haight-Ashbury.

What does that mean? I tried to decipher it: Hate-ash-berry?

According to the reporter, sporting a gray crew cut, irresponsible
young people had virtually taken over that area. He mentioned how
both women and men wore their hair long and dressed in outlandish,
flowing clothing. Worse yet, he reported, this group of rebels scorned

society and our government. They protested the war in Vietnam. All they believed in was the counterculture, their music, and free love.

Free love? Wasn't all love free?

My eyes remained glued to the fuzzy colored screen with its strange greenish glow. The camera panned to a young woman. Dark blond hair hung about her face. Metal glasses with perfectly round, dark lenses perched on her nose. An infant was nestled tightly against her chest, bound with a colorful scarf. A glorious, open-mouthed smile lit up her face.

"Drugs such as LSD, amphetamines, marijuana, and heroin are taken by these young people. Some call them flower children because they often hand out flowers to complete strangers on the street. But because of their illicit drug use, these young Americans are fast becoming known as the acid generation."

Acid? I had not heard of this drug. I knew little about marijuana and had never smoked it. I had heard I would become a drug addict if I did. Some of the wilder boys at school boasted about smoking weed. I had heard some even inhaled model-airplane glue.

"They're falling down in the streets," the flustered reporter claimed.

Wildly dancing couples swayed in the next clip, hair whipping about their heads, their faces euphoric. Bare feet stomped and hands clapped. They hugged each other and laughed as they grinned at the camera.

"Ugh, they look dirty to me," Mindy said.

"Me too. They're dope fiends," the channel changer chimed in, sniffing with disdain.

"They are not Christians," Mindy huffed.

I studied the happy faces on the TV screen. I wished I were dancing in the street somewhere. I wanted to be out in California, laughing and handing out flowers.

"They look happy to me," I blurted out. The girls' faces turned to look at me, eyebrows raised.

"I wish I was there." I shocked them silent as I wondered out loud if the joyful girl with the baby on the screen was married. I felt a prick of jealousy and yearning and quickly stood to leave.

"See y'all later." I left the room, their innocent eyes burning holes in my back.

ᕬ

A few days later found me leaning against the wall in the clinic hallway.

"It's painless and over fast. Doctors don't want to spend a lot of time with us charity-case girls," Abby assured me. Her hair was parted straight down the middle and woven into two long, tight braids, and her warm breath tickled my ear. Embarrassed twittering filled the hallway as girls waited to be looked over and weighed in.

When my turn came, I entered the room and stepped nervously on the scale for the nurse. A harried intern glanced at me. He pushed his glasses high on the bridge of his oily nose and studied my chart, pointing to a stool. My legs dangled after I climbed onto it. The nurse taking my blood pressure pressed her lips together in a tight smile as I covertly glanced at the intern's slicked-back brown hair and earnest face. To my surprise, he looked as young as the boys in my high school.

But Abby was right: It was quick and painless—no pelvic exam, just a glance at me and my chart. I felt healthy and strong and thankful that I wasn't plagued by the issues some of the girls suffered. The intern announced that my weight was fine and I was in good form.

I never uttered a word and was flooded with relief as I was whisked out of the exam room and they made ready for Abby. She winked as I passed her. I adored her impish, crooked smile.

Many a night, alone with my thoughts, I tried to wrap my mind around what was happening inside me. I had never seen a drawing or photograph of a fetus. Pregnancy and its mysteries had never interested me until now, when it was happening to me. Unlike many girls I knew, I seldom fantasized about being a mother.

Alone at night, I cradled my growing bump with my hand as I imagined this baby, this tiny stranger. Would he love me? Could I do this? Then there it was: a swish of movement deep within.

Something was happening. A tender feeling wrapped itself around me. My undeniable bond with this tiny being seemed to grow stronger every day. I couldn't bear thinking about what the future held, so I didn't.

Chapter 13

Almost every day, I dutifully wrote letters to Mama and Grammy. All the thoughts I had not been able to verbalize poured out onto those pages. I mailed my dispatches with the conviction and determination that I had learned my lesson. I wrote detailed stories of life happening around me, leaving out circumstances that would cause them worry, always hoping to sound cheerful despite being dreadfully homesick.

Mama, never much of a letter writer, surprised me when she answered some of my notes with news of home and my younger brothers. Her messages were short and to the point, and she often threw in a barb about Grammy. She never mentioned the baby but sometimes added at the end of her letters that she hoped I was feeling okay.

I wrote back on my white lined notebook sheets, asking for more stamps and paper as my supplies dwindled.

"It's okay if you can't send them. I'll be fine," I added at the bottom of the letter. Guilt filled me whenever I asked for anything, but I had no money and no way to get such materials for myself.

Grammy, an avid letter writer, wrote to me every week. Her chatty letters documented the weather, her garden, her garden club, and church news. She filled me in on the general gossip about our circle of relatives and friends, often including a line assuring me not to worry, "because everyone thinks you're at your grandma Effie's, honey."

As always, I played the role of peacemaker between Mama and Grammy, even in the form of my letters home. I constantly worried about one of them feeling slighted if I wrote more to one than to the other.

I also wrote to my adored cousin Mark, who was attending the University of Southern Mississippi. He never failed to answer, even though he was busy learning to be a freshman. His witty, brilliant letters were a treat, describing life on campus and filled with words of endearment. I would race to my room when they arrived and wait to read them privately, as if he were my secret lover.

In his scratchy, dreadful handwriting, he composed vivid descriptions of what he had discovered in his research at the library, explaining what was happening inside me, along with information about each phase of my pregnancy.

By the fifth month, the fetus's teeth are already beginning to form within his jawbone. He may have some hair on his head, including eyebrows and eyelashes. Fingernails have grown to the tips of the fingers, and he can clench his fists. The fetus is about four to five inches long.

I soaked up the descriptions of what my baby looked like and how he was developing. I reread them over and over. This was the only information or education about my pregnancy that I received from anyone during this entire time.

Before I go, Laura, remember this: You are not the first young woman to accidentally get pregnant, and you won't be the last. You are a good person, and I love you and I believe in you. You will get through this. I'm here for you.
Always,
Mark

Chapter 14

Sundays, we had chapel. We all squeezed into the small room, fanning our overheated, ripe bodies, only half listening to the kindly old minister drone on. He and his wife were always present during the week too. Rehabilitation was a huge priority, but without any counseling or classes, we only had Sunday chapel to do the trick. "Go forth and sin no more" was the prevailing theme.

Weekdays consisted of breakfast, laundry detail, lunch, and afternoons free to write letters, read books, relax, and have supper. I watched with fascination as my belly blossomed outward into the shape of a bowl. And I was starting to feel accepted as I slowly made more friends. Walks with Pepper or afternoons we spent commiserating in her room helped the days fly by. We worried about our lives after we left this place. We wondered what our babies would look like. We learned we could give our babies a crib name and fussed over the options.

It was another lazy afternoon. Pepper sprawled on her bed, daydreaming out loud.

"I like the name Timothy. It's a strong name." She smiled. "I just know my baby is a boy."

"I know mine's a boy too." I rubbed my belly. "I just read a book about Scotland. There was a King James. They called him Jamie."

"Laurie, you and your books," Pepper chided me.

"James. Sounds strong, like Timothy does," I countered.

"And you could call him Jamie." Pepper clapped her hands. "The name Jamie works for a girl too. Just in case you're wrong."

"I'm not wrong," I said. I patted my round belly and the newly named Jamie.

We had jumped over that hurdle. Now our babies would have something only we would know we had given to them. After all, a crib name was the only thing we could give them.

~

One morning, an unexpected package was waiting for me in the mail. I hurried to my room, silently cheering that Ella was nowhere in sight as I peeled off the brown paper wrapping and excitedly pried open the box. Mama had sent everything I asked for. There was a notebook and envelopes; a roll of five-cent stamps; and, as a surprise, two brand-new books: The Source, by James Michener, and In Cold Blood, by Truman Capote. Five Hershey bars were tucked inside the box. Another surprise was a colossal box of candied orange slices, my favorite. My mouth watered. Mama had remembered.

There was a note—"Maybe you can share with friends. Love, Mama"—and, in an envelope, five one-dollar bills. I was rich.

This care package was so unexpected, so generous. I laughed out loud and felt a silly grin plaster itself across my face as I quickly stashed the cash and chocolate bars and headed down to the courtyard, carrying the box of candy, my new Truman Capote book tucked under my arm.

Some girls received packages from back home, but few shared their contents. Packages seemed to arrive daily for Taylor. After opening them, she'd brag about her new jewelry, new clothes, expensive chocolates, and fresh fruit. Just yesterday, she had received a crate of fresh strawberries from her parents. She greedily devoured every berry while we sat watching her, our mouths watering.

I pushed open the back door, and there they were, Abby smoking in the middle of the group while Taylor held court. Their improvised fans stirred the warm, smoky air as Taylor dramatically threw her body into telling one of her outlandish stories. Her audience sat spell-bound as ever.

I sat down next to Abby and waited patiently for Taylor to finish her story, then opened the box and pushed it in front of Abby. Inside I was a puddle of nerves, but I managed to blurt out, "Hey, y'all, I got some goodies here."

That got their attention. Abby's eyes twinkled. "Hey, girl, I love me some orange slices!" She grabbed several and passed the box.

"Where'd you get these?" Taylor peered into the box and picked through it, her nose wrinkling as if she smelled a stink. She grabbed a handful.

"My mama sent them. She knows I love 'em," I bragged, wanting Taylor to know my mama sent packages too.

Taylor stuffed three in her mouth at once.

God, for having all that money, she sure never learned any good manners.

"Pass them dis way, you piggy," one of the girls sneered at Taylor, who pointedly ignored her and held the box farther away from her.

Bonnie grabbed the box, daintily picked out a sugary slice, and sucked on it, lifting her brows and rolling her eyes, pretending to swoon.

"Hey, pass the box this way, ya hear?" a girl complained, and Bonnie obliged, snickering, "Y'all are the piggies. Oink, oink."

"Can I have one?" shy little Sadie asked, ducking her head like we might take a swing at her. She always joined us outside but never said a word unless spoken to. Rumors about how she had gotten here in the first place were rampant.

"Sure, Sadie. Take as many as you want," I coaxed her gently.

"What do y'all have there? I want some." Pepper's roommate,

Shirley, whined as she rounded the corner, trailing her offensive odor of Sweet Honesty perfume and too few showers.

"Have some, Shirley." I felt gracious offering my candy to her.

Soon all the girls had plucked a few candies out of the box and returned to comparing stories. They threw a few thank-yous my way, surprising me and warming my cheeks.

Relief flooded me as I observed the enjoyment a box of jellied orange slices could create and how those simple sweets had delighted this unruly group. The box emptied fast, but I didn't care. I knew I was winning points with the toughest girls in the Home; plus, the chocolate bars lay hidden safely in my room.

Thank you, Mama.

That night as I snuggled under my covers, tossing and turning, my mind kept thinking of Mama. The good times and the bad times. I had been a bookworm of a little girl with blue eyeglasses perched on my nose, insecure about most things. I remembered Mama brushing my hair.

"Can I have a ponytail with pink barrettes in my hair, like my friend Lucy, Mama?"

Mama would lift my hair up, study it, and state, "Your hair is curlier than Lucy's, and your ponytail will flip up so cute at the ends."

I'd proudly sported my flipped-up ponytail, complete with a red ribbon bow, to school.

The next day, Mama grumbled when I asked for a ponytail again. "No. Not today. You're sweaty and your hair is stinky. Go brush it."

Years later, when I was a teenager, Mama and I would put up each other's hair in pink sponge rollers. I would teach her how to rat-comb her hair for the newest bouffant styles. She bought me Dippity-do, a slimy hair gel, when I begged for it, and we experimented with it, giggling at ourselves in the mirror while trying out new styles on each other. I felt lucky to have a young, pretty mama who wanted to be modern.

But then, just as often after we styled our hair, she would look at me, shake her head, and sigh. "I pity your husband when you get married. He'll see the real you in the mornings, when you first wake up." She cackled like she had said the funniest thing in the world, and I laughed along with her, hiding my hurt feelings. In my heart, I knew Mama loved me. And she was right. My hair was straight and limp, and I did sweat when it was hot.

Chapter 15

Ella remained testy with me during the day, but to my surprise she began confiding in me late at night. She told me that she was twenty-eight years old. I was stunned. I had guessed she was older than most of us, but that was really old. I listened to the story of her hard life and started to understand the sad person she was.

"You're lucky you get letters, Laura. You have a family that cares," she admonished me one night when I complained about my relationship with Mama. "I have no one to turn to. My family disowned me after all this. Fine with me. I never want to see them again." She grew agitated.

"Have you tried writing to them? Maybe they're sorry now," I suggested.

"That ain't happenin'. I never want to see my family again."

"Did you tell your baby's father?" I asked cautiously.

She let out a harsh bark. "That's the last thing I want. This here"— she pointed to her stomach—"is because I believed the married jerk."

"Married?" I whispered.

"Yes, married. Don't act so shocked, for God's sake, Miss Goody Two Shoes." She frowned at me.

"Does he know?"

"Hell no. And he never will. Martin was my boss. He lied to me, and later I found out he was fiddlin' with all the girls in the office. The bastard." Her eyes were glassy with unshed tears. "I got here on my own, and I'll leave on my own, without his help and without his kid."

I flinched at her anger. She made it sound like I was a spoiled princess when she told me about her life and her family. She was right, though: My life *was* better than hers. Late into the night, I listened to her sadness with a pinch of guilt as we shared my chocolate bars.

"I never wanted to have a baby. I don't even like babies. This has ruined my life. I had to quit my job. I have nowhere to turn." She wrung her hands. "You'll think I'm a monster, but I tried to get rid of it. I took quinine. I drank a drink with turpentine stirred into it. I threw myself down stairs. I punched my stomach over and over. Nothing worked."

"I don't think you're a monster." I looked straight in her eyes. I knew only too well the fear of people finding out, along with not knowing what the future held.

"I don't have the guts to kill myself. I wish I did."

I was speechless and thought of what I had waiting for me at home, a family I knew loved me and I hoped would continue to. Ella didn't have any of that.

Her eyes glistened. "I hate Martin. I hate how he ruined my life. I hate this place, and I hate this kid too." Each night she vented, and I listened, worried when her anger grew violent.

Soon, her due date had passed, and Ella was awfully uncomfortable. I cringed when she ranted that she couldn't wait to get rid of this brat. I had never heard anyone talk about an innocent baby the way she did, but I didn't judge her. Who was I to judge?

By the end of the week, I was half listening as Ella complained about her pains and was engrossed in my magazine when she began moaning. She worsened rapidly, and I began to sweat along with her, begging her to go to the clinic downstairs. Finally, she agreed to let me walk her down, and I was relieved when they kept her there.

"Good luck." I reached for her, but she had already turned away.

The next morning after breakfast, I walked over to the clinic to check on her. The nurse in charge assured me Ella had been taken to a nearby hospital and would be delivering soon. I was stunned. She hadn't had the baby yet? It had been hours.

Our suitemates were in my room when I went back upstairs. Word spread like wildfire among the girls when one of us went into labor. They all agreed Ella was the most sullen, grouchy suitemate, and they didn't hide the fact that they were glad she would be leaving soon.

"Yes, she's pretty miserable, y'all, but she's been through a lot," I said.

"Humph! Haven't we all been through a lot? She's hateful." They all agreed, putting me in my place.

∾

The next morning, I stopped by the clinic. Ella had been brought back to the Home and was resting in the recovery room after delivering a baby girl. I was stunned at how haggard and pale she looked when I entered.

"Hey, Ella, how ya doin'?"

She reached out her hand. Hiding my surprise, I grasped it. I had never seen her like this.

Her voice was weak. "God, I feel so beat up. It was awful. Pure hell. Did you see her?"

"Not yet. But I'll go look through the nursery window. I bet she's pretty."

"I wouldn't know. I don't want to see her." She pulled her hand away from mine.

Turning away from me, she exhaled a low, heart-wrenching wail. I quickly looked down at my belly where my lap used to be, embarrassed for her. This girl never exhibited any emotion except anger. She would probably slap me if I hugged her, but when I looked back at her tortured face, I couldn't help myself and reached again for her hand, holding it tight.

As Ella sobbed, she didn't pull her hand out of mine like before. Instead, her viselike grip prevented me from moving an inch.

"I'm so sorry." Tears filled my eyes, and I felt a distinct kick in my belly, reminding me my baby was still safe inside me.

Spent from weeping, Ella wiped her runny nose and wrecked face with the corner of the sheet. She straightened herself, grimacing. "Hell, my whole bottom is on fire. Even my ass hurts. I can't wait to leave this damn place." That sounded more like the Ella I knew.

She began to tell the story of the delivery. It was worse than she had imagined. The doctor was a hateful old man. They didn't give her painkillers. "Probably punishing me because I'm not married," she reasoned out loud.

Then a wicked smile lit up her face. "I kicked that bitchy nurse twice."

It sounds barbaric, even for Ella. It can't be true. She must be exaggerating.

∽

Later, when I looked through the nursery window, I saw the new baby girl, with a swatch of black hair and a tiny red face. A hunchbacked, elderly nurse's aide flitted about from bassinet to bassinet, and muffled cries filtered into the hallway.

As I stood there, an unnerving feeling came over me. The space around me seemed to darken. I looked over my shoulder and jumped. Miss Felton had silently walked up and stood so close to me my skin prickled. A heavy scent of Juicy Fruit gum, along with flowery talcum powder, made me dizzy.

"Oh, my. The little ones are fussy today," Miss Felton murmured.

I forced myself to stand still and not bolt. "Yes, ma'am."

Standing side by side, we watched the babies complaining loudly.

"Laura, how's your laundry job?"

"It's good, Miss Felton."

"We have more than enough girls in there, and I think it's time to move you to a different job. Maybe the nursery. You're bright and trustworthy, and I remember that you have younger siblings. Have you ever been responsible for watching over babies or children?"

I felt my cheeks heat up. *Miss Felton thinks I'm bright and responsible? Work in the nursery?* Folding sheets was easy, and I had thought I would do that job forever. It was frightening to think of being responsible for newborn babies.

"Um, yes, last summer I had a job working for a military family as a babysitter. There were three little ones. A baby a year old and twins who were five." Words spilled out of my mouth as my body overheated. She stood so close I could see the broken capillaries on her face.

She studied me, her head tilted. Waiting.

I continued, "Three boys. Kind of like my three brothers back home." I straightened my shoulders as I painted a story that wasn't entirely true, because I failed to mention that I had been beside myself every day. The twin boys were monsters with perpetually runny noses who cheerfully smeared snot across my arms when I attempted to capture them to wipe their messy faces. The baby cried all day and pooped in his soggy diaper constantly. The family's small military-issue duplex stank of urine and spoiled milk.

That job had helped cement the idea that the last thing I wanted was to be married with a bunch of babies. After I graduated from high school, I would go to college or move away to some big city like New York and become a writer. I'd date rich, handsome men and dance the nights away in disco clubs, dressed in miniskirts and sequined tops. Or just maybe Clay would become a famous rock star and I would live a glamourous life married to him, not one that included screaming, smelly kids.

I left out the fact that the harried young mother showed up early one day, something she had never done. She was furious to find Clay sitting with me on the front steps.

She sprang out of her brown Chevy station wagon, her face distorted with an angry frown. Holding the dripping baby on my hip, I nervously tried to explain that my boyfriend had just stopped by minutes earlier, but I couldn't get out much of an explanation before she had a hissy fit and began screaming in my face.

"How dare you have boys over to visit? I made that rule perfectly clear. What kind of girl are you, anyway?" she roared, spittle hitting my cheek.

The baby wailed as she jerked him out of my arms. Clay bolted, and I stood there alone. She continued to yell about how she'd report me to the school summer work program that had recommended me. She stamped her foot, and her baby screamed more loudly.

Before she turned away, I saw angry tears filling her eyes. "I'll have to think about retaining you. I'm shocked you're that kind of girl. Leave." She marched up the steps, not bothering to ask where the twins were.

Mortified, I walked three miles home, worried the whole time that I had blown my first real job. I conjured up a story about the mother's not needing me any longer to tell Mama.

Scared to face my employer, I simply did not to show up to babysit the next morning. So much for my first real job. Nor did I tell Miss Felton about the job I held for the rest of that summer. It consisted of lolling around the pool at the resort where Clay worked, working on my tan, drinking gallons of sweet iced tea and the occasional illegal gin and tonic from the overly friendly bartender. But, most important, keeping Clay happy had filled my summer days.

I smiled at Miss Felton. "Yes, ma'am. I know how to take care of babies."

Chapter 16

Oh no. I'm late.

Tonight I was starting my new job in the nursery, on the late shift. Bolting out of bed, not stopping to brush my hair, I raced down to the first floor and knocked timidly on the door. A tall woman opened it.

"Sorry I'm late," I stammered.

Her face was unreadable. She wore her unruly curls in a knot at the very top of her head, and ringlets fell across her wide forehead. Thick black-framed glasses hung on a chain around her neck. She smelled of starch and baby lotion. I had never stood this close to a Black lady and was afraid I would disappoint her. Would she think I was some spoiled, silly white girl?

ॐ

"You the new girl?"

"Yes, ma'am. I'm Laura."

"I'm Miss Jones. Okay?"

"Okay. Sure. Look, I'm sorry I'm late." I apologized again.

Her dark, liquid eyes glanced my way. I took in the heavy fringe of her eyelashes.

"Come on in here. We got lots to do." She shook her head as if I were already a hopeless case. "On my watch, everything runs smooth as glass. Understand?"

"Oh, yes, ma'am."

Another girl, her hair held back in a bright yellow triangular head-scarf, sat in a rocker, feeding a baby spread across her mountain of a belly. She nodded at me, and I realized it was Shirley, Pepper's roommate.

"First off, you walk in here, you wash up."

I turned to the sink, quickly rinsed my hands in cold water, and grabbed a rough brown paper towel.

"No." Miss Jones pushed my hands back into the sink. "Like this. Scrub those hands with hot water, and your arms too. Scrub 'em good. Here, with Phisohex soap. It kills the germs." A frown darkened her features as she pumped a load of milky fluid from a green bottle across my hands.

Miss Jones shoved a hand brush at me. "Brush under them fingernails too."

I scrubbed my hands hard, until she nodded approval.

"Next, you always put on a clean smock." She pointed to sterilized smocks stacked neatly on a shelf. "We got uniforms too. You gonna want to grab some to work in."

"Yes, ma'am." I pulled a stiff white smock over my clothes.

"Every time you come in this nursery, you scrub up. You hear? We don't want no germs brought here to these babies."

"Yes, ma'am." I nodded and followed her into the nursery. Miss Jones showed me where the formula-filled bottles were kept. Neat stacks of diapers and linens lined the shelves. Lastly, she led me into a dimly lit area filled with bassinets. Shirley stood over a baby, changing a tiny diaper.

"You know Shirley?"

I nodded. *Too well.*

Miss Jones explained, "Shirley's not gonna be here on nights no more. That's where you come in, Laura."

"Yes, ma'am." I gulped, glancing at a baby bundled in a thin flannel blanket. Abundant, thick black curls poked out of the blanket.

"Lordy, just look at all that hair." Miss Jones chuckled.

"Okay, now, this here is Lucy. See her little birth card?" She pointed to a small card taped to the side of the bassinet.

Lucy? Ella's baby girl.

"I'm gonna teach you how to change this precious child's diaper."

"I know how to change a diaper." I jumped at the chance to impress Miss Jones.

She gave me a sideways glance. "Uh-huh. Well, watch me anyway. This is the right way."

Miss Jones expertly changed Lucy's miniature cloth diaper. "Now pick her up. Careful. She's brand new."

As I lifted Ella's baby girl, my heart lurched. She was light as a feather but surprisingly sturdy and warm. Praying I wouldn't drop her, I lowered myself down into a rocker.

"That baby won't break." Shirley chuckled at my discomfort.

Miss Jones gently placed a bottle in my hand and guided it down to Lucy's perfect pink mouth, and she immediately started sucking for all she was worth. "Such a good baby," Miss Jones cooed.

My eyes never left that miniature round face until she fell back to sleep. A lump expanded in my throat as I realized Ella's baby girl was perfect and poor Ella had never even seen her. I wished I could hold Lucy all night and never let her go.

Hours later, when I left the nursery, I thanked Miss Jones. Though my head was spinning and my nerves were frayed, I strangely felt wide awake and happy.

"You're welcome, child. You gonna work out fine—just be on time tomorrow. Oh, and Laura, you can call me Delli." Miss Jones almost smiled as I waved and quietly closed the door.

I grinned all the way down the dark hallways to my room.

I didn't realize it that night, but I had met a woman who would

become one of my dearest friends at the Home. I would soon
learn in Delli's presence that I wasn't a miserable, wayward girl.
Welcoming and kind, she was totally dedicated to her job of caring
for her tiny charges and as eager to teach me as I was willing to
learn. Her bearing acted as a soft blanket covering me with kindness and acceptance.

In the still of the night, we sat rocking and holding babies long
after they were fed, and we traded stories. Delli told me about her
life outside the Home. I rambled on about my life back home in
Mississippi, soon learning I could tell her just about anything. One
night I confided in her that I worried my parents would never love
me again.

"They love you, sugar. Just worried for you, that's all," Delli assured
me.

"I don't think so, Delli. My mama is beside herself. I think she
hates me."

"This will all work out, Laura. Your mama don't hate you, honey
child."

Adapting quickly to caring for the infants, I treasured the sheer
joy of holding a new life and rocking each little one to sleep. The
fact that I had known some of their mamas made it more endearing.
Searching Lucy's deep-blue eyes, I saw Ella and it broke my heart
each night that she would never know the miracle of this baby girl.

My own tiny baby, nestled safe inside me, rolled and stretched as
I rocked others, filled with a feeling I had never imagined. Nothing
in my old life seemed to matter. Sometimes I wanted my nights in
the nursery to last forever. I learned I was good at taking care of
babies, and I genuinely loved my job. I could be a good mama. I just
knew it.

One night, laying a baby across my chest and shoulder, I rocked back and forth, humming Petula Clark's song "Kiss Me Goodbye." Oh, how I loved that song. My baby kicked hard, and I smiled.

Somehow, I'll keep you. I startled myself. The thought seemed so sharp and loud that I worried I had shouted it.

I looked up sheepishly as Delli walked through the nursery, quietly humming a hymn. The longing to keep my baby hit with such an impact, I had to force myself to act normal, biting my lip until I tasted blood so that I wouldn't cry or maybe scream.

I refused to let myself think about the sadness involved with leaving these precious infants here. Protecting my heart, I avoided thinking that the baby I carried safely in my own body would be a tiny bundle in one of these bassinets. If I did, I knew I would never stop crying.

Chapter 17

After a week of late nights in the nursery, I escaped the gossiping girls on the patio and headed back to my room, eager for a sorely needed nap. No sooner had I fallen into a deep sleep than I heard a loud rapping at the door. I pulled the covers over my head. Working the night shift had turned my world upside down, and I had enough trouble sleeping as it was. I would ignore it.

Whoever it was jiggled the doorknob.

"Go away!" I shouted.

"Hey, Laura. Get up. Tina needs you."

My eyes flew open. Pepper needed me. I hadn't seen her much this week.

Jumping up, I jerked open the door, and there stood Shirley, peering past me into my room. She told me Tina was in labor and asking for me. I closed the door in her face as she tried to push her way into my room. Instantly wide awake, I pushed past the fatigue, hurried into my shoes, and rushed down the staircase toward the clinic.

A kind nurse greeted me. "Your friend Tina will be happy to see you."

I rushed into the labor room. Pepper grabbed my hand.

"Hi, Pep, I'm here." I squeezed her hand.

"Oh, Laurie, I hate this," she whimpered. Her frightened eyes looked huge, and immediately I felt a sick pang of fear.

114

The nurse told us it would be a while and then turned to me, explaining that she had already prepped Tina, so I could sit here and keep her company. She bustled out of the room, and there we sat. Pepper seemed in her own world, not talking but obviously hurting. I sat next to her bed without any idea of what to do.

Prepped? What the heck is "prepped"?

"Are you in a lot of pain? It looks bad. What's 'prepped'?"

"It was awful. You don't want to know." She let out a soft moan. "The cramps are getting worse, Laurie."

"This will be over soon. You'll be fine, Pepper. I just know it."

I nervously chattered away, hoping to cheer her up, and talked for both of us for what seemed like hours. I stopped pretending to be cheerful when her pains worsened, because I doubted my own words that she would be fine. Would she?

"You're doing really good," I lied.

Pepper moaned more loudly.

I jumped. "I'll get the nurse!" I hurried out into the hall.

"She needs you. Sorry, please come." I apologized to the nurse on duty, preoccupied with her *Redbook* magazine. An open bag of M&M's lay on the desk in front of her.

How can she be reading a magazine at a time like this?

"Be there in a minute." She glanced up, her smile radiant. "Doctor's arriving soon."

God, Pepper's dying and no one cares. How can the nurse be so calm?

Not long after that, an aggravated older man with a balding head and a grumpy bedside manner hobbled into the room, ordering me to wait in the hall. A few minutes later, he emerged from the room and spoke to the nurse as he shook off his wrinkled suit jacket and loosened his tie. I noticed the nurse had stashed away the magazine and M&M's.

Slinking back into the room to keep watch over my friend, I wet a washcloth and patted her face with it. Mama's cure-all. For hours, Pepper continued to turn and twist her body, sometimes weeping pitifully. My mouth was dry, my stomach growling, but I couldn't leave her. My heart ached as I watched her, unable to help.

When will this end? God, it takes forever to have a baby.

Nobody bothered to tell us anything. It seemed as if the staff had allowed me into the room to babysit poor Pepper, who was getting louder by the minute. Never one to show emotion or cry out loud, here she was crying, moaning, and scared to death. Tossing and turning, she grabbed my arm. "Laurie, get the nurse. Please. Please." It was terrifying. Her black ringlets dripped with sweat. Each time she strained, I panicked.

I bolted out the door and yelled for the nurse, who patiently pointed a finger in the air, indicating "one minute."

Where is the damn doctor? The baby is coming, I just know it.

My teeth chattering, a feeling of nausea overwhelmed me and I ran back to Pepper's side. Sitting helplessly, watching her, I was scared to death. Something must have gone terribly wrong. What if the baby was dead? What if Pepper was dying?

Finally, after what seemed like an awfully long time but was probably mere minutes, the distracted doctor hurried into the cramped room, nurse behind him, and shooed me out of the room again to wait in the dim hallway. There was a frantic flurry of activity as they rolled Pepper across the tiny hall into the constricted delivery room. I stood against the door frame, invisible, starving, and thirsty, realizing there was nothing more I could do. Primal fear washed over me, and I shivered, sorry I had ever promised to stay with Pepper.

Eager to escape, I headed down the hall just as the nurse stepped out of the delivery room.

"Would you like to stay with your friend Tina and witness the birth?" she called out cheerfully to me.

God, no! I shuddered. But a weak "sure" came out of my mouth.

Positioning me close to the doorway, she quickly turned back into the small, crowded delivery room. I had a clear view of the back of the doctor's shiny head and wide back. Pepper lay in front of him on the delivery table. She was completely still, quiet now, and the nurse stood beside her, holding a black contraption over her face. Her legs were spread wide in stirrups, draped with sheets. The doctor was inches away from her, peering between her legs, speaking calmly to the nurse. They appeared at ease and almost jovial.

Oh my God, how embarrassing. If Pepper knew they had her spread out like this, she would die. I'll never tell her.

Mortified, I wanted to look away, but couldn't. I was mesmerized, frozen in my tracks.

"Here we go." The doctor spoke loudly, his voice rich behind his surgical mask. His grumpy attitude at once gone, he seemed almost giddy as he took what looked like a shiny metal object to Pepper's privates.

What is that? She looks different down there. Poor Pepper, she looks deformed. Wait, what am I looking at?

I had never seen another woman's vagina, especially one with a bloody episiotomy and a baby's head crowning. I hadn't realized that the routine practice was to shave a woman's vaginal area and perineum. I simply reasoned Pepper must be different down there.

No wonder Ella's bottom was on fire, I thought. The raw episiotomy alone was enough to make me feel faint.

Everything happened so fast. Before I could blink, a perfectly formed, exquisite baby boy whooshed out of my friend's body, along with a rush of fluid. His tiny head was covered with a mass of bloody black curls. A waxy white substance covered his squirming red body. His mouth opened like a baby bird's, and he let out a marvelous yowl. It was that phenomenal sound of life only a newborn baby makes entering this world, and it melted my pounding heart. Tears sprang to my eyes at that glorious music.

Meanwhile, during all the action, Pepper lay silent, drugged and half asleep as the doctor and nurse congratulated each other on this easy and perfect birth. I leaned against the door frame, laughing and crying at the same time, watching them at work as they explained to me that now they were waiting for the placenta to be birthed.

Oh, wow. Oh, God. This is a miracle. My knees shook. All the blood and fluids didn't make me queasy at all because the beauty of the moment was all that mattered. What I had just witnessed was life-changing. This was the real deal. I had witnessed birth.

As the gory placenta was emptied from Pepper, I gasped. The sights and sounds of the night vibrated in my very core. The nurse had bundled up Pepper's baby and headed to the nursery, and now I was free to go, but first I grabbed for Pepper's hand.

"You guessed right, Pepper. It's a boy and he's perfect and he has so much black hair. Timothy is gorgeous."

Pepper's lips curved up in a tired smile, but her sad eyes made my heart clench. Wandering the hallways to my room, I no longer felt tired or hungry. Adrenaline pumped through my vibrating body, and I knew I would never be the same after this day.

My arms could not wait to wrap around that beautiful baby boy tonight at the 2:00 a.m. feeding. I laughed through my tears, sounding like a maniac. My heart was exploding.

If I feel like this, how must Pepper feel?

Back in my room, I had time to rest before my shift and quickly wrote a letter to Mama. I had to tell her about the miracle I had witnessed.

Dear Mama,

Tonight, I was present when a baby boy was born. Mama, he is so perfect, and it was a miracle to watch his entry into the world. I'm still crying. How can I put it into words? I do know this. I want to keep my baby. Can you please change Daddy's mind? Could you help me raise the baby, but not as your baby, as mine? I'll find a job and I will work hard. I will not ask for anything else. I promise. I can't leave my baby. It will kill me. Mama, you should have seen the precious baby boy my friend had. She named him Timothy. We'll call him Timmy.

I don't know why I said okay to leaving my baby. I don't care what people say. I only agreed with Daddy because I knew I had hurt him, and you were not there to help me talk him into keeping my baby. Mama, you need to help me. I'm begging you.

Timmy's tiny scrunched-up face and his beautiful dark eyes, so new, so wise, played over in my mind nonstop.

In the morning, I reread my letter. I realized I had to rewrite it because it would only upset my parents. God knows, I had upset them enough already. I never mailed it.

Chapter 18

During the last week of April, the dining hall rang with chatter and soft laughter as we girls amused ourselves. We stopped our gossiping when a staff member walked to our table with a new girl in tow and introduced me to my new roommate.

Lizzie was petite, barely five feet tall, with a frail frame. She wore her bleached platinum blond hair in a bouffant upsweep. Her makeup was meticulous and her smile, stunning. Tiny as she was, her extra-large personality shone through. She reminded me of a miniature Dolly Parton, minus Dolly's famous bosom. Her pint-size maternity top almost hid the fact that she was pregnant. She seemed like an angel, all goodness and light, and my lonely soul warmed to her immediately. I watched in awe as her magical smile lit up the room.

"Hey. Welcome. Here, have a seat." I moved to make room for her, wanting her all to myself.

"Why, thank you. Don't mind if I do." Lizzie glowed, immediately comfortable with everyone at the table. She was interested in hearing who we all were and our stories. Her sweet demeanor was instantly contagious.

That afternoon, I learned Lizzie was seventeen and her due date was four months away. I learned the father of her baby was her high school sweetheart, Bobby Lee. He was a high school football hero whom everyone in her small hometown adored. His family had turned her away and forbidden him to marry her. We marveled that our high schools had played football games against each other and compared notes on which games we had both attended, laughing about the fact that we might have brushed shoulders.

"I just know we were at those games at the same time." Lizzie's white teeth sparkled in her wide lipsticked smile.

"I know. It's crazy." I grinned at her, checking out her perfect hair and manicured pink nails. "Do you like to read?" I asked.

"Not really." She smiled confidently.

We were improbably compatible, despite our differences, and I adored Lizzie. I took on the role of big sister and advisor to her as I explained how the Home operated and what I had learned so far, taking delight in amusing her with stories of different staff members, the girls, and the rigid rules as I helped put her things away in our room.

"Laura, I have to tell you a couple of secrets." Lizzie sat down on her bed, patting a spot next to her.

"Sure." I sat down, folding one of her frilly tops, overjoyed that I finally had a roommate who was fun and seemed to love to talk as much as me.

"First off, my real name is Lizzie. I kept my real name."

"My real name is Laura." We squealed and hugged each other, gloating and thrilled that we were both brave enough to buck the system. Rebels without a clue.

"Please don't tell anyone, but I'm gonna try to keep my baby. They think I'm giving it up, but to hell with them. I'm not leaving here without it." She was adamant. Her face flushed deep pink.

"How? How can you keep your baby if you told them you're leaving it?"

"Bobby Lee will marry me. I just know it. I'm working on it. I am not leaving my baby. But you gotta promise me right now you won't say anything to anyone. Promise me." She peered into my eyes, extending her hand, fingers curled into her palm, with only her little finger jutted out.

"Okay, it's our secret. I promise," I said, curling my little finger with hers, sealing our commitment and new friendship with a pinky promise.

∿

"Laura, you must promise me you'll take extra-special care of Timmy," Pepper told me after her son's birth. "Please."

"Oh, Pepper. I adore him. Of course I'll always take good care of Timmy."

"I hate that Shirley works in the nursery and takes care of him." Pepper looked over her shoulder and whispered, "She's nasty."

"Don't you worry. She must scrub up to her elbows and wear a smock when she feeds the babies. Plus, I always check on Timmy. I cuddle and rock him as much as I can."

Pepper left her room only for meals. She kept away from the other girls and was practically a recluse, alone with her studies. She avoided the nursery window and was eager to get back to school and forget this place. Eventually her stiff, stylish mother arrived to pick her up and take her home to Texas.

The morning before her mother arrived, Pepper and I cried in each other's arms. "Promise you'll write to me about Timmy. I hope he gets adopted soon. Please watch out for him, Laura."

"I promise."

∿

It was true. I was obsessed with Timmy. His wise almond-shaped eyes were fringed with thick, long lashes and peered into mine as if he knew me. As I rocked him after feedings, I quietly sang Beatles songs, watching his perfect pink lips purse at me as he blew little milk bubbles, his belly full. He looked exactly like Pepper, and that thrilled me most of all. I dreaded the day he would be adopted, yet my heart knew it would be best for him.

∽

At the end of April, I was thrilled when I got a letter from Mama saying that she and Daddy would drive the two hours and come take me to lunch on Sunday. I was also excited I'd be leaving the Home for a few hours.

That morning, I dressed with care and sat at the front of the building, waiting for them to arrive. When they drove up, I ran into the lobby to sign myself out and grinned as I opened the door of their car, scooting into the back seat.

"Hey." I giggled.

Mama's eyes were glassy as she smiled and reached for my hand. I held on tight. Daddy turned his head to look at me, his face breaking into a wide smile. "Hey, hon."

I had worried he would never smile at me again.

"We thought we'd grab lunch and go somewhere after. Maybe walk around? Do you need to shop for anything?" Mama sounded happy.

"Can I have a po' boy and a stuffed crab? I'm starvin'!"

"Yes, whatever you want."

During our meal of the delicious shrimp po' boys and stuffed crab, Mama and Daddy told me news of my brothers and Grammy. They mentioned not one word about the baby who was growing inside me. Not a peep about Clay.

After lunch we walked through Audubon Park, and I felt as if I was the luckiest girl in the world. Watching families strolling by as we sat on a park bench, I hoped we looked like any other normal family: a father, mother, and pregnant, "married" daughter out for a

Sunday stroll. My head held high, I attempted to look as nonchalant as possible, wishing I had a fake wedding ring, like some of the girls at the Home. Now I knew why they wore them when they went out.

Mama glanced at my stomach. "You're showing a lot."

I nodded, trying to hold in my stomach, and attempted a smile.

Just then, a tiny girl with a balloon skipped past us, all pink frills and strawberry curls. Her proud mama and daddy followed, pushing a stroller with a new baby nestled in lacy fluff. I looked away, but not before I saw Mama's stricken face glance at the baby. Daddy was sitting on the bench, his hands clasped on his knees, looking down at his lap, his forehead furrowed.

My eyes followed the exquisite little girl as she continued skipping farther down the path. *Could my baby be a girl?*

Mama looked in my direction, and I quickly removed my hands, which had been draped across my belly. Jamie kicked excitedly inside me. I wished we could talk about him, but that would hurt them even more. Instead of sharing anything about the tumbling going on in my body, I told them stories about the other girls and how we were all good friends.

I explained how we all made visits to the tiny market across the street from the Home and always bought sweets and Cokes. I left out the fact that I sometimes bought cigarettes too. Mama had always said, "Only trampy women smoke, and besides, smoking causes wrinkles and makes your clothes stink."

Each time I felt the tension becoming uncomfortable, I would slyly change the subject to something I knew they were comfortable with. If I upset them, they might not come again.

By dusk, delivered back to the Home stuffed and satisfied, clasping a bag of chocolate bars for me and cookies for Lizzie, I felt tears threatening. Mama handed me a sack filled with a new paperback book and some shampoo and soap.

"Oh, here. Your Grammy sent this too." Mama rolled her eyes and handed me a second sack. "Another top and some headbands. I told her you don't need more stuff to find a place for."

There weren't any long, drawn-out hugs or tears. Stoic as ever, I felt humbled by my parents' visit and the gifts. I knew I was hardly worthy of their attention and both the monetary and the emotional expense of their visit. Mama hugged me, Daddy waved, and, with a lump in my throat, I turned my back, opened the door to the Home, and went inside without a backward glance.

Up the stairs I ran and swung open the door to our room, calling out to Lizzie, "Look—cookies for you, and we have a big bottle of Prell shampoo and Dove soap."

She beamed her brilliant smile. I gushed about what a fine day it had been and how happy I was as we sat cross-legged on our beds. But while we devoured the sugary cookies, I secretly felt hollow and hurt. *My parents pretended like Jamie wasn't real, and I went along with it.* It felt wrong that we couldn't talk about my baby.

Chapter 19

Routine prevailed for us girls at the Home, revolving around meal-times and our various jobs. There were a few lazy and shiftless girls, but for the most part no one argued about our jobs. After all, this was our chance to prove that we were decent young women worthy of this second chance, and working really did make our days fly by.

Many an afternoon found us outside in the courtyard, vying for comfort under the covered concrete slab. Girls delivered their babies and left soon after, returning home to their old/new lives without their babies. Then, like magic, new girls arrived, some with stories, some too damaged to talk at all. Most eventually joined in the cama-raderie of our secret sisterhood, which helped to keep us sane.

Our cravings for sugar were next to fanatical as we headed across the street to the little grocery store. Those evenings we lost our shy-ness, laughing and joking like the typical teenagers we still were. As a group, we felt invincible. Besides, the inhabitants in the neighbor-hood ignored us, for the most part. They were conditioned to seeing pregnant girls come and go out of the Home.

Sometimes we walked to a close-by bakery to buy hot, fresh donuts. Following the delicious smell of butter and sugar, we stopped and spoke to the children playing on the sidewalks. We discussed which of the old row houses and Creole cottages we would like to

live in one day. As we waddled up and down the sidewalks shaded
by the ancient oaks, we dreamed of our future selves after we left
this place.

Nights were the worst. When I was unable to sleep, a movie reel
of my life would play in my head, never failing to leave me physically
aching for home, for my old life with family and friends. Cradling my
stomach with my arms and whispering to my baby, I would feel silent
tears wetting my face. My mind often wandered back to the previous
summer. Closing my eyes, I could smell the briny air of my hometown. I almost felt the tender gulf breeze lifting my hair. I could see
the gray pelicans perched on the posts of the piers and hear seagulls
squawking.

"Let's go to the island and walk to the other side. We can spend
the whole day alone," Clay urged me one day. A group of friends was
headed out to one of the outlying islands that pepper the Gulf Coast.

"I don't know." I hesitated. I was thrilled to think of spending a
whole day alone with him on the island but afraid of how it would
look. "What will everyone say if we don't stay with the group?"

"Who cares what they say?" He laughed and kissed me. That was
all it took.

He had brought a little tent to protect us from the unrelenting sun.
Frosty, illegal beer, bitter and sharp, tingled in our mouths. I didn't
like the taste but loved the buzzy, blurry way it made me feel. And
nothing had ever tasted better than the soggy ham sandwiches I'd
packed. Over and over that day we rushed into the waves, full and
dizzy, laughing, unable to keep our hands off each other, before we
ran back to lie in the shaded seclusion of our tent. Clay wrapped his
arms around me for hours as we whispered our dreams to each other,
until the unbearable heat forced us back out to run into the water.

What glorious days those were. We waited until the last boat
headed back to the mainland. Painfully sunburned and in love, I was
so smug, so sure he had eyes only for me.

Another time, Clay suggested, "Let's go to New Orleans, instead of that dumb dance you want to go to."

"New Orleans? Are you crazy? How? I can't."

"Buddy and Cash are going. We'll hitch a ride with them. Just tell your mama you're going to sleep over at Nancy's. Please?" He nuzzled my neck and laid his head on my chest.

The idea of being alone with him far from home warmed me from head to toe. So I lied to my mama and went along with his plan. Once again, alcohol colored the trip, helping my guilt fade away as we drove along the dark highway toward another forbidden adventure.

That warm, humid night, walking up and down Bourbon Street with the three boys for the first time, I quickly understood why the Crescent City was dubbed Sin City. Loud, colorful partygoers staggered through the streets; music blared everywhere; prostitutes on the corners leered at us as we walked past, arm in arm. I got my first glimpse of seminude dancers in fishnet stockings and stilettos standing outside the entries of loud bars and dark, sinister clubs. Along with deafening music, the harsh stench of wood-planked floors drenched in old alcohol, years of ground-up cigarette butts, and stale perspiration flowed from the open doorways. I was dumbfounded by the sweaty, sleek bodies; thick, pancake makeup–plastered faces; and outlandish wigs back-combed ten inches high.

Those vile-looking women reached long glittery arms toward the boys. "Come on in here, handsome. We know how to give ya a good time, Sugah." They lifted naked breasts toward us, sequined pasties covering dark nipples.

I had never imagined a world like this. A shiver of fear ran through me the whole night, along with a clear feeling of being all grown up and wanting to prove to Clay that none of this bothered me. Clay leered at the nearly naked women. How could I compete in my green suede A-line skirt, black tights, pumps, and button-down blouse? He laughed, calling back, "Sorry, ladies, not this time. I'm with my girl," thrilling me and putting my mind at ease.

The rest of that night is a blur. We walked the French Quarter for hours, venturing into a maze of the city's oldest streets and crumbling alleyways. The smells of urine and vomit were disgusting, but I held on to Clay's arm, laughing and cringing at the lewd jokes he and Cash made.

The four of us ended up at a party in a decrepit apartment filled with what seemed like hundreds of wild partygoers, most older than we were. We drank a mysterious purple brew, laced with who knew what, from flimsy paper cups. A beautiful red-haired woman beckoned us into a dark hallway. I closed my eyes as someone lowered my body onto a dank mattress covered with coats and clothing.

Waking up in a fog the next morning, I lay on my own bed back home, fully dressed, with only the vaguest memories of that party. My new suede skirt was ruined, streaked with blue and magenta paint. I would have to throw it away before Mama saw it. As I stripped off my blouse and bra, I gasped when I realized brilliant, colorful flowers had been body-painted across my breasts.

Lying in my bed at the Home, I still squirmed when I remembered that morning. I had no memory of how the paintings had happened, and Clay had assured me he had no memories afterward either. Recalling that time, I felt my aching sadness change to anger, then numbness, then back to anger at how discarded I felt.

∾

The callus on my middle digit hardened as night after night I wrote countless letters, pouring my heart out, sharing my dreams. Many mornings I would read them only to tear them up. I would plan on ways to explain to Mama and Daddy how we could keep the baby. I would scheme about how to get in touch with Clay.

Wouldn't he change his mind if he saw me?

Seconds later, I would decide I hated him and hoped I never saw him again.

ⱺ

May was a long month. Time stood still in our little world. Many of the tough girls who had held court in the enclosed yard when I had arrived had already given birth, relinquished their babies, and left. Most had gone without saying goodbye, glad to be rid of this hard time in their lives. Taylor was one of them. Without her leading the pack, there seemed to be less anger and sarcasm among the residents. The new girls were a far gentler group, but we still smoked, gossiped about staff, complained about our jobs, our aches and pains.

Bored and always hungry, we planned intrigues, such as slipping into the kitchen late at night, opening the walk-in fridge and stealing food, mostly ice cream. We craved fun and excitement as much as we did sugar.

Sometimes we would sneak off on unofficial outings, catching the streetcars and riding down to the French Quarter, oohing and aahing over the stately mansions along St. Charles Avenue. I would fantasize, imagining Clay becoming a famous rock star and taking me to live in a gigantic white estate with our golden child. The magical essence of old New Orleans held me captive.

One bright morning, fed up and drained from feeling like a prisoner, I gathered all my courage to do something I had never done. Slipping out of the building, I began walking quickly down the street, my spirits lifting as a cool breeze carried the scent of freshly baked bread. I nodded to an elderly couple walking arm in arm past me, their faces rosy and sweet. I stopped at a designated corner, simply opened the back door of a white '65 Rambler sedan, and scooted in, grinning from ear to ear. Red vinyl seat covers scorched the backs of my thighs.

Nancy's letter had set a scheme in motion. She missed me and wanted to visit with her boyfriend, Aaron. Letters flew back and forth as we formulated a plan and decided on a place to meet. Afraid to ask if I could have friends visit me and risk being told no, I had allowed the adventure of sneaking out to see my best friend overshadow my fear of getting caught.

Dressing carefully that morning, I sprayed Aqua Net with a heavy hand over my back-combed hair and tied on a red headband. I carefully applied makeup with the advice of Lizzie, who was in on my secret rendezvous. Catching my reflection in the bathroom mirror, I smiled and thought, *Not bad.*

It was exciting, just like the "old days," when Nancy would drive to my house and toot the horn and I'd run out and jump in her car. We would sing along with the radio, gossip, and head to a party or just cruise the beach, looking for any new adventure that awaited us. How carefree we had been. How cocky.

Smoothing my maternity top over my belly, I quickly thought, *Who am I kidding? This is not like the old days.*

∾

After I hurled myself into the back seat, Aaron took off with a squeal of the tires. We all laughed out loud.

"I did it! I escaped!" I was jubilant. "It really wasn't that hard. I should escape prison more often."

Nancy howled along with me. "Yeehaw, Laura. You did it!" she hollered.

Just the thought of seeing old friends had filled me with excitement for days, but after laughing and congratulating myself in the car, I felt a bit shy. Was I imagining it, or were both of my friends discreetly checking out my full-blown pregnant body?

As we drove out of the neighborhood into downtown New

Orleans, I pointed out places of interest as if I were their appointed tour guide. We stopped at a greasy spoon, one of the hundreds that dotted the Crescent City, and gobbled up sloppy, dripping hamburgers and extra-salty french fries. Icy cold malts tickled our throats.

While we giggled and enjoyed ourselves, Nancy filled me in on all the gossip at school and quiet Aaron chuckled now and then. It felt normal and comfortable to be able to laugh with friends; still, worry sat heavily on my shoulders the entire time.

What if they figure out I'm missing? Will they call Mama and Daddy?

As we walked through City Park, I regaled them with stories of the Home and my situation, as if it were just a small bump in the road and living there wasn't all that bad.

"What are the other girls like?" Nancy asked.

"Oh, they're mostly fun. I like them. Wait. I take that back. Some are not fun. Remember I wrote to you about my first roommate?"

"She sounded like a class-A loser." Nancy rolled her eyes.

"Just another pitiful girl in trouble, I guess. Like me."

She looked at me, nodding her head sadly.

"It's not so much the girls; it's the place. It's, well, like an institution. Old people run it, and sometimes it gives me the creeps. Other days it's okay, but it does get boring."

The soft, humid breeze surrounded us, and the glossy leaves shimmered above us. Nancy and I sat down on a bench as Aaron walked away, smoking and gazing over the park. I took this opportunity to ask what I had been dying to ask.

"Have you heard from Clay? Did he go to Vietnam?"

"No. Haven't heard a word."

"I wonder if he wrote to me at the house. Mama would have told me, I think."

"Don't worry about him. He let you down, and he's with someone else now, Laura." Nancy frowned. "You still thinking he'll come around?"

My head ached. "No," I lied.

Aaron ambled back to the bench in time to hear us talking about Clay, and he mumbled something under his breath.

What does he really think of me, his girlfriend's pregnant, unmarried friend locked away in an institution?

Later that afternoon, I said a bittersweet goodbye, waving as they drove away. Now I felt more alone than ever. *They're heading back home to their lives and leaving me here. Who am I kidding? I'm not who I was, and they know it.*

The street was quiet and empty as I walked purposefully back up the uneven sidewalk and stoically into the building. The front doors closed like a steel trap behind me.

Later, I pleaded a headache when Lizzie asked if I had had fun with my friends. Where had we gone? What had we eaten?

"I feel sick. I can't talk. It was too hot today. I need to get some rest before I go down to work my shift. Sorry, Lizzie," I squeaked as I lay down on my bed and rolled away from her puzzled face. Squeezing my eyes shut, I was still and silent, waiting to hear the door shut quietly as a hot tear slipped down my face.

∾

All the while, the Mamas & the Papas crooned on the transistor radios. "California Dreamin'" and "Monday, Monday" constantly filled the airwaves, along with "Ruby Tuesday" by the Stones, Lizzie's favorite. The Supremes belted out "Baby Love" as we sang along, and the Beatles seemed to sing every other song.

"Hey, girls, I read that there's a town in England named Ryde and there's an unwed mothers' home there. That's what this song is about," Harriet, a studious girl, commented one afternoon after the DJ announced that the Beatles' "Ticket to Ride" was up next.

"That's just a stupid rumor, Harriet." One of the older girls laughed.

Another girl chimed in, "Hey, maybe one of the Beatles' girlfriends got herself in trouble and that's why they wrote this song."

"No way, stupid. None of the Beatles would do that." Harriet jumped to John, Paul, George, and Ringo's defense.

"Well, whatever it's about, it's a good song." I winked at Harriet.

We all happily began singing together that we had a ticket to Ryde.

We swooned over bands and idolized band members. We knew all the words to the top hits and danced with abandon when the mood hit. Still, no matter how late we stayed up on Saturday nights, Sunday mornings found us lined up in the pews of the in-house chapel, eyes drooping, hands folded over our swollen middles, shampooed heads bent in prayer.

I struggled not to yawn as I listened to the lessons taught by the kind old reverend, who always strove to teach us wayward young women life lessons we could use when this time was over. While he'd say an extra-long, fervent prayer about redemption, I'd look around.

Here we sat, young, fresh, some beautiful, some plain, some wealthy, some poor. All round and glowing with pregnancy, along with an aura of despair. Desperate to understand what was happening. Desperate that our families forgive us. Desperate to feel loved.

❧

As we huddled on the patio, most conversations centered on "back home," and some girls boasted about how forgiving their parents would be when they returned, unburdened by the unwanted child. A few alluded to violent, angry parents. Most did not speak about their baby's father without remorse, yet some did with pure hatred. Still, a few girls planned to reconnect with the fathers of their babies and assured us they would marry those boys and have other children.

A tall, graceful girl named Susan Marie seemed so dedicated to her rat of a boyfriend that it drove me nuts. I watched her one afternoon on the patio, preening and going on and on.

"I write to Tyler every day," she simpered. "He's too darn busy to write back." She sat back with an angelic smile on her pretty face.

She sounds like a simpleton.

"He's on the football team. He's gonna graduate in two years from Auburn, and he promised he'll wait for me. He can't have a baby tying him down right now, with all his sports and stuff, so I have to respect that. Don't I?"

"God, he sounds like a class-A jerk to me," Lizzie fumed. "Why you'd have anything to do with him after he put you through all this, I'll never know."

I was glad Lizzie called Susan Marie out, but if I was honest, would I ever want to see Clay again? If he came to get me, would I go with him and forgive him for denying me? Yes, I would.

Chapter 20

One stormy afternoon in late May, I was thrilled when I called home and Mama said she and Daddy were planning another visit that weekend.

The next morning, Lizzie and I headed downstairs to breakfast and I chirped about how I hoped Daddy would take us to the French Quarter after lunch.

"Ooh, the Vieux Carré. Lucky you, Laura." She pretended to swoon.

I couldn't have asked for a better roomie. Lizzie was a shining light, always positive and exuberant. We often talked about her continued communication with her true love, Bobby Lee, and she'd fill me in on their plans of how they would keep their baby. I envied her.

I'm beginning to believe she might pull it off.

That night, as I fed the babies in my charge and listened to Delli's nonstop stories about her children and home life, my mind wandered, still worried about how to approach the subject of keeping my baby with my parents. Our rockers softly creaked as the tiny bundles drained their sterilized bottles of formula.

"Yes, sirree, my baby boy, Roy Junior, he's somethin', all right." Delli shook her head and rolled her eyes. We both chuckled as the tiny fuzzy-haired baby girl snug across her chest let out a loud, long burp.

While daydreaming, I had missed Delli's entire story about her youngest child, Roy Junior. He was always her favorite subject, but she spoke with fierce love about all five of her children and confided that she was "still dizzy in love" with her teddy bear of a husband, Big Roy.

"Delli, what happens when a girl refuses to leave her baby?" *There, I said it out loud.*

Delli's liquid eyes widened. "Now, honey, I don't get involved in that."

"I'm asking for someone else," I lied through my teeth.

"I guess you can talk to Miss Felton or Miss McKay about that, honey." She stood up, moving over to the other side of the nursery to gently tuck in her bundled baby. "No, I can't help with that, Laura."

"I . . . I want to ask, um, my mama and daddy about keeping my baby," I confessed.

"Oh, child. I don't know what to say." Her sad eyes glanced quickly at me and then back at her task at hand. A whimper became a wail in the corners of the nursery. We still had four infants to feed.

Feeling brave, I continued, "I know one girl who says she'll keep hers, no matter what." I clasped my tiny ward close to my heart. She squirmed and stretched. I held her more tightly, inhaling her baby hair mixed with the scent of formula.

"I promised I wouldn't tell who it is, so I can't tell you. But I think she'll do it. She's determined."

My heart was pounding. I tasted blood as I chewed my lip. We silently walked past each other, I to change the next baby in line, she to test a bottle and settle down in a rocker with her complaining baby. Her face was set in a stern frown as she began humming the old hymn "I Go to the Garden Alone."

I come to the Garden alone, while the dew is still on the roses . . .
And he walks with me and he talks to me and he tells me I am his
own and

The joy we share as we tarry there, no other has ever known . . .

I loved that hymn. How many times had I stood next to Grammy in church, sharing a hymnal and singing those beautiful old words of faith and devotion?

Delli's charge started squirming and refusing his bottle. She hummed louder and tucked him back against her chest. "This little boy, he's hungry, but he's got some temper." She laughed softly, changing the subject, gently nudging the nipple of the bottle against his pink lips. "He's a live wire, this little one." The agitated newborn settled down in her arms as she kept up her humming. Subject closed, we continued to rock our babies.

෮

Sunday arrived, hot with thunderclouds. I was in a high mood at chapel and waited patiently for my parents to arrive midmorning. Standing next to me, Lizzie peered out the window. Eager to introduce her to my folks, I rushed to Daddy as he walked up the sidewalk.

"Hey, Daddy!" I gushed. "This here's Lizzie, my roommate."

"Hey." Lizzie stood ramrod straight, extending her hand, smiling her most gorgeous smile.

My shy daddy smiled, greeting her in his quite bashful way. "Hello, Lizzie." Turning to me, he said, "Your mama's waitin' in the car, Laura."

Lizzie and I hurried down the steps to the car parked at the curb. There sat Mama, staring straight ahead. She jumped when I pulled open her car door. "Laura, you scared me to death." She frowned and then noticed the small blond girl behind me.

"Mama, meet Lizzie, my roommate."

"How do you do? Thank you for the cookies you sent." Lizzie beamed.

Mama quickly gathered herself and returned a flustered smile. "Nice to meet you, Lizzie. I'm glad you liked the cookies."

Mama's discomfort was unmistakable, but Lizzie rattled on. I swear she glowed when she said how happy she was that we were roommates and told Mama how much fun we had together. Mama sat speechless with an empty smile on her face, all the while probably wondering, *How can these silly girls be happy at a time like this?*

Hanging out the car window, I waved wildly as we drove away.

"Where to, hon?" Daddy turned to Mama. I hadn't seen him this carefree in a long time.

"Just somewhere to eat, Billy. I don't know where," Mama snapped at him.

"Anywhere is good for me," I chimed in, thrilled to be escaping for the day. But as I fanned myself, my happiness slowly deflated in the tense atmosphere of the car.

I hung my arms over the front seat between my parents. "Lizzie's nice, huh, Mama?"

"I guess. How would I know? I just met her." Mama's answer was flat, and she continued to face away from us. Her terse answer and attitude filled me with dread.

After our rocky start, we stopped at a small New Orleans eatery, and as I gorged myself on fried seafood, Mama sat staring at me, her face blank.

Daddy made an effort to lessen the tension. "Grammy said to tell you Miss Latil's been real sick. She asked me to drive her over to visit the old lady last week. She asked about you. Grammy told her you're doing just fine. She told her you're enjoying time with Grandma Effie."

"That's good." I helped myself to another roll.

He glanced over at Mama, who remained motionless, looking straight at me, not eating her gumbo, her mouth set in a firm, straight line.

"Eat your gumbo, Ann. It's good." He winked at me.

Mama was silent, her eyes boring into me.

I squirmed, wiping my mouth with a napkin. "What, Mama? What's wrong?"

"You eat like you're starving. You need to get a grip on yourself. How much weight have you gained?"

Immediately, I put my napkin down. Heat crept up my cheeks, and I looked down at my seven-months-pregnant belly. Who would have known my body could stretch like this? I'd become heavy and cumbersome. My fingers looked like sausages. My ankles seemed like an old lady's. I felt like a stranger lost in a different body.

"I don't know. I don't want to know. The doctor says I'm doing good. Some girls are on special diets." I chattered on nervously. "But I'm not." I pushed away the dish of bread pudding that Daddy had ordered for me. My appetite dissolved.

"Well, you better watch it. Even your face looks puffy. You'll have a hard time taking off that weight, and you won't be happy," she warned.

"I can always diet." I looked away. A lump lodged in my throat. "Mama, do you like making me feel bad? You're the one who said let's go get something to eat."

Never one for confrontation, especially between Mama and me, Daddy stood, leaving our booth to pay the bill. As I watched him walk to the front of the café, my eyes filled with angry tears.

"Stop that crying." Mama clenched her teeth. "You're overreacting. I'm just warning you before you get fat. You want that?"

"I'm sorry. Maybe I do eat too much." I wiped my eyes with my crumpled napkin.

"You do."

"I'm hungry all the time," I whispered.

"I'm just telling you for your own good." She dramatically pushed her bowl of untouched gumbo away from her. "You don't want to look like your cousin Nelda, do you? It can happen before you know it. You'll see. You'll be sorry."

This was nothing new. I had heard this lecture since I could remember. Poor Cousin Nelda was heavy and had been since she was a baby. Mama always warned me that I would soon become just like Nelda every time I took a second helping of food or poured an extra glass of milk. I was exhausted from that lecture and wanted to scream at her to stop. Instead, I changed the subject. I blurted out, "Mama, Lizzie's gonna keep her baby."

That got her attention. "That's not very smart of her. She has no idea what's ahead of her. How on earth does that silly girl plan on taking care of a baby?"

"She's gonna marry her boyfriend after she has it."

"Humph, so, her boyfriend wants to marry her? What's he been waiting for?" Mama gave me a knowing look. I shrank back in the booth.

"Don't tell anyone. I wasn't supposed to tell." I squirmed. Now I was a traitor to my friend and wished I could take back my words.

"Who would I tell?" Mama stood up and turned from me, but not before I saw angry tears in her eyes.

"Mama." I scrambled awkwardly out of the uncomfortable booth and hurried toward her. "Mama, wait."

She continued walking to the lobby toward Daddy, who waited patiently to drive us to the Vieux Carré.

As we walked the steamy sidewalks of the bustling French Quarter, I noticed that it was much tamer in the daylight than when Clay had brought me here at night the summer before.

We strolled past St. Louis Cathedral, taking in the colorful sights of New Orleans. The sights and sounds of this exotic old city still fascinated me, and in no time my hurt feelings from Mama's cutting remarks dissolved.

We peered through the tiny panes of a dusty window in a decrepit old shop on a dank side alley, deciding to enter for a bit of relief from the blazing sun. I spotted a tray of rings and stood marveling at the miniature hand-painted flowers circling each of them.

"Would you like a ring, hon?" Daddy stood next to me. "Come on. I'll get it for you."

"It's pretty, Laura. Billy, get it for her." Mama's voice was light.

Maybe I was forgiven for eating too much.

Before we headed back to the Home, we sat quietly over frosty mugs of vanilla ice cream and root beer. It had been Mama's idea to get ice cream. The icy air-conditioning felt like heaven as I slipped my shoes off under the table to rub my swollen feet against the smooth, cool tile floor. The coating of velvety ice cream in my mouth was divine. I wanted this moment to last forever. If we continued to avoid the elephant in the room, perhaps we could still laugh and talk to each other.

Mama turned back to me as we pulled up in front of the building.

I kissed her offered cheek. "Mama, I'll try to watch my eating."

"I'm only telling you for your own good."

Daddy handed me two sacks. "Bye, hon." He touched my shoulder gently. "We'll be back next month."

Tears threatened as I reached for his hand. He pulled me awkwardly into his arms, and I inhaled deeply, savoring his comforting scent. Too soon, he released me.

Sorting through my treasures that night, Lizzie and I giggled. There was a round container of rose-scented talcum powder with a fluffy puff, and the infamous candied orange slices.

The second sack, from Grammy, contained another new maternity top with a matching babushka, one of the little triangular scarves that were all the rage. She had included a note, writing that she would miss me on my birthday. As always, she asked no questions about my predicament and made no mention of the baby. That secret was even a secret between us.

She had enclosed a program from church, along with a glossy black-and-white photo of herself with Mark. In the photo, she wore one of her flowery "going to church" hats and looked as elegantly put together as ever in her light nubby suit, complete with white gloves and a set of pearls. Mark wore a dark jacket and striped tie. My chest tightened.

"Look, Lizzie, this is my grammy with my cousin Mark. Maybe this was taken on Easter?"

Glancing at the photo, Lizzie smiled. "He's handsome. Your grammy looks so nice." She turned back to the mirror. "Do you think I should do a side-swept hairdo?"

Just then, my baby kicked hard. "Wow, Jamie's wild tonight!" I laughed, holding my belly.

"Getting your attention, huh? He must have loved that ice cream float. He wants more!" Lizzie giggled.

"Smart baby," I agreed.

I lay awake for hours that evening, staring out at the dark night through the window. My eyelids heavy, my mind wide awake. *Will my life ever feel normal again? Will Grammy forgive me?* I promised myself I would make her proud when I returned home.

I poked at the tiny fist or foot that pushed me from the inside. It pushed back. Trying to imagine how a baby could be folded up inside me, I comforted myself, wrapping my arms around my middle, loving my private, special bond with this tiny miracle. I already loved him.

Chapter 21

Warm, sultry days didn't keep us girls from congregating out on the concrete slab, the awning over our heads keeping the harsh sun from frying us. We sat lazily fanning ourselves, slapping at bugs and mosquitos, and gossiping for all we were worth.

Since I worked in the nursery most nights, I usually slept late in the mornings, waking for lunch and visiting with the girls in the afternoon. Many of them would ask me to take extra care of their babies after they left the Home. I always assured them I would and did my best to pour extra love on their babies.

Abby, like Pepper, had begged me to watch over her precious boy. He was a big, healthy baby with round cheeks like Abby's.

"Laura, please hold him as long as you can and rock him extra long," Abby pleaded when she prepared to leave. She had named her baby boy Bobby.

"Abby, I'll take good care of your Bobby, and I'll write to you about him too. Okay?"

Her jaw was set, and she closed her wet eyes tightly, nodded her head at me, and turned away.

Every promise I made to my sad departing friends, I kept. All the while, I wondered who would take special care of my baby and snuggle with him when I left.

ல

Huge black clouds hung low in the sky. Thunder rumbled in, and then stifling humidity dripped in the air. As soon as I felt as if I would explode, a breeze would pick up, the clouds would part, and the sun would appear, causing steam to rise from the ground. It was that type of miserable day when three of the other girls and I were sitting outside, fanning ourselves, slapping at bugs, and reading magazines. I had wrapped a wet towel around my neck and was thinking about heading inside for a cool shower as sweat trickled down between my breasts.

The ever-present transistor radio played music by the Beach Boys. "Good, good, good vibrations," Lizzie sang along quietly. I hummed, my nose stuck in a paperback. I didn't even glance up when a girl whispered, "Hmm, who is that?"

"Hey, y'all," one of Miss Felton's pets called out as she led a new girl toward us.

I glanced up in time to see a statuesque blond swiping long corn-colored bangs out of her eyes. She smiled shyly as she was introduced.

She's perfect. Like one of those California surfer girls.

The Beach Boys played on as we tried to appear nonchalant, our eyes feasting on this new girl, who looked like one of the models in our *Seventeen* magazines.

The most amazing thing about her was that she didn't look pregnant at all. Her calico peasant blouse hung straight over a flat stomach. She rocked stylish, low-slung hip huggers that ended at her feet in huge banana bell-bottoms. Her rough, Mexican-style leather sandals were stylishly frayed, and bright orange polished toenails peeked out from them.

I felt like a walrus with my dorky glasses, oily skin, lank hair, and enormous belly. Her name was Hanna. Even her name was exotic. She mentioned that she was twenty years old and a college student. Mama would have said she was old enough to know better than to get pregnant and not so smart for a college girl.

She was from far away in California, and her grandma Mimi, who was a resident of New Orleans, had brought her here. She claimed not to have known she was pregnant until just a few weeks before. And this was the best part: She said she was due in a month.

What? One month? That's impossible. Look at her.

We glanced around at each other with knowing eyes. Our doubting faces spoke volumes.

Hanna fit in with our outside group instantly, spending the hot, humid afternoons outside on the patio, recounting her story. Her accidental and seemingly phantom pregnancy was the product of a one-night stand. After too many sloe gin fizzes, she had taken some pills a friend gave her.

Pills? Again, we all looked around at each other. *What kind of pills?*

She read our minds. "Uppers."

She had no memory of the boy she had been with. Couldn't remember his face.

Right afterward, she had been afraid she was pregnant, but when she never grew a tummy, she thought maybe she was wrong. Her periods ceased, and eventually she began to feel sensations in her lower abdomen, but never enough to alarm her.

"I was going to classes and feeling great. Everything was groovy. I never saw the guy again, so I kind of forgot about that night. Then I started getting these awful feelings in my gut. Like, you know, major gas pains."

We all laughed, nodding our heads.

"I took laxatives and felt better. Well, hell, I felt great. But then I had the worst heartburn. I couldn't eat anything without my stomach blazing. I was bloated and miserable. I started feeling pressure and jabbing movements in my stomach, ya know? Scared shitless!"

We all moved in closer, our eyes huge.

"I kept thinking it was cramps. Still no period. I took Midol all the time. *Nothing* worked."

We were mesmerized by her story and how expressive this pretty girl was, with her sharp California slang. Plus, we loved her other stories of beaches and bands and smoking grass on campus. She sparkled when she spoke, and she laughed often.

Hanna confided in a girlfriend, who insisted she go to a doctor. After all, she might have cancer or some other dreaded disease.

"I was so scared. I kept thinking, *How can I tell my folks I have cancer?*"

Her bright blue eyes shimmered. We all held our breath.

"My friend and I were stunned when the campus doctor told me the results of my test. It was worse than cancer. I was pregnant. My parents would never forgive me. They'd make me drop out of school. My life would be over."

We fell in love with Hanna and became her ardent fan club. As I listened to her, Jamie rolled over and I thought how impossible it would be for me not to realize there was a baby moving and kicking inside me.

Not wanting to tell her parents, she tearfully called her grandmother in New Orleans, who, after dropping the phone and almost fainting from shock, gathered herself and became the voice of reason that Hanna needed.

"Mimi told me to calm down. She told me we would figure this out together. She said she didn't care how it happened—let's fix it." Hanna smiled up at us as she rubbed baby oil and iodine on her long tan legs. We were spellbound watching her, waiting with bated breath for the next part of her story.

Her Mimi told her it was best that her parents never learn the truth. Together, the two of them concocted a story. Mimi called her son and his wife.

"It will add so much to Hanna's life to meet wonderful old families and learn the ways of her Southern relatives. Y'all know how I feel about California—Hanna needs to know there's more to life than suntans and music. My word, who knows what else is going on out there? I keep hearing about those wild runaways in San Francisco. No culture there. Plus, I'm not getting any younger, my dears, and she would be such a great help to me. Please, my darlings, let me have this gift of my granddaughter for a summer."

It worked, and that was how she ended up at the Home, sheltered by Mimi, who understood and supported her. Hanna felt at peace and was perfectly willing to give up this child she had not even been aware of until recently—and, incredibly, after only a few days, she did appear to be growing a belly. Delivery was closer than she or any of us realized.

From that time forward, over the years, whenever I heard the rare news story of a woman saying that she had delivered a baby after not realizing she was pregnant, I thought of Hanna. I knew it was possible; I had seen it with my own two eyes.

Hanna's stay was the shortest of any resident the entire time I was there. In less than two weeks, just when she should have been acclimating and getting a handle on the Home's routine, she experienced a short labor and in record time delivered a perfect six-pound baby girl.

The baby was a round little package with a pink rosebud mouth and a mass of straight straw-colored hair. She looked like a porcelain baby doll. Hanna named the golden bundle Sunny because she was born on a Sunday.

Three days after her baby was born, Hanna left us. She had added a bit of exotic fun and sunshine to our dull, routine days with her stories of the West Coast, along with her exuberant interest in all our lives. She left me California dreamin' more than ever.

As we said goodbye, she and I exchanged addresses and she told me her real name. As we hugged, we promised to stay in contact and to write to each other, and we did just that for a couple of years, until life got in the way.

Chapter 22

The eve of my eighteenth birthday found me trudging glumly down the hallway to the pay phone after dinner. Birthdays were never a big deal at our house. When we were small children, we had parties with friends and cousins, balloons, presents, and cake, but once we became teenagers, our parents treated birthdays much like any other day, except that Daddy would swing by Uncle Paul's bakery on his way home from work to pick up a cloyingly sweet decorated cake for the lucky birthday boy or girl. Oh, how I loved that icing.

Standing alone in the dark hallway that evening, twisting the phone cord around my hand, I listened as the phone rang repeatedly.

A polite phone operator broke in. "There seems to be no answer at this time."

Where were they?

My calls were not frequent. It was expensive to call long-distance in those days. I hung up and leaned against the wall. I hesitated dialing Grammy, because I knew she couldn't afford collect long-distance calls.

Could I have been more homesick? I missed Mama's red beans and rice and Daddy's perfect biscuits. I missed drinking hot tea with Grammy from her bone china teacups. I even missed my bratty younger brothers. I wished I could argue with them right now and boss them around until they went tattling to Mama.

A new girl sauntered up to the phone. We nodded to each other, and I walked away, dreading another evening of endless chatter with the girls. Lizzie always had a posse of friends in our room, trying new hairstyles on each other, polishing their nails hot pink or white, and dazzling each other with their stories. I didn't have it in me to join them tonight.

"Wait up!" The girl down the hall surprised me. I turned as she hurried toward me.

"No answer." She shrugged. I didn't know her or want to know her, so I remained silent, my face set.

"Want to walk over and get an RC?" she persisted.

"Uh, no, I'm headed to my room. I work night shift tonight."

"Oh, come on. You'll feel better getting out of here for a minute. I'm buying." I heard a speck of desperation in her voice. "I'm Kay."

She'd tied her dark hair back in a low ponytail with a pink paisley scarf and wore a tight top that stretched across her middle. Her eyes twinkled, and her lopsided smile was contagious.

"Okay, let's do it." I felt better just saying the words. We headed out the door, hurrying across the street to the mom-and-pop market before it closed for the night.

Within no time, we had an RC cola for her and a Barq's root beer for me and made our way to the empty patio area. Kay offered me her pack of Salems, and we smoked in the balmy air, swatting at mosquitoes as they munched on our bare legs. The smoke burned my nose and chest but felt good too. My icy root beer slid down easily, cooling my insides.

I cheered up as Kay bubbled on about her life in Alabama. She leaned toward me, waving her hands in the air when she wanted to make a point. As I settled in to listen to her story, my hopeless sadness began to ebb away.

Like so many of us, she had believed a boy who said she was the prettiest little thing in town. That boy claimed he loved her, but then, as with most of us, that boy wanted no part of a real-life baby when she accidently became pregnant. She wasn't bitter. She, like me, had been consenting. We had messed up and we were all too willing to take on the shame of our pregnancies and not put total blame on the fathers of our babies.

I told Kay that my grammy was born and raised in Alabama too and that I traveled with her every summer on the Greyhound bus to her hometown to visit our relatives. I told her about my uncle's farm and my favorite girl cousin over there, how we had run wild and free as little girls and how now, as teenagers, we hung out at the one and only Dairy Queen in that small farm town. How just last summer while I was visiting, the high school boys, after working on farms all day, used their daddies' trucks to haul a bunch of us clandestinely to Dauphin Beach at night to cool off. I loved visiting Alabama.

"I would die if my Alabama family knew I was here," I said, staring at the night sky.

Kay was getting a bit misty-eyed. She loved her family and longed to be with them. I agreed it was hard being here. I learned that she loved books almost as much as I did. We discussed books we'd read and bands we liked. I was glad I had taken her up on the soda and smoke. Under the stars, I could almost forget about graduation and my birthday.

"I better get in. I'm being eaten alive by these damn mosquitoes tonight, and I have my shift. I'm never late."

"It's still early," she protested.

"Well, Lizzie, my roommate, will be wondering where I am."

"Do you always worry so much about stuff?" She lit another cigarette.

"Yeah, I guess I do."

"You should try your call again."

I had not planned on it, but thought, *Why not? It's not that late.*

Inserting the dime in the phone, asking the operator to place a collect call and held my breath.

On the first ring, Mama picked up. "Yes, I'll accept the call," she told the operator.

"Hello?" My eyes welled up at the mere sound of her voice. "Hey, Mama." My voice caught.

"Laura, why are you calling this late? You scared me half to death."

"I have to work the night shift. It doesn't seem that late to me." Holding my breath for a minute, I worked up my courage. "Mama, do you know what happened tonight?"

"No, what?" she asked, her voice cautious.

Tears filled my eyes, and I choked out, "My class graduated. It was tonight."

Caught off guard, she sat silent for a minute. Then she said, "Well, you can't worry about that. What's done is done. Why on earth are you letting this upset you? You knew you wouldn't be there."

I imagined her sitting in her recliner with Teddy, that vicious little dog who ruled the house, in her lap. He tolerated only Mama. Silent tears slid down my checks. The hallway was dim, and a lone girl walking past gave me a wide berth, her face turned away. The wall inches from my face, I held my side.

Mama's coolness infuriated me. "It's still sad, Mama."

"Well, you need to pull yourself together. It's water under the bridge now."

Straightening up, I wiped my face with the hem of my top. "Tomorrow's my birthday," I mumbled.

My mama's voice cracked. "I know that. I know that." She started to cry, bringing me to fresh tears again. "Oh, Laura. Silly. Of course I know it's your birthday."

"I'm sorry. I didn't mean for you to cry, Mama." But secretly, part me was glad. I needed her to cry along with me. We each held our phone receiver, unable to talk. I swallowed hard, holding in a sob.

After a while, she cleared her throat. "I got you a card but haven't had a chance to mail it yet. You can't worry about what's already done. Pull yourself together. You did this, and now look at the mess we're all in. I don't know what else to say."

"I'm sorry. I just . . . Well, I wish things were different."

"Stop thinking about the graduation. Stop thinking about stuff you can't do anything about. You're always so emotional. You'll make yourself sick. You always overreact."

"I'm so sad," I mumbled. "I wanted to graduate."

We sat silently again for a while.

Mama finally said, "You need to forget about it and go to bed now. You need to rest, you hear?"

I exhaled. "I have to work tonight."

"Well, go wash your face and lie down. Tell them you can't work tonight."

"All right." I knew I'd never do that.

"Okay. We love you, Laura. You hear me? You go on now and forget about graduation, because what's done is done."

"Bye, Mama."

I leaned against the wall, the phone at my ear, listening to dead silence.

Why had I called? For a few minutes, I allowed myself the torture of visualizing my classmates celebrating after graduation. I imagined them laughing, sloe gin in the boys' flasks, the girls preening in their brand-new dresses, fancy parties full of hugs and joyful celebration. Did any of them wonder why I was missing?

I would forget this phone call. I would not let myself feel this pain again.

It doesn't matter. What's done is done. Mama's right. I knew this would happen.

Chapter 23

"You're doing fine. Probably less than a month to go." The young red-haired intern spoke into a pad of paper on the counter, ignoring me. It was June and another clinic day. Out of the corner of my eye, as I straightened my skirt, I watched him scribble.

"Um, thank you," I offered in a shy voice as I rushed from the room. *Less than a month?* My head spun.

I hurried down the hall, waving at one of the nurses' aides, rushing past the nursery window, catching the eye of a girl rocking a baby, and grinning at her, laughing out loud.

Less than a month.

Outside on the patio, Lizzie and Kay sang along with the Rolling Stones. The New Orleans radio station WTIX must have played "Ruby Tuesday" thirty times each day. As I plopped down in one of the rusty chairs, everyone looked up at me.

"I love this song, I really do." Lizzie's voice was clear and sweet as she sang the lyrics and Kay joined in.

Hands resting atop my rounded belly, I caught my breath. "Guess what, girls?" I paused for dramatic effect. "That doctor said I have less than a month."

Lizzie stopped singing midverse, her eyes huge.

"Wow, lucky you!" Kay laughed gleefully, clapping her hands. "You're gonna be home soon, Miss Lucky Laura."

Lizzie pouted. "Not lucky for me. I don't want to lose my room-mate. How can it be? But okay, okay, I'm happy for you because I know you're just miserable, honey." She looked down at her growing belly and began to rub her back, muttering, "I didn't like that doctor today."

"I liked him. He was nice to me. Lizzie, I'm not that miserable. I'm okay, just wish I could get comfortable at night. Look at this." I lifted my leg, displaying a bloated ankle that looked like it belonged to some old granny, not me.

Kay lit her cigarette. "I don't have any aches and pains. I feel great so far. Thank you, Jesus. All y'all are full of aches and pains. I never heard such complainin'. Lordy!"

Lots of backs ached. Kay was right. All we seemed to do was complain. If it wasn't our backs, it was heartburn, or food, or the heat. Simply knowing my time was just around the corner helped any discomfort I had disappear.

I had a secret: I liked being pregnant. I felt healthy and strong. But I'd never have dared to utter those words out loud—nobody had anything positive to say about gaining weight or watching stretch marks or varicose veins mar her body; no one was happy to be in this situation. An even bigger secret was that I wanted Jamie to stay inside me forever.

Many a night, Lizzie and I whispered for hours about her keeping her baby. I admired her spunk and continued to hold on to a desper-ate hope and secret fantasy that I would do the same. I daydreamed of walking through the front door of my childhood home, all smiles, a tiny bundle in my arms. I would be wearing a stylish red jumper and black tights—very mod. My hair would look lovely, sprayed into a shiny flip, just like Marlo Thomas's on *That Girl*. My perfect baby would be wrapped tight in a yellow-and-white crocheted blanket, a tiny pale blue cap sitting atop his beautiful baby head.

My fantasy always ended there. What happened after I walked

through that door was a mystery. I even had a similar dream, always waking from a sound sleep, heart thudding, my pillow stifling my sobs.

I couldn't wait to be home. On the other hand, how could I leave if it meant leaving Jamie? I kept my worries buried deep, never daring to speak them out loud.

∾

"I've decided I'm naming my baby Ruby if it's a girl and, of course, Bobby Lee Junior if it's a boy." Lizzie sat painting her toenails in the center of her bed, humming her theme song. Had I ever been more tired of a Rolling Stones song?

It had been a quiet evening for us, and I cringed as I watched the nail polish bottle tip precariously on Lizzie's bedspread.

Why do I have to be the worried "mother hen" all the time? I'm not reminding her again about the polish spilling, and that's that. She'll have to deal with it.

But I couldn't help myself. "Watch that polish, Lizzie. It's about to spill." I peeked over the paperback in front of my face.

"Who cares?" Lizzie huffed. "I hate this ugly brown bedspread. Back home my comforter is fluffy and pink. I have stuffed animals lined up across the pillows. They're all pink too. Every one of them from Bobby Lee. You worry too much, Laura." She grinned, her face covered with a pasty green beauty mask that promised to leave her already perfect complexion glowing.

"No. I don't worry too much." I threw my book down. "You don't worry enough. Someone has to be responsible around here, and it's always me. I'm damn tired of it, Lizzie."

"Ooh-wee. Someone's in a snit today." She gave me that infuriating smile again.

How she managed to look adorable with a ghoulish beauty mask drying in clumps on her face and fat sponge rollers clamped all over her head annoyed me to no end.

Without saying another word, I left the room. No denying it, Lizzie was getting on my last nerve. It seemed like I was constantly fidgety and overheated. My ankles and feet throbbed. I couldn't soak in a bathtub, since we had only a miniature shower, barely large enough to squeeze our oversize bodies into. I couldn't reach around my middle to paint my own toes, much less repaint them over and over like Lizzie.

I had only three weeks until my due date, but it seemed like three months when I thought about the long, blistering-hot days ahead. I tossed and turned every night, the air-conditioning making only a dent as the oppressive humidity and heat index of the Louisiana summer radiated down on us. I seldom sat out on the patio anymore, and staying cooped up in my air-conditioned room with the smell of mildew and layers of old hair spray had made me only more irritable.

I found Kay alone on the patio.

"Hey, girl. What y'all doing tonight?" she called as I waddled toward her.

"Lizzie's painting her toes again and trying a new beauty mask," I huffed, grimacing as I sat down gingerly on the warm metal. Even my bottom hurt. "I'm doin' nothin', as usual. I'm sick of this place."

"You sound mad as a hornet, girl. You okay?"

"I'm fine. Only tired, I guess." I stared up at the black night sky.

"Want a smoke?" She leaned over, her pack extended.

"I need to stop. I can't smoke when I go back. My mama and grammy would die if they saw me smoking a cigarette. Nobody smokes in my house."

"Really? Huh—everyone smokes in mine. Even my ninety-year-old granny, Bunny." She quietly hummed "Ruby Tuesday." "Lizzie's got me humming that song all day long." Kay's voice was tender. "She told me her plan. She wants to keep her baby."

"You think she will?" I reached over and helped myself to a cigarette from her pack, forgetting I planned to stop.

"God knows. She's pretty determined. She's a little spitfire." She
looked up at the dark sky, blowing smoke rings. "Knowing Lizzie, yes,
probably." Kay's voice was tinged with amusement.

We sat still while crickets and millions of bugs serenaded us.

In that moment, I realized I truly did hope the best for Lizzie. I
loved her and would cheer for her no matter what. "She's brave. I'll
give her that. I hope she keeps her baby, and I hope Bobby Lee mar-
ries her."

Mosquitoes sucked the blood from my elephant ankles. A few
trills of laughter came from the girls' lit windows surrounding the
courtyard. Faint sounds from the neighborhood swirled in the dark,
along with insects adding their serenade to the night. A car horn
beeped; a tinny radio played Dixieland music. Occasionally a conversation was loud enough to be audible as the neighbors walked the
sidewalks surrounding us.

Here we sat, smack in the middle of this old city, hidden and
invisible.

Chapter 24

Mail arrived the next morning, and that always cheered me. I quickly peeled open the first letter. Written on lined notebook paper, Mama's distinctive cursive read:

> *Dear Laura,*
> *I have been busy. We are all fine. Your brothers are out of school now. This summer is miserable—hot and muggy. At least you have air-conditioning there, so that is good.*
> *Your daddy and me are coming to see you next Sunday. I hope you are okay.*
> *Love,*
> *Your mama*

Only three more days and they would be here to visit. This time, I would be sure not to upset Mama. Just the thought of a good meal in a restaurant and an outing made my day. And just maybe we could talk about Jamie.

Grammy's card was lovely. Always frugal yet creative, she had drawn pastel flowers on a piece of paper with colored pencils and taped it on the front of a slip of heavy paper. Inside she had written a sweet verse about how she was thinking of me.

To my sweet Lady Bug, the note began. I traced the words with my finger. Her handwriting was rough, with a few misspelled words scattered throughout the letter. She had taught herself to read and write as a young girl on a sharecropper's farm in Alabama in the early 1900s.

I do miss you so much. I hope your halth is good. Church servus
was a nice one Sunday. Miss Elenore fell, hurt her back. Say a
prayer. It's sure hot here but I still work in my garden every day.
You will be home soon Honey.
I love you so,
Your Grammy

My eyes welled. I peered out the front of the building. The rain splashed on the dirty sidewalks, and the muddy gutters were filling with debris. Still miserably hot, gloomy, and tiresome.

It won't be long before I'm out of here. Soon. Very soon, I consoled myself.

ॐ

Sunday morning, the room was dark and gloomy and thunderclouds hung low in the sky, but my mood was light and sunny as I showered and pondered what to wear for my parents' visit.

Lizzie came rushing into our room, a new friend in tow. "You sure look pale, Laura. You feel okay?" She hovered over me, redoing my hair, spritzing away at my head with her can of Aqua Net. "Your hair's gonna fall if you don't spray more. God, I sure hate summertime."

Poor Lizzie—she only wanted to help, but watching her new friend boldly thumbing through my magazine and enduring Lizzie's unwanted fiddling with my hair caused my chest to tighten and my neck to burn.

"Ugh, Lizzie, Lizzie. Stop. Stop sprayin' that stuff. I'm chokin' here."

I coughed and pulled away, waving the strong fumes from my face. "I don't care if my hair falls. It's just my mama and daddy coming to visit. They don't give a hoot about my hair."

I glanced in the mirror. A tired, irritated girl, dark circles under her eyes, sporting an enormous belly, stared back at me. Even my largest maternity top stretched tight and uncomfortable across my body now. No amount of hair spray would help me look better, I thought, as I wiped the glue-like spray off the lenses of my glasses.

"Sorr-*y*, Miss Grumpy. I swear, I can't say anything—you're all over me. I was just tryin' to help you look presentable." Lizzie had had enough of me too. "Come on, Vicki, let's get out of here and go to your room. Someone"—she looked pointedly at me—"is hateful today." She huffed as she and the newest member of her fan club stomped out of the room.

Good riddance.

Mama and Daddy arrived earlier than usual. Daddy's eyes widened and I didn't miss the look on Mama's face as they watched me waddle out to the car. My middle had enlarged rapidly this past month. No doubt Cokes and chocolate bars had contributed.

Once we were in the car, Daddy glanced back at me with a grin. My heart leaped with love. Mama sat staring quietly out her side window.

Here we go. She's miserable. I felt even worse now. *I wish Daddy had come alone and left her at home.*

Scattered showers pelted the restaurant window as we sat eating our lunch, but when we walked outside the rain had stopped and the air seemed a bit cooler. We headed to Audubon Park, planning to stroll among the lush, shaded trees. Today the park was virtually empty, and the air seemed to grow more oppressive with each step.

"Can we sit down?" I folded onto the first bench we came to. "I don't feel so good." Sweat beads broke out all over my face, and waves of nausea swept over me.

Mama quickly sat next to me, vigorously fanning me with her white handkerchief. She put her hands on my shoulders and searched my face. Her touch and kindness would have brought me to my knees if I hadn't been sitting.

"Billy, look at her. We can't stay here. Laura, are you okay?"

Daddy stood over us. "We have to take her back."

"No, no. I just need to rest. Please don't take me back," I begged. "It's so hot. I ate too much. I'll be okay; I just need to catch my breath."

"Billy, she can't stay out in this heat. We need to go somewhere with an air conditioner." Mama was on the verge of frantic. "Laura, do you think it's time?"

Time? "Uh, no." I hesitated. *We're talking about the baby coming. We never do that.* I added cautiously, "No, I think I'm just overheated, maybe?"

"Let's go." Daddy started walking away, and we stood up and followed, my knees wobbly. Mama held my arm, her face set and worried.

༃

"Okay, girls, I'm going in and getting us a room. I'll be right back," Daddy announced, as we pulled into a gravel parking lot close to Lake Pontchartrain. The motel was painted a dusty mustard yellow, with blood-red trim peeling around the windows and doorways. TRAVEL STOP INN, the sign read. A neon sign in the window blinked: V-C-NCY.

"You can take a bath and cool off here. That's what you need." The concern in Mama's eyes almost made my distress worthwhile. This was the Mama I longed for.

"I'm feeling better. I got overheated is all. But to tell ya the truth, I'd love a bath."

The icy air in the simple room brought immediate relief. It was darkened with blackout drapes and carried a faint smell of damp carpet and old cigarettes. The wall-unit air conditioner droned steadily and dripped slowly into an aluminum bucket. Between the two double beds, the requisite Gideons' Bible sat on a squat night-stand. Best of all, there was a large bathroom with pink and black tiles and a long, narrow bathtub along the wall. The faucets dripped steadily, and a harsh brown rust stain ran from the spigot to the floor of the tub.

That ugly bathtub looked glorious to me.

Daddy left us and came back carrying a plastic tub filled with ice, and three bottles of RC cola. He settled into a chair across the room and began working on a crossword puzzle as Mama filled a towel with ice, instructing me to recline on one of the lumpy beds with the towel across my forehead while she ran a tepid bath.

"After your bath, you'll lie down and take a nap. Then you'll feel better." Mama helped me into the bathroom.

As I carefully immersed myself in the lukewarm, velvety water, delighting in the lemon scent of the tiny bar of hotel soap, time stood still. I thought about how this was the last place I had thought we'd be when I'd woken that morning, but it had turned out to be the best place.

"You okay in there?" Mama called through the closed door. "Did you lock this door?"

"Yes, Mama. I'll get out in a minute."

"Laura, you unlock this door. You could faint in there."

"I will. Just give me some time, Mama." I didn't move. She would have to wait.

"I worry if this door is locked."

"Please, Mama. I need this time alone. Please."

A tear trailed silently down my face as Jamie jolted me with a pow-erful kick. It was as if he wanted to remind me he was there as my heart was breaking. Could he really know my moods? He was part of me, after all. I pressed my hand on what was either a tiny foot, fist, or elbow pushing outward and creating a bump on the pale, blue-veined sphere that pushed up out of the water.

Will I ever look normal again? Maybe now I should ask them if we can keep the baby. Maybe Mama will understand. She can make Daddy agree.

I'll never know how long I stayed in that tub, but it seemed like hours of pure bliss, because privacy and a bath had been impossible for months. After my fingers and toes shriveled and I had assured Mama several times I was "doing fine," I heaved my bulky body out of the water. I would never take a simple soak for granted again.

℘

As I pulled myself from a deep sleep, my parents' hushed voices murmured. How long had we been in this the motel room? I lay still and disoriented.

"She's better now, hon. Just overheated. She'll be okay," Daddy whispered.

"I know, Billy."

Was Mama crying? "I don't like to see her like this. She must be so uncomfortable in this heat. Poor thing. She looks awful, and that baby must be huge."

I stiffened.

"It's obvious she has no idea what she's in for." Mama sniffed.

"Well, we have to take her back. It's gettin' late."

At that moment, I felt cherished by parents, who whispered so as not to wake me. Who had sat quietly for hours in this dark room, allowing me to rest. I couldn't let them down. They had continued to love me after I had disappointed them in the worst way. I simply had to do what they wanted me to do.

Chapter 25

" I t's horrible. I can't stand to think about it."

We girls had been repeating those words all day long after we heard the news that the movie star Jayne Mansfield had been killed in a horrific car wreck. She had been performing in a nightclub on the beach right in my hometown and was headed back to New Orleans on the highway when the horrendous accident happened. Her children, the only survivors, were in that car as well. The rumors were rampant, and the descriptions of the accident became more gory by the hour. We kept glued to the radio and newspapers, unable to stop talking about it.

"What are ya gonna do when you go back home, Laura?" a friendly girl, Linda, asked, changing the subject. She sat fanning herself with an old church fan, her ginger hair rolled in two-inch steel rollers. "You're lucky. You can forget about all of this after you have the baby." She smiled at me, all sugar and spice.

Something told me there was no forgetting this place, this time, or this baby inside me. "I can't even think about what I'm gonna do when I leave here. I guess I'll get a job," I mumbled.

We all sat silent in our own world among the constant hum of insects. Lizzie changed the station on the transistor radio. The Association was singing their hit song "Cherish," soothing us with the soft and wistful lyrics. First one girl, then another, hummed along, and soon we all began to sing.

Each in our own thoughts, we listened as the song played on. Tears wet my eyes, and a profound sadness clamped itself around my shoulders. *We are all broken.*

As the song came to an end, I heard a few sniffles and felt a heavy sorrow for all of us. No one made eye contact, but slowly the mood lightened and the girls began to chatter.

"Hey, did y'all know Mama Cass named her baby girl Owen? I think it's kinda cute for a girl. Different. Mama Cass wasn't married, ya know. That didn't stop her from keeping her baby. I read that in a movie magazine."

"Ewww . . . Owen? For a girl? I hate it." Lizzie was disgusted. All the girls agreed.

I stood and stretched. "See y'all tomorrow. I'm going up to my room."

As I walked away, the girls' voices, soft and fuzzy, called out gentle "good nights" in the moist night breeze. A riverboat's horn blasted a lonely sound on the Mississippi in the distance.

My departure was close, and part of me dreaded leaving this sisterhood of girls. All our conversations revolved around "when we get out of this place" and what would be waiting for us when we got home. We dared not say it out loud, but we all knew life would never be the same.

ॐ

Later that night, I slowly walked the peaceful, dim halls towards the nursery. Delli had been another surprise in my life. I could not remember ever feeling awkward with her. The difference in our skin color meant nothing to me now. How ignorant I had been. This kind woman had taught me powerful lessons by example, by accepting me, and through her unjudgmental character. She loved all life, new and old, and a powerful, serene aura flowed from her.

I washed up before the feedings. Delli touched my shoulder shyly, and I turned around to face her. "Yes, ma'am, you're 'bout to pop," she said. "Won't be long, Laura."

Washing up, I chuckled. "Well, I don't think I can get much bigger, and I'm weeks past the first due date the doctor in Mississippi told my mama." I tugged at my uniform, which pulled across my girth. "Guess nobody knows for sure, because I sure don't feel like I'm having a baby tomorrow."

"It's soon. I'm always right about that. I'm gonna miss you. You're a good girl and a hard worker."

After I had my baby, I would probably never see her again. I would miss laughing together every night and how we shared treats, along with stories. I'd miss our easy banter and how she had never made me feel worthless or stupid. I had poured out my heart to her about my life. I had cried to her about Clay. She always listened. In turn, I felt as if I knew her husband, Roy. I knew her kids' names and could describe each of them. I knew her worries; she knew mine.

"Delli, maybe we'll see each other again. I could come back and visit you. I'll write to you. Promise you'll write back."

"Well, honey chile, I don't think you're ever gonna want to come back here. And I do understand that." She gave me that radiant smile of hers. "We're from different worlds. And you know what? It's okay, child."

"I'm your friend, Delli. I'll always remember how good you've been to me. Always."

"I'll always remember you too, Laura."

The babies were starting to stir and make their newborn whimpers, hungry and restless. A shrill wail broke the peaceful moment. "We got us some hungry cherubs to feed." Delli shook her head playfully and grinned as we both hurried into the inner nursery to do our jobs. The subject was closed. The moment was lost. She was all business again.

Changing the diaper of a chubby red-haired baby boy, I cooed and he stopped fussing. His wise newborn eyes peered into mine. His tiny mouth twisted in a half smile, or maybe it was gas. Who knew? All I knew was that my heart clenched when I looked at that miniature heart-shaped face. "You sweet baby boy, you, little Andy," I whispered, holding him close.

I never worked in the nursery again after that night.

Chapter 26

I woke early on July 7, feeling determined to take on the world. "Good, good, good vibrations." I sang the Beach Boys' song softly as I thought about my day ahead. It was time I made a change. I had been lazy. I would head down to breakfast and then come back to my room and look over my long-forgotten correspondence courses. I would buckle down and complete them. Yes, I would stop hanging out and gossiping with everyone and wasting my days.

By the time I had eaten breakfast and listened to all the goings-on at our table of chattering girls, I had forgotten any plans to turn over a new leaf. We were going on an outing. Schoolwork could wait.

Our plan was to head out for a walk, jump on a streetcar, and head downtown for a few hours before anyone realized we were gone. It was exciting, a little dangerous, and just what we needed to escape another routine, boring day.

Lizzie and I left the dining room, eager for a new adventure. Halfway up the stairs, I stopped. Vibrations pulsated through my thighs, with enough pressure to make me pause. A dull heaviness weighed me down with each step.

"Come on, Laura. Step it up." Lizzie looked down from the landing.

"I feel kind of weird, like my legs are hurting right here." I rubbed the fronts of my thighs. "Today's my due date. Did you remember?"

"Good grief. You look fine. Come on, let's get ready. The girls will leave without us."

In the room I hesitated, doubt chewing at the edges of my mind. "Lizzie, I probably shouldn't go today. I mean, what if the baby does come? It's so hot. What if I get sick like I did last week? What if—"

"Do you have a backache? 'Cause that's what you get when you go into labor. All the girls say that," she called from the bathroom.

"Um, no backache."

"Well, then that's that. You're not in labor. And if you get sick, we'll come back. I can't stand this place one more day. I'm so dang bored I could scream!" From my vantage point, I could see Lizzie waving her arms around dramatically.

"But last time it was hours before we got on the streetcar coming back. Remember? We got lost. I shouldn't go anyway. I have to get back to my studies."

"What? Studies? I can't believe you sometimes, Laura. You pass up fun for the worst reasons. Well, I'm going, so you just stay here and study your little heart out. You're gonna be jealous when we get back." She continued making last-minute touches to her stiff bouffant hairstyle.

Pulling the correspondence courses out of the box under my bed, I pretended to pore over them as she left with a gleeful, "You're gonna be sorry. We'll miss you. Toodle-oo."

A growing heaviness had filled my lower pelvic area within a couple of hours, and the muscles in my thighs tightened painfully. Uncomfortable and a little worried, I tried to rest on my bed.

Maybe these were those false labor pains, Braxton Hicks contractions. All of us girls knew about them. How embarrassing would it be if I went down to the clinic and they told me I wasn't in labor?

I tried to read my schoolwork, but I daydreamed instead, thinking of the time I started my period. How Mama had told me I was now a woman and could have babies when I got married. I had been twelve and happy because now I would be like the girls at my junior high who bragged about having already started. Mama was so happy for me. She let me stay home from school and took me along with her to her coffee klatch at Miss Lena Mae's that morning. We celebrated my becoming a woman with a fun lunch of fried shrimp in paper boats, salty french fries, and icy root beer at A&W. Now look how things had turned out.

I couldn't sit still, get comfortable, or forget the constant ache in my upper thighs.

Could this be labor? It's not so bad.

By noon, mild contractions started. I was becoming anxious and felt shaky inside. Hidden away in my room, I ached. My back didn't hurt at all. Was Lizzie right? If my back didn't hurt did that mean I wasn't really in labor?

I rubbed my mountain of a belly, gently pushing down, trying to get a kick or some movement from Jamie. He seemed awfully still.

He isn't moving. Please, God, make sure he's okay.

Lizzie and the girls wouldn't be back until suppertime, so I decided to wait. Lizzie would know what to do.

At three o'clock, in the bathroom, I noticed a small spot of blood on my underwear. Reality slammed me. As I showered, I doubled over when a raft of new, steady cramps hit me hard. Fear hovered over me, but I felt oddly detached.

Out of the shower, I made my way down the hall. At this point I didn't care if I was wrong about this being labor. If they sent me back to my room, I would laugh it off.

At least they'll know what to do, and maybe they can give me some medicine for the cramps.

But my head knew. These were not plain old cramps. Jamie was coming. As I headed down the hall, a small girl named Betsy smiled as I passed her. Her smile left her face as she stared at me.

"Hey. You okay?"

Sweat pooled under my arms and beaded across my forehead,

but I tried to sound carefree and made an effort to stand up straight. "Yeah, I think so. Hey, if you see Lizzie at supper, can you tell her I had to go to the clinic?"

"You in labor?" Betsy's eyes were huge. She stared at the belly hanging in front of me as if it might explode.

"I think. Maybe? Not sure."

"Well, I'm sure! Lordy! I'll walk with you, and, oh yeah, I'll tell Lizzie. Where is she now?"

"Not sure," I lied.

∾

After one look at me, the nurse on duty steered me toward the labor room. "Okay, dear, undress now, and here's a gown. Let's get you in bed. I'll be right back." She had a kind, no-nonsense way about her, and I was finally at ease. This nurse would know what to do.

And this isn't too bad. Uncomfortable, but I can handle it.

After wrapping a black sleeve around my arm and taking my blood pressure three different times, the nurse's forehead furrowed and she was all business.

"Try to relax, dear."

A contraction grew as she inserted her fingers inside me to probe about.

"Ahhh!" I was ashamed for crying out, but the pain sliced me in two.

"Well, my dear, you are definitely in labor and dilating nicely. You should have come down sooner," she scolded gently, as she removed her gloves and wrote something in my chart. Heading out of the room, she threw over her shoulder, "Will be right back. Just lie quietly, dear."

Tears slid down my cheeks as she swished out of the room, leaving me completely alone. Solid fear gripped my gut as another contraction wormed its way up my thighs and into my pelvic area. This was getting serious.

Be brave.

Amid the waves of contractions, the nurse kept coming in and out of the room and taking my blood pressure repeatedly. By the time a doctor arrived, I was dying of thirst, as well as scared to death. Feeling as if my bladder was about to burst, I kept thinking I should get up, but the nurse sternly forbade me to get out of the bed and shoved a bedpan under my hips, leaving it there while she stood in the hall, conferring with the doctor.

She removed the uncomfortable steel pan, and the doctor returned to administer another painful exam. She replaced the pan in one fluid movement as the doctor grumbled and mumbled, peering into my eyes with his own red-rimmed, muddy brown eyes. His heavy black eyebrows grew into a single line across his forehead, giving him a frightening, angry appearance. I wondered if I was keeping him from his supper.

"You're comin' along there, girl. Stay calm. You'll have this baby tonight." His voice was rumbling and deep, and I immediately knew he wasn't irritated, just concerned. He checked my blood pressure again and started to leave the room but then stopped and said, "Don't worry. You'll do fine. You're built to have babies."

"Built to have babies"? Not a compliment, in my opinion. It made me sound like a broodmare. But I shoved down the humiliation.

The next thing I knew, the nurse was gently shaking me, explaining that they needed to transport me to Baptiste Hospital in New Orleans. She didn't say why, and I was beyond asking questions, because the pains had resumed with a vengeance.

"Here, dear, let me help you sit up." The nurse pulled me to a sitting position. A loud groan issued from somewhere deep inside me, startling me as a powerful contraction took control of my body. I gagged as nausea consumed me. I started heaving bile all down my front.

I feared I might be dying. My teeth chattered uncontrollably, and my hands and feet felt numb. Then everything went blank.

Chapter 27

I have no memory of the ride to the hospital. Of being admitted. Of signing anything. I have no idea who left me there. All of that is a mystery. No matter how hard I strain my brain to remember, I have not retained a minute of that lost time.

The next memory is crystal clear. I wake up in what appears to be a large, impersonal hospital. Glaring lights, loud noises, someone moaning. I'm in a long, narrow hallway on a gurney, lying on a cold plastic pad that crunches and squeaks underneath me with every movement I make. Injured or sick people, their faces twisted and hurting, sit along the wall, slumped in hard wooden chairs.

A child is whimpering, an old Black man is praying out loud to Jesus, and a woman is sobbing. Someone is speaking rapidly in a foreign language and although I do not understand what he is saying, I hear the desperation and fear in his voice. The common denominator of everyone in the hall is that we are all miserable, in distress, or in pain. We look anywhere except at each other. Neglected and alone, I stare up at the ceiling, trying to breathe. The plaster above me is cracked in places, and I see black mildew spreading like spiderwebs across the cracks.

Time crawls on; the cruel contractions continue relentlessly. I'm trying to be brave, pressing my lips together and doing my best not to make a sound. There's no one at my side to comfort me. No one speaks to me. Medical staff walk past me without a glance. Tears track down my face. I have never felt this frightened, this abandoned.

Once again, my memory fails me. I'll never know how long I was left in that hallway. I clearly recall being completely alone in a dim, windowless cubbyhole of a room. I'm in a high, narrow hospital bed, and metal safety bars surround me, making it impossible for me to roll off the bed or even climb out. The bars are painted a pale hospital green. The thick paint is chipped. I watch my fingers clasp those bars tightly as I strain with each contraction.

A tall nurse pushes into my room, rolling a cart filled with dangerous-looking contraptions spread across it. She is vast, filling the small room with her presence. Her sleeves are rolled high, revealing massive arms. Silently, she goes about her business of positioning a stainless-steel bowl next to me on the bed and pulls away the top sheet, shoving my hospital gown up to my chest. I shiver with fear as frigid, stale air makes contact with my overheated, damp body.

With a grim face and no explanation, she quickly swabs cold water from my waist down and in between my legs, abruptly pushing them apart. I see the flash of a straight razor gleaming in the dim light.

Oh God . . . Oh no . . . Is she cutting me to help the baby come out? I remember the bloody mess of Pepper's episiotomy.

I cringe, staring at the ceiling, biting my lip, steadying myself, preparing for the worst. Still not speaking, she proceeds to suds my most private parts and then expertly shaves my entire pubic area in minutes. I am mortified. The contractions continue to encircle my middle, and I squirm, twisting away from them.

Next, this silent woman pushes me roughly, rolling me onto my side and shocking my senses as she unexpectedly pushes my buttocks apart and rams a ridged probe into my bottom. I try to pull away, groan, and thrash some more. Her heavy hand splays on my side, clasping me so tightly and hard that I can't move.

She is pushing a frigid fluid inside me, seemingly never-ending gallons of it, and I worry I might faint. I have never had this happen in my life. Along with the contractions, I have never known such pain.

After I feel as if I will burst, the monster nurse jerks the apparatus out of me, simultaneously shoving a bedpan under me. I am humiliated, hurt, and confused, and now I experience the added indignity of my bowels emptying into the metal bedpan.

I did not witness any of this when I sat with Pepper in labor. She was prepped long before I went to her room. At that time, I had no idea that a prebirth enema was standard procedure in hospitals for laboring mothers. It seemed cruel, barbaric. No young ladies talked about such things in detail, and there was always an air of mystery surrounding this part of labor, even at the Home. Was this part a secret? Had I not listened?

I'll never know whether I simply thought the nurse was indifferent and uncaring or whether she was simply a brute. I do know she was brisk and businesslike and gave me no words of comfort or encouragement. An aura of anger and disgust radiated from her. Either she hated her job or she hated me.

Gathering the courage to speak as she cleaned up her supplies to roll out of the room, I begged her desperately for water. She turned away silently and walked out, never to return.

∾

Cries and moans emit from all the rooms surrounding me. Shrill female voices curse and yell. The sounds ring loudly in my ears, and the more deafening they become, the quieter I become, shrinking away from this reality that must be hell.

What did I expect? I deserve this. This is what happens when you screw up.

At my lowest point, what seems like a dream unfolds. Mama walks through the door. Tiny and disheveled, she gazes at me on the bed, rolled into a ball. My tortured face and damp hair tangled in clumps must be a sight, because her face betrays her horror.

Is she real? I blink my eyes, and yes, she's real. I break into sobs of relief.

"Mama, Mama. Help me. I can't do this." I claw toward her with outstretched arms.

"Shh, Laura, get ahold of yourself." She reaches through the bars to touch my shoulder. "Quiet, now. I'm here."

"I can't do this! I can't! Why didn't you tell me?"

"You need to calm down." She starts crying along with me.

"Mama, it's bad. Why didn't you tell me?" I demand.

"I couldn't tell you. You wouldn't have believed me anyway." She held my hand. "Now, try to calm down. It'll be over soon." Her hand is warm on my shoulder, and although her voice has become matter-of-fact and terse, I see in her sad eyes the same fear and sadness that I'm feeling. But there's something else there too. Shame, embarrassment, something. Is it because of the fuss I'm making or simply that I'm in this place and the disgrace of it all?

I wish I didn't have to see that look on her face. I wish she wasn't here.

When another contraction grips my body, I roll away from her.

I never heard anyone at the Home say that her mother was with her during labor. Years later, I reflected on this act of love. Receiving a call alerting them that I had gone into labor and had been swooped off to a city hospital, Daddy and Mama dropped everything and made the two-hour drive to be near me.

I imagined Daddy pacing nervously downstairs in the waiting room while Mama frantically asked for me at the admissions desk, demanding she see me. A shy woman in unfamiliar places and circumstances, she searched for and found me in the belly of this enormous hospital. In those days, it was not routine practice to allow family in labor rooms, but my determined mama had bullied her way into mine, all five feet of her. She was going to see her daughter no matter who she had to fight with. Now, here she stood at my side as I labored to bring her first grandchild into the world, just to give him away. Like mothers and daughters throughout time, we suffered this pain together.

Soon an overworked, disgruntled nurse bustles into the dimly lit room, surprised to see Mama. "Sorry, ma'am, nobody is allowed in these rooms. Even mamas. You have to say bye now. We'll take care of your girl."

Mama doesn't argue with her. Her hand still resting on my shoulder through the pale green bars, she whispers, "You can do this. Be brave." Another contraction spirals, ready to slam my body as she presses my shoulder, turns, and leaves the dark cave of a room.

Nobody enters after that as I whimper for help, frightened to death something is wrong.

I remember only pain, until another overworked nurse enters the room. She doesn't explain anything, simply inserts a needle in my arm, leaving me moaning one minute as the hot sting spreads all the way up to my shoulder, and only a dull blackness after that.

∾

Where am I? What happened? God, I'm so thirsty.

My eyes slit open to bright yellow light. I detect an astringent, antiseptic smell, along with the strong scent of bleach and the weight of heavy, stiff sheets covering me. I lie on my back as my consciousness pushes cobwebs from my brain. Foggy and parched, I lick my dry lips. Have wads of cotton been forced down my raw throat?

My hand reaches for my baby. There's no hill of a belly, only a flat, empty sack where my Jamie lay yesterday. A panicky shiver runs through me.

I don't even remember giving birth. Where is my baby? Did he die? Crushing grief floods me.

My last memory is excruciating pain and confusion in the labor room. Jamie is gone, my body deflated. Heaviness closes over me. I can't think or move.

Is my baby alive? Is it a boy? A girl?

Struggling to push open my heavy eyelids again, I take in my surroundings. Sunbeams glow and pour through tall windows. Everything is fuzzy white and pale yellow, the colors of gelatinous eggs. Without my glasses, I experience my world as a blur, but I see a group of women propped up in beds that encircle this room, facing each other.

Am I dreaming? Invisible, I observe these laughing women. They speak softly, smiling at one another. They cluck, nodding their heads, each telling her own story. I swallow as I watch them pour water from pitchers. The tinkling sounds of ice splashing into pale green glasses are torture. They sip nonchalantly. They all seem much older than I am, and smarter. Their chatter goes on relentlessly. No one is paying me any mind. As I listen covertly, I realize they are talking about their babies and their deliveries. And their husbands.

I am not like these women, so confident, so full of laughter. I close my eyes, and a hard lump fills my dry throat.

Where is my baby?

"Well, our new little mama's awake." The loudest woman in this group of new mothers announces. "Lord, you were out, sugar, and I mean *out*." Her strong New Orleans accent and grating voice announces the type of woman she is. One of those women who take charge whether asked to or not. One of those women who always asks inappropriate questions. The type everyone steps back from. She scares the hell out of me.

What will she ask me? Will she ask if my baby is a boy or girl? What will I say? Will she ask if my husband is excited about the new baby?

Horrified that I will have to make conversation with this woman, I'm saved by a nurse who strides into the room and heads straight to my bed. Her hair is a fiery pile of red curls flattened by her white cap. Hundreds of freckles decorate a wide, smiling pink face. Thick black-framed glasses perch on her nose.

She chortles, "I sure am happy to see you're finally awake. I bet you're hungry as a mama bear."

"Thirsty," I croak. "Ma'am, my glasses?" I whisper.

She quickly produces my glasses from a white sack under the nightstand.

"I can't see a thing without mine either, sugar. Blind as a bat." She smiles. I place my glasses on my face, grateful to her because now I can see clearly and even more so because she's saving me from having to make conversation with the gawking women.

As she bends over, I breathe in her scent: cigarettes, soap, Juicy Fruit gum. She begins cranking my bed up to a semisitting position and promptly sticks a thermometer in my mouth. Next, she takes my blood pressure. "Still a teeny bit high," she mutters to herself. The room has gotten quiet, and all eyes seem to be on me. Heat climbs up my neck and cheeks.

Pushing on rubber gloves, she pulls the sheets off me as she simultaneously whips a curtain around my bed. She peers between my legs and without a pause removes bloody pads from under me, replacing them with fresh, clean ones. The metallic scent of blood fills my nostrils and wafts about me. My face blazes.

"Do you need the bedpan, honey?" She seems to study my eyes.

"No, ma'am," I mumble, as she bundles up the mess from my bed.

"We don't want you getting up out of bed to go to relieve yourself in the ladies' room yet. Too soon. Understand?" She removes her gloves, tucks the stiff white sheets tightly around me, and, without waiting for an answer, whips the curtains back again, exposing me to the room.

All business, she grabs a pitcher on my nightstand and pours water into one of the green glass cups. "I'll get you some food up here. Want some juice first?" She's studying the chart on a clipboard attached to the foot of my bed, making notes. She's a whirlwind.

Does that chart say I'm an unwed mother? Does it say I can't see my baby? That I'm an unfit mother?

It must not, because she's still smiling.

Cool tap water slides down my throat, and I nearly cry with relief. I reach for the pitcher to pour more. Screwing up my courage, I whisper, "Um, ma'am . . . my . . . um, my baby?"

"Oh, we'll be bringing them out soon."

Them? My mouth drops open.

She turns and announces to the room, "Ladies. Ladies. Feeding time in a few minutes."

Then, turning back to me, she smiles. "Your baby boy is doing fine. I'll bring him to you. You feel up to feeding him?"

Choking on my mouthful of water, I say, "Oh, yes, I know how to feed him."

My heart soars. *She said my little boy is fine. I just knew it. He's a boy.*

The women are all atwitter now, talking among themselves. Turning away from them, I feel my insides tremble. Blood silently gushes out of my body, warm and sticky, pooling onto the new pads.

An uninterested aide enters the room and pushes a glass of orange juice at me. I gulp it down. The juice is frosty and golden, like pure sunshine. I feel stronger, more alert, as I fully wake from my drugged stupor.

I lie back, eyes closed. *If they think I'm sleeping, no one will ask me questions.* I turn my head away from everyone, eavesdropping on their happy chatter.

A tall aide enters the room. "Flowers for Mrs. Hammond," she calls out.

"Oh, my Joseph. He's an angel," Mrs. Hammond shouts. Through slitted eyes, I watch as the aide carries a massive vase of pink hydrangeas over to the brash woman's bed. It completely covers the small metal nightstand. All the new mothers ooh and aah.

Minutes later, cries of newborns echo from the hall. My eyes open wide, and I watch as nurses enter, pushing bassinets, wheels clicking. The nurses begin pairing the babies with their mamas, all business. I pull myself up, sitting as straight as I can. My heart pounds so loudly, I'm sure everyone in the room can hear it. I chew the inside of my mouth, afraid I'll cry out loud as tears spring into my eyes.

A petite blond nurse with a pixie haircut walks straight up to the foot of my bed, checks my name on the chart, and bends to pick up a tiny bundle from the bassinet. I swallow a sob as I glimpse a blue-and-white flannel blanket, frayed and pilled, obviously laundered a thousand times.

My heart stops. My arms reach out.

"Here's your mama," Pixie Nurse chirps to the bundle. She places it carefully in my arms.

This is Jamie. This is my son. This is my baby boy. This is a miracle. This is me feeling like I have never felt in my life.

It feels so right as my arms cradle my solid, seven-pound boy, swaddled tightly, sleeping soundly. I have held and cared for countless infants in the nursery for months, but nothing has prepared me for holding my own son, my flesh, my blood. Tears steadily wet my face as I study the miracle in my arms.

His face. His face. I know the curve of his cheek, the furrowed forehead. His lips.

Soft, downy cheeks; almond eyes with almost transparent lashes lying on those cheeks; tiny, perfect pink lips; pale fuzz on his head; and peachy seashell baby ears. He has my nose. What's this? A pale bruise on the right side of his face and a red dent on the left temple. Is he hurt? I hug him close, feeling the weight of him, breathing in his new-baby scent.

My son.

Holding him is exquisite joy, exquisite pain.

Suddenly I realize the nurse has been standing over me impatiently, trying to explain that I am to "give him his bottle. He probably won't take much. Too sleepy yet. He's still so new. But let's give it a try."

She's tugging at my arms, telling me I'm holding him too tightly. To relax. "Loosen your grip there, Mama. He's not going anywhere," she jokes. I flinch.

I pull away from her and hug him more closely. I assure her that I've fed lots of babies and know what to do. I want her to leave us alone. I won't meet her eye. Rebuffed, she scurries away.

"Oh, Jamie. It's you. Hey. I'm your mama," I whisper. I am giddy. I am in love. The activity in the room swirls around us, yet we are alone. My heart soars.

Jamie lies half asleep in my arms. His eyes are silvery slits, and he couldn't care less about eating. His little face twists into a newborn grimace, but finally he latches onto the brown rubber nipple. I watch with fascination as his mouth works at sucking, stops, seems to drop off again, sucks, and stops, and his eyelids flutter.

He seems plain worn out. I jiggle him gently, along with the bottle. Oh so gently I tease his lips until he puckers them in a teeny "o."

I'm mesmerized. *He is perfect, this son of mine. I know this tiny boy. I've felt his every move within my body for the past five months.*

The conversations around the room break into my consciousness.

"Yeah, I nursed my last girl. Damn formula's so expensive. How do y'all afford that stuff?" Mrs. Hammond is holding court again. Looking up, I observe some of the women breastfeeding and others holding bottles.

"Well, I've read there's better healthy stuff in formula. Makes sense to me. Plus, I hate sore titties," one new mother interjects, and the other bottle-feeding mothers nod.

For a quick moment, I am one of them. I cannot stop smiling, my wet eyes directed on my son. We have a bond. He is the one to whom I have told my darkest secrets and desires for months. He is real. He's here with me.

Jamie unlatches from the bottle, his dark-bluish eyes roll back and forth and he seems to focus on me for a second; then they close again. He sighs, and his baby lip lifts, crooked and unquestionably beautiful.

In the nursery, Delli would have chuckled and said, "It's just gas." I know differently. This has to be his first smile for his mama. Formula rolls out of the side of his baby mouth, puddling under his chin. His eyes close again, and he's asleep. His little breaths are soft huffing noises. I marvel all over again at the beauty and perfection of him.

Delli says that "all babies are a gift from God, regardless about their beginnings." If I didn't believe in God before, I believe now. This child is certainly a miracle and meant to be.

I think he's prettier than any of the other babies in the nursery at the Home.

I slip my finger into his mouth, and he sucks, causing a solid pain in my chest. Contractions squeeze my lower gut, hurting, but in a good way. My breasts tingle, ready to do easily what they were made for. His miniature fingers curl instinctively around my finger.

His hands. How I love them. They are my hands, my fingers. I hold him more tightly and gently spread him across my legs, loosening his blanket. My desire to see his sweet, solid body is feverish. I have never felt this pull, this love, and it jolts me with such intensity that I feel as if I may explode.

"Your first?" I look up at a sweet-faced blond lady sitting across the room from me. She is holding her baby at her breast, serene and delicate, exactly like a painting of the Madonna. Glowing sunshine streams in from the window behind her, creating a halo over her fair hair. Lazy sunbeams drift across the space between us.

"Um, yes, ma'am," I answer, barely above a whisper. My hands protectively cover his tiny body.

I long so badly to say it out loud, I can't help myself. "Jamie. His name is Jamie."

"Oh, that's a fine name. This here is Lucille Marie—for my mama, who is Lucille Lorraine. Little Lucy. My mama's called Big Lucy." She adoringly watches her daughter tugging at her breast. "Another girl. We have four little darlings, but my husband wants a boy before we stop." Her bright pink lips stretch wide over large pearly teeth.

Inside I shake. I feel unsteady and a bit unhinged.

I return her smile shyly and look back down at Jamie, determined not to make eye contact with the woman any longer. *Stop talking. Next thing I know, she'll ask about my husband.*

After peering at Jamie's downy body and marveling at his velvety brand-new skin, the stubby remainder of his umbilical cord, and the gauze pad that lies over it, I adjust the tiny diaper from which his wee frog legs poke. My hand strokes his ten curled baby toes.

"You are perfect," I whisper again, expertly wrapping the blanket around him, snugly, just like Delli taught me. As I hold him tightly in my arms, he sleeps without a care. I try to rouse him, gently kissing his smooth head. I wiggle his tiny foot. He squirms but sleeps on.

Staring at him and memorizing his face, I blink away tears. His face scrunches. I laugh because he resembles a miniature old man. Where minutes before I thought he looked like Mama's family, now I see Daddy's side. He bears no resemblance to Clay. But babies change. His downy fuzz is colorless and closer to blond than my dark color.

I jump as Mrs. Hammond bellows across the room, "Your baby's still sleepin'? That's the damn twilight shot, girl. You shoulda told 'em not to give you that. I had that shot with my Joey Jr., and he took two days to finally wake up. I hate that shot. My next two babies, I said, 'No, sir. Do *not* put me out.'"

Mrs. Hammond is staring hard at me, her baby clamped to her huge fleshy breast.

"Didn't someone tell you about that shot?" She seems astounded; her left eyebrow shoots up on her forehead, merging with her dark, unruly hairline.

My cheeks are slabs of heat. Instinctively I know this woman is trying to advise me, to be helpful. She sounds harsh only because she is more than likely the product of a loud and boisterous New Orleans family. I want to trust her. I also know she is beyond nosy and will grill me if I let her. I shake my head and look down at my son again.

Don't make eye contact. Be brave. I shift my weight and turn away from her.

I inhale Jamie's round forehead again. The scent of my son is exquisite. I could sit here with him in my arms forever, at peace, regardless of the contractions continuously squeezing my belly or the raw scent of the blood pooling under me.

His bottle forgotten, Jamie sleeps soundly against my heart.

All the women are listening and asking questions as Mrs. Hammond rails on, the expert on anything and everything. Their conversations are background chirping, like insects in the night. They mean nothing to me. All that matters is my son. I'm in my own heaven, holding and loving my boy.

❧

Too soon, Pixie Nurse stomps into the room, heading straight for my bed. She glares at me, brow furrowed.

Is she angry?

Panicking, I stumble over my words. "He only took an ounce. He doesn't want to wake up. I'll try later. I'm just holding him now." Her face frightens me; my eyes beg her to leave. I continue babbling nervously. "Sometimes new babies don't want to eat."

"I'll take him now. He needs to be changed." She grabs the bottle, reaching abruptly for my son.

"I can change him." I continue to clutch him.

She bends closer, hissing at my forehead, "You're leaving soon, missy, and he was supposed to stay in the nursery. I'll take him now. Time's up."

Her infuriated voice startles and embarrasses me. *She knows.* I see it in her eyes. She thinks I'm a monster. A slut. An unfit mother. Not even a mother. Not worthy of holding and feeding my son. Jerking away and turning from her, I clasp Jamie even tighter.

The red-haired nurse with the black glasses has entered the room and walks directly to my bed. Like a flapping white stork, she hovers over me. She takes in the scene unfolding before her eyes: Pixie Nurse, hands on her hips; me, pressing my baby against my chest, eyes pleading.

The other women are silent now. Crackling tension fills the room, and all eyes turn to the drama unfolding in our own tiny universe. An infant cries out, instantly hushed by a nipple. Eager for the unknown story, like vultures they wait. I know what they're thinking: *Why are they taking her baby so soon? What did she do?*

Stepping aside, Pixie Nurse smirks as the red-haired nurse smiles patiently at me. Bending close, she smiles softly and says for all to hear, "What a sleepy little man. We'll take him back to the nursery, and maybe when he wakes you can try to feed him again." Then she leans even closer to my ear and whispers, "Let's not have any problems here, honey."

Before I can protest, she swoops Jamie expertly out of my arms and shuttles him away. A hard emptiness fills me. Blood pumps in my temples. My ears roar with static.

The women resume feeding their babies, studying their perfect newborns' faces, and for once they are stunned silent. I turn away from them, roll toward the wall, eyes closed.

I'm no better than scum. I'm not worthy of my baby. I close into myself and tamp down the shame.

Chapter 28

That afternoon, after another feeding when my son is not brought to me, after being probed by nurses, my flaccid stomach massaged and pummeled, my blood pressure taken twice, bloody pads routinely pulled out from under me and new ones stuffed between my legs, I lie silent and numb. Offered a bedpan twice, I refuse.

I will not use a bedpan in front of these women. I will die first.

A young intern, practically a boy, walks in. Bright red acne peppers his wide cheekbones; his Brylcreem-slicked black hair hangs limp and greasy across his forehead. He flushes visibly as he glances around the room. His tired gray lab coat is creased and wrinkled. Pulled from a dirty clothes hamper? Dark smudges sit under his weary eyes. His disheveled and awkward appearance does not instill confidence.

Pixie Nurse struts at his side, official and stern. He is clearly uncomfortable, and she is unmistakably in charge. Silence fills the room once more. I feel the women's eyes boring into me, their breath held.

As Pixie Nurse directs the boy intern to the foot of my bed, the silence rings in my ears. He stares at my chart, his lips pressed firmly together; the minutes stretch on forever.

Does it say "unwed mother"?

Looking up, he stares straight into my eyes and his lips lift into a weak smile. In an unexpectedly deep voice, he asks permission to "check" me. I am mortified knowing he will look under the covers at my bottom and my gory pads. The sharp scent of my own blood down there fills my nostrils.

Before I can answer, he is lifting the sheet and poking my stomach. The skin on my face burns hot. I grit my teeth. I don't want him looking at me. He quickly drops the sheet and glances at me. "Miss, you have what we call a deep episiotomy. Couldn't be helped, I'm sure. It'll heal fine over time. Keep yourself clean down there. Get checked in six weeks or so, and no sex for eight weeks. Absolutely no sex, okay? No more babies for a while. Ya hear?"

Clean down there? No sex? What kind of girl does he think I am?

Looking at the nurse, he orders, "Make sure she knows about sitz baths. She's gonna need them." He nods to the nurse, jots something on the chart, hands it back, and flees the room without another glance at me.

No food arrives. Hunger pains stab at me, along with the insistent cramping. Light-headed, flustered, I feel feverish. I wonder, *Do I have the flu?*

After emptying the water pitcher on my bedstand, I continue to feel parched. No one refills the pitcher. Afraid to ask for anything, I lie silent. Nobody explains what a sitz—or was it silts?—bath is because nobody speaks to me. I seem to have an invisible bubble around my bed. My ears roar.

Meanwhile, the other mothers are cleaning up and primping for visitor hour. For their husbands. They're in high spirits as another bouquet is brought in for one of them. The cloying scent of lilies fills the room. They pointedly ignore me. I am an outcast.

∾

My heart hurts, and tears continually flood my eyes. Jamie is all I can think about. I force myself to try to remember his birth. It's useless. I recall nothing past the long, agonizing wait in the hallway and then Mama coming into the labor room and the violent contractions. *Was that a dream? Did she come to my room?* Giving birth to my son is a white void.

Maybe they shut me up. I was upset and making a fuss. It's my fault I got that shot.

I strain again to remember, puzzled that those hours are gone from my mind.

Maybe Mrs. Hammond is right. I should have said "no shot." Who knew? Where are Mama and Daddy? Did they go home? Do they know I have a baby boy?

Against my will, my eyelids close as I slip into a deep sleep. The sounds around me lull me. I long to sleep forever, and struggle to wake when I hear the red-haired nurse pulling the curtain around my bed again.

Before I can say a word, she explains in a hushed voice, "Honey, we're gonna get you up and try a walk to the bathroom and get you ready to leave." She searches my face. Her voice lowered, she explains, "They'll be here soon to take you back, and your baby too." I see pity in her eyes.

Chapter 29

Before nightfall, I'm back at the Home and in the clinic. The nurse is kind. She brings me food and encourages me to drink water and then drink some more. She hovers over me for a while, checking and rechecking my vitals. She helps me slip my gown down around my waist and wraps a long length of cloth around my breasts. "Here, honey, this'll dry up your milk. Never hurts to be extra careful. You don't need that problem." Soon my chest is bound and rigid.

Lizzie and two other girls visit, telling me they saw Jamie through the nursery window. "He's so pretty." We avoid talking about the fact that I will be leaving him soon. They chatter nonsense and soon swoop out of the room. I hear their cheerful voices disappearing down the hall.

"Honey, you need to rest. This will help." The nurse is so kind. A needle pricks my arm.

Thank God I'm back here. No more questions to answer. My head falls back on the stiff pillowcase. Though I'm weary, foggy, and sore, my mind is chaotic and adrenaline zips through my veins.

I try to summon the guts to ignore the nurse's warning to lie quietly; I want to walk down to look through the nursery window at my son. It's not that far. A desperate longing to hold my baby has taken over my entire being. I struggle to keep my eyes open, but deep murkiness imprisons me, putting me out like a light. My last thought is of the baby boy down the hall, and my last hope is that Delli is the one holding him, feeding him, tonight.

∾

The next day dawns with buttery sunshine spilling through the window. A jumble of nightmares and a mosaic of memories of holding Jamie fill my head. I am fragile, sore, and weepy. I look up as the door whooshes open and a bubbling, ponytailed, very pregnant girl adjusts a breakfast tray on the side of my bed. In a voice ripe with a deep Louisiana accent, she singsongs, "Time to rise and shine."

The unpleasant mingled scent of antiseptic and crisp bacon makes me queasy, and all I can think about is Jamie. He's real and he's here.

In the small bathroom, I wipe away the dried blood that coats my thighs and bandage myself with another industrial-size Kotex pad, splash cold water on my face, and try not to study my wretched self in the mirror.

Miss Felton stands next to the bed when I open the bathroom door.

"Good morning, Laura. Up and moving around. That's good to see."

"Thank you, ma'am. I want to see my baby, please."

"Not yet. The baby is fine. That's not your concern right now, my dear." She watches me as I struggle to sit down on the bed, gingerly lowering my poor, sore bottom.

"Your parents called." Her voice is condescending again. "They want to drive over today and take you back this afternoon. My, they're in a rush to take you out of here. Ready for you to be home, that's for sure."

Her statement shocks me wide awake. "Already? I don't think I'm ready to leave. I don't feel so good," I plead.

Not yet. Not yet. I'm not ready to leave here. I can't leave Jamie.

"You're correct. You are most definitely not ready. There are a few issues to see to first." She cocks her head.

"Are they headed here today? What did they say?"

"Well, it seems they're determined. I told them it was impossible today. I let them know we have to take you to our attorney's office in the morning, so they must wait until tomorrow afternoon." She peered at my chart, never making eye contact. "I told them you may need an extra day. Your father was insistent when I told him that. He got rather put out and, well, to be honest, almost rude." She sniffs. "Also, just so you know, it's best you don't go back upstairs. Your belongings will be brought down, and you need to rest for two or three weeks. Doctor's orders."

Relief courses through my veins.

"Your chart shows you've had excessive bleeding and your BP has not stabilized. It's troubling."

Her words strike fear in my heart. "Is that serious, Miss Felton?"

"Simply a few complications, but from the looks of you, we should probably have a doctor check you before you're released. You should see a doctor after returning home as well. We cannot be held responsible if you leave too early. I know your parents are eager to get you back, but it's Sunday and they'll have to wait until it can be arranged. Period."

She sniffs again and continues her tirade.

"You are not well, Laura. I'll let your roommate know to pack your things for you." She folds her arms across her chest. "Oh, and, Laura, many girls donate their maternity clothes when they're released. It's a kind thing to do for the less fortunate new girls. Smart too. After all, you won't be needing them again anytime soon, will you?"

Miss Felton turns and takes her leave. Over her shoulder, she warns, "It's best if you do not go to the nursery yet. I'll be back to fetch you tomorrow morning."

I want to be with Jamie. I want to stay with my friends here. I'll call home and tell my parents, "Please don't come yet. Miss Felton says I'm not well." I will beg if that's what it takes.

Getting out of bed, determined to fix this situation, I head down the hall. There is no nurse at the desk, not a soul in sight, as I walk to the pay phone and call. The phone rings forever.

Come on. Answer. Where could they be? Church? No, Mama said she'll never go again.

"There's no answer, ma'am." I hear the operator's velvety voice, and I hang up quietly.

I slowly make my way to the nursery, my bottom burning. *Please let Delli be there.* Searching for Jamie at the window, I feel my already revved-up heart knocking frantically in my chest.

Where is he?

Miss Blue, one of the weekend nurse aides, walks around the corner. She gives me her gentle smile and opens the door, peering out.

"Hello, Miss Laura. Sugar, you doin' okay?"

"Hey, Miss Blue. May I see my baby, please?"

"In a while, honey. I just got him fed, changed, and back to sleep. He's a good baby. Maybe you can feed him next time he wakes. I'll bring him to you." She looks me up and down. "You feel poorly, don't you?"

"Oh, please, Miss Blue, I'm fine. I feel all right. I just need to hold him. His name is Jamie." Shaky and hot, I feel sweat beginning to bead all over my body. A wave of nausea blasts through me.

"You don't look too good. You pale as a ghost. You need to get yourself back in that bed, sugar."

A loud commotion surprises us as laughter fills the hallway. A posse of girls pushing playfully at each other rushes toward us. There's Lizzie, leading her fan club. She squeals when she spots me, and grabs me around the waist, almost knocking me over, hugging me for all she's worth.

"Whoa, not so tight." I wobble, unsteady on slippered feet.

"Quiet, girls. The babies are sleepin'." Miss Blue frowns, pushing the door shut, shaking her head. She peeks out of the window once more, with a final glare at Lizzie.

"What a w-i-t-c-h," Lizzie whispers, rolling her eyes.

Their peals of laughter set me on edge. Now I'm the one glaring at them. I don't want any trouble. I don't want Miss Blue to associate me with troublemakers. I only want to see Jamie.

"Shh!" They all back away, chastised. The last thing on earth I want to do is entertain Lizzie and her friends, yet I'm helpless in her presence. My head pounding, we make our way back down the hall.

"Where were you?" the nurse demands as I arrive back in my room.

"Calling my mama. I'm sorry."

"Only one visitor, girls." She shoos the girls out of the room, and Lizzie stands her ground defiantly.

A trickle of blood is worming its way down my leg.

Oh God. When does this stop?

"I'm sorry. I need another pad." The nausea is back.

"Honey, get up there in the bed. I'll get your supplies." A worried frown creases the nurse's forehead, and she shoots Lizzie a look. "You must leave now. No visitors."

❧

Another shot and many pad changings later, I'm told I need to stay off my feet and stay in bed. Once again, I slip into a coma-like sleep within minutes.

Oh, how I love that shot. Almost instantly I'm woozy, forget all my problems, and feel no pain. I seem to float in and out of dreams, hallucinating at times, seeing myself from up above, lying stiff and still, as if I were dead.

I have disturbing dreams of Jamie, an older Jamie with red hair, sitting on a rug on a wood floor, holding his arms out to me. I dream of Lizzie, parceling out to the girls the pretty clothes my grammy sewed, her hair in an outrageous, foot-high beehive style, her lips painted bright magenta.

I cry in my sleep, waking myself. My hand automatically rubs my soft belly, bringing more loneliness and pain. Ashamed and horrified at what I'm about to do, I bury my sobs in the hills of my pillow, hugging myself.

Hours later, I drag myself out of bed, making my way down the darkened hallway and stopping at the nursery window once more. *Where is Delli?*

A different aide looks up, recognizes me, and nods.

I ask through the window, "Can I come in?"

"I'll bring him down to you," she promises, and turns her back on me.

One of the new girls from the kitchen is heading down the hall with a metal tray laden with food, balancing it with the help of her belly. "Hey, you the one who just had your baby? I got your supper here. You goin' back to the room?" her backwoods voice calls out.

My throat closes and tears threaten, but I nod.

"I'll walk with you. You lookin' at your baby?" She has stringy blond hair and angry acne. Her pale, spindly arms strain to balance the tray. I feel older and wiser by decades. I continue to stand at the window, craning my neck to see Jamie. She peers in with me. I glance sideways at her. She has many months to go.

"See my son?" I point towards his bassinet. "The one next to the wall. See? I named him Jamie. He's beautiful," I boast quietly.

"I can't see that far. I don't even like babies. Better get to eating— your food's gettin' cold. It's good too. Roast beef, gravy, and potatoes. Oh, and apple pie. They do feed us good here."

We head down the hall, the backwoods girl prattling on the entire way. I'm anxious and irritated. She reminds me that there's no way around it—I will never be anyone else. I will always be the girl who got in trouble, backward and damaged. I'm just like her, and that thought makes me cringe.

Rudely ignoring the silly, jabbering girl, I pick at my dinner silently, feeling mean, not caring. She eventually slithers away. Pushing the congealed food away, I watch as the nurse offers me another tiny white paper cup. Three pills of various colors like sparkling candies lie in the bottom of the cup, and I swallow them dutifully. There is no resistance on my part, just numb acceptance.

I'm leaving my boy. I let that thought sink in, allowing myself to feel a raw, deep ache. Final thoughts weave through my foggy mind: *I'll sleep for a while, then get up and go down the hall to him. I have tomorrow.* Jamie's tiny face plays out behind my closed eyelids as I welcome that dark cavern of drugged sleep.

No one brought Jamie to me that night. The building could have collapsed, and I doubt I would have woken up. I doubt I even rolled over once. My sleep was like that of the dead, complete lights out. Jamie was one day old.

Chapter 30

ace smashed into my pillow so hard the side of my cheek ached, I forced one eye open. The stiff pillowcase smelled of soap tinged with the sharp scent of blood. I had chewed my lip until it bled across the case. I ran my tongue around my mouth, feeling bits of loose skin. The vivid dream I was having was still fresh in my clouded head: It was a spring morning. Mama was in my bedroom, sitting on my bed, pushing my shoulder gently, softly singing the pop tune "Wake Up Little Susie." "Time to get up, Laura. You're gonna be late for school." She smiled sweetly, and I felt loved and taken care of.

My next thought was of Jamie.

Cleaning myself up as best I could, I could tell that the bleeding had slowed down. I was stronger but still sluggish. I peered at myself in the small mirror on the wall and quickly looked away.

I look old.

There were rumblings outside the bathroom. I cautiously opened the door a crack and peered out. Flat fried eggs glowing with grease and a puddle of grits congealed on a tray sat next to the bed, and in the entry to the room, Miss Felton, gray head bent, was intently comparing notes on a chart with the nurse.

The door clicked when I tried to quietly close it.

"Laura? Are you okay in there, dear?" Miss Felton called out in her simpering drawl.

"Yes, ma'am, I'm fine. I need some more time is all."

Why can't they just go away?

"Well, we're leaving within the hour. So please try to hurry yourself along, now. Understand?" Miss Felton's version of concern colored her voice.

"Yes, ma'am." I opened the door, peering out at her. "But where are we going?"

"I told you yesterday. Downtown. To the attorney's office. We need to get you there and back. Your parents are insisting they will be here to pick you up this afternoon." She looked none too pleased. "We have much to do." She sniffed.

"But I want to hold my baby," I demanded.

"I'm not the one rushing this, dear."

"I need to see my baby."

"Of course. If we have time. The baby is not your worry right now."

"I don't think I'm ready to do all of that. You promised I could hold him. They said they would bring him last night, and no one did. Please, Miss Felton." My head spun as I grasped at reasons not to leave. "I feel faint—"

Turning from me, she interrupted. "Laura, that is exactly why you must hurry now." She gestured toward the disgusting tray. "Eat some toast. I'll return in thirty minutes to get you, and please do not dilly-dally. Mr. Hill, our attorney, is doing us a huge favor meeting us today."

She muttered something about things slipping between the cracks, unreliable employees, and irritating workers who made extra work for everyone. As I watched the back of her head disappearing down the hall, her ever-present black bobby pins drawing a haphazard pattern across her graying bun, the nurse plucked at my arm.

"Time to eat. Miss Felton was not happy that I let you sleep in."

I tried to swallow a bite of cold toast spread with oily margarine. Looking across the room, there was a paper grocery sack overflowing with my books and belongings. Grammy's blue suitcase sat in the corner of the room. The peach gingham dress that I had worn when I entered the Home five months earlier hung across the chair. My beige pumps sat side by side on the floor.

I sank into the chair. The thought of unwinding the tightly bound cloth around my chest and struggling into a garter belt, then tugging on nylons, exhausted me. But there was no way around this. I would have to get dressed sooner or later.

After a sponge bath at the sink, I struggled with my coarse, thick, hospital-issue sanitary belt attached to a massive Kotex. It was as cumbersome as a huge diaper. I began digging through the suitcase for a bra, panties, cotton garter belt, nylons, and my lacy half-slip.

I looked down at my lap. It resembled a pile of dough, and I cringed as I pulled my panties over my stomach. This was the era of Twiggy. No teenage girl wanted to look the way I looked.

I stared in the bathroom mirror and tried back-combing my stiff hair into a reasonable hairstyle. Robot-like, I continued to look at my reflection, never allowing myself to stop and think about what lay ahead of me. I could not think of my baby down the hall. I could not think of signing a paper that would take him away from me. I could not think of going home. If Mama and Daddy came to get me today, I would plead with them to let me take Jamie back with me, or maybe they would let me stay here longer with him.

Vanity compelled me to smear lipstick on my pale mouth, but makeup couldn't correct my drawn face or the smudged circles under my eyes. I stepped back from the mirror, hating what I saw, and immediately scrubbed off the lipstick, then worried I was leaving the rough white towel smeared with bright pink stains. Peering at myself, I realized I looked haunted.

෴

I must have shut down at this point, as I have absolutely no memory of my ride through the New Orleans streets and downtown to the attorney's office. Who drove me there? Was it Miss Felton? If anyone sat with me, held my hand, supported me, I have no memory of it, but surely someone must have stayed with me.

What I do remember is a dim, musty elevator, lurching up several floors, and a cluttered office. I sat across from an older man, who appeared seedy and unkempt. A heavy rust-colored ashtray on the desk between us overflowed with reeking cigarette butts. That stench mixed with the smell of mold turned my stomach. I recall a shiny brown business suit but no face. His head in my memory seems huge, round, with no features.

A massive window looked out across the city. I stared out at ominous clouds, at buildings, at nothing. The attorney pushed a white sheet of paper across the dark desk for me to sign. If he offered an explanation of what I was signing or what this document entailed, I have no memory of that. I do remember hesitating. I do remember quivering, my hand shaking, my knees weak, and Daddy's stern words playing over and over in my head. *You have to do this, Laura. Your mama cannot raise this baby. If you care about this child, it's for the best. You will go back to your life, and you will forget about this.*

During my time at the Home, there was little, if any, conversation among the girls regarding this part of our stay. Each day we wobbled in a surreal existence, one foot in front of the other. Were we numb by this point, knowing we did not have a voice? Lizzie was the only one who was always adamant that she would not sign any papers.

If you care about this child . . .

I love this child.

Taking up the offered ballpoint pen, my fingers curling tightly around it, I pretended to read the typed words on the stiff document. My vision blurred with unshed tears. The words made no sense, even when I tried to reread them. Exhausted, numb, my ears roaring, I felt my entire chest cavity aching.

I can't.

I can still clearly see the pen hovering over the paper, my fingers white where they grasped it; the attorney, holding a fancy gold lighter to his cigarette, sitting silently, eyes watching me, smoke circling his oversize head.

It's for the best. You can't raise this baby. If you care about him . . .

I thought of Daddy. His sad eyes when I cried. Of Mama. Of Grammy. I thought of Clay. I thought of Jamie lying in his bassinet in the nursery.

Time stood still. The attorney's fingers drummed lightly on the desk, irritating and erratic. He cleared his phlegm-filled throat. My stomach lurched.

You made this bed. You cannot raise a baby. It's not fair to Jamie.

Maybe I can come back here with Mama and Daddy after I talk to them. Maybe I can undo this.

I signed the paper.

My world spun. My face impassive, heart drumming, I watched as the attorney reached for the document, checking my signature. There was the sound of a dark, phlegm-filled chuckle and then he looked into my eyes.

His words would stay with me the rest of my life. Words I remember verbatim.

"Firm, strong signature. *You* know what you're doing, girl."

His deep, smug voice stung. Was he implying that I wanted to do this? I knew what signing these papers meant, but I hated signing them. I despised him, but I detested myself most of all.

My world collapsing, I heard no comforting words, no explanation that there was a time frame in which I could have changed my mind about the adoption. I would learn that forty years later. But that day, the attorney said nothing about that. He simply pronounced his arrogant observation.

It was as if he had spat on me.

∾

The ride back to the Home from the attorney's office is also a blank. Is it because I buried that traumatic morning so far down in my heart and soul that I cannot for the life of me bring back some of the missing details?

Often over the next fifty years, I wondered why huge chunks of my memory during that awful year eluded me while other memories were crystal clear. I read once that the brain seems to have a protective mechanism and when it is overwhelmed, shocked, or traumatized it will actually suppress those memories.

∾

The next thing I recall is bittersweet, painful, and raw. Once back, everything moved so fast, my head spun. Mama and Daddy were waiting there to take me home, but first the promised holding of my son happened. I was settled into a rocking chair in the nursery, and Jamie, bundled in a tight white swaddle, was positioned in my soft lap. The nurse was kind. She knew this was my last opportunity to hold my baby before I was released from this place.

I marveled at the exquisite tiny human in my arms, where he belonged. His wee fingers wrapped around mine. Salty wetness dripped onto my lips. The too-tight garter belt ate into my flesh. The snug bra did nothing to stop the tug deep in my breasts.

Jamie's eyes were half-open slits, and he oh so softly huffed baby breaths at me. I studied his face long and hard. The heft of his body, his downy skin, and his wispy hair mesmerized me. My chest ached as I whispered my love to him. I wanted to hold him forever or simply die right there, with him in my arms.

Please, God. Please never let me forget his face or the feel of his tiny body in my arms.

∾

How long did I sit, holding my son nestled quietly in my lap? Thirty minutes? Forty? An hour? I have no recollection of his being taken from me. My memory simply goes blank after seeing Jamie held tightly in my arms.

My next complete remembrance is of standing in the lobby. Mama and Daddy were both there. Daddy had signed me out, and Mama looked lost standing next to me, her hand tentative on my arm. Although they appeared stoic, they also looked ravaged, shell-shocked, and older than when they had left me here five months earlier. I hated that it was I who was personally responsible for my mama's swollen red eyes and for the haggard look on both their faces.

Grammy's blue suitcase had already been stashed in the trunk, along with two brown grocery sacks filled with the minutiae of my stay. Time was ticking. Daddy was impatient, shifting from foot to foot. Lizzie and a few of the girls had come to tell me goodbye, with tears and hugs. Members of a secret sisterhood, we murmured promises to keep in touch, never doubting we would.

My forehead against the glass, I stood with my parents, the three of us peering at my son in his bassinet. My thoughts tumbled out. "Daddy, I think he looks like you."

Daddy's mouth tightened, but he nodded his sad smile at me, then quickly turned away, his eyes glassy.

Mama seemed to be shrinking next to me. I whispered, "Isn't he pretty, Mama? I named him Jamie."

Her hand grabbed for mine, and as we both trembled, I held on to her hand for dear life.

"He's a beautiful baby, Laura." Her voice broke, and my heart lurched to hear her so sad. I grabbed at that doubt and hurt in her voice like a lifeline, blurting, "I've been thinking, Mama. I can't leave him here. I'll figure it out. I'll take care of him." I grabbed her arm and turned from the window, facing her.

She stiffened and turned away, reaching for Daddy's arm. Neither said a word.

"Hon, time to go." Daddy's face was a mixture of grief and awe as he looked at Jamie through the window one last time. I would never see that look on his face again. Mama's face was set, broken.

Miss Felton stood next to her, all business. "Jamie is a fine, healthy baby, Laura. Always remember that you did the best thing for your child. He is in good hands. God will watch out for him, and he will be with a fine family. Now you can go back to school and back to your life and God will guide you. We all wish you and your family well."

She smiled and added, "It really is best for everyone." I knew she was trying to comfort me and put me at ease, but I looked away from her.

For months, I had lived in a fantasy world, thinking that somehow this moment would not come. Mama would demand we keep Jamie. Daddy would relent because Mama always got her way. Clay would miraculously appear out of nowhere and proclaim his love for me and our baby. Maybe I would sit down on the floor and refuse to leave. Anything but this.

There was no knight in shining armor. There was no savior. And nobody heard me.

I begged, "Daddy, please can I stay one more minute? I have to look at him one last time."

Allowed to go back, I watched as a girl walked to the window with Jamie. I knew how she felt. Working in the nursery, I had shown many a new mother the precious life she had brought into this world as she said her final goodbye. My vision was blurred, between my fresh tears and my glasses, spotted with dried tears. I studied Jamie's face. I knew this was making it harder. I knew Mama and Daddy were waiting anxiously in the lobby, but I was paralyzed.

Lizzie stood next to me, squeezing my shoulder. "I'll check on Jamie every day, and I'll write to you." Fresh tears trailed down her softly powdered face.

How can I stand this? How I can I stand myself? I need to let him go to a better home, to a mama and daddy who are married and will give him all he needs. I won't be here tomorrow, waking up to my job at the nursery, Jamie safe inside me.

As I walked toward my parents, I put on a brave face, but I was broken. Part of my heart, my body, and my soul remained with Jamie. I would never be released from this place, this time. I had no doubt he would be with me forever.

Chapter 31

The silence was toxic as we pulled onto the old highway and the city of New Orleans disappeared in the rearview mirror. Threatening black clouds hung heavy in the sky. Jagged bursts of lightning splashed haphazardly on the horizon. Daddy, facing ahead, gripped the steering wheel for all he was worth, driving away from Jamie. His jaw clenched repeatedly. Both Mama and Daddy's mouths were set firm in a thin line. Her arms folded across her chest, Mama sat holding on to herself for dear life. Neither one of them uttered a sound.

He's their grandson, for God's sake.

Reality sank in deep as I melted into the back seat. Wailing sobs sat close to bursting inside me. Covering my mouth, I swallowed the lump lodged like a rock in my throat.

Troubled silence built within the steel trap of the moving car. Unspoken grief permeated each inch of space, suffocating and unyielding.

I want to die.

"Do we want to stop at White Palace, get somethin' to eat?" Daddy's voice startled me. He sounded artificial and loud.

Mama sprang toward him, barking, "No, Billy, I just want to get Laura home. She needs to get to bed. We're not stopping."

"I just thought—"

"Well, stop thinking. Just drive home." Mama glared at him.

"I thought she'd feel better if she ate. I thought—"

"Stop thinking!" She screamed at him. The silence was so thick, it was murderous.

They talk as if I'm not here. Eat? I never want to eat again. I hate them.

Tears gagged me, and fury replaced my sadness as the miles whipped by. Mississippi pine trees lined the highway. Staring at those trees, I wanted to scream, *Turn the car around. I don't want to go. Take me back to my son.* The words caught in my throat. My heart pounded harder, and I couldn't even wipe my face, wet with tears and snot. *Oh, how I hate my weak self.*

The silence stretched on, along with the miles. Mama eventually turned back to look at me, her voice high and strained. "Your Grammy will be happy you're home. She's driving me crazy with her questions. God, she's a royal pain." She strangled out a harsh laugh as if she was entertaining me. Even at a time like this, Mama had to bring up her disdain for my beloved grandmother.

God forbid Mama try to comfort me. Can't she imagine what it feels like to leave your two-day-old son and never look back?

The uncontrollable, primal sobs that I had held in for days finally burst out of me. Lightning flashed, and driving rain pelted the windshield. Mama turned back around and stared ahead, her shoulders shuddering as she sobbed too. Daddy drove on, eyes on the road, knuckles white.

Never-ending pine trees, bridges over masses of water, and semitrucks on the highway flew by. This was not the joyous trip back to my old life that everyone else in the world seemed to think it should be. I couldn't even remember my old life right then.

Gradually, my tears slowed. I was spent, and every bone in my body ached, but soon that was replaced by rage and I screamed arrogantly at the backs of their heads, "I can't wait to see my Grammy. She's the only one I care about."

Those first words out of my mouth since we had pulled away from the Home an hour earlier were pointedly meant to hurt Mama. Now, as a keening came from deep inside me, Mama whipped around, looking at me in the back seat, her own angry eyes swollen slits.

"Stop, now. Get ahold of yourself. We'll be home soon, and your brothers won't understand you being this out of control." Her face was flushed bright red with shades of purple.

I only wailed louder.

"Stop!" she yelled. "Stop!" Turning away, she began crying again, the subject closed.

As if on cue, torrential rain poured through the clouds, harder than ever, and the windshield wipers seemed deafening as the downpour lashed the glass. We were alone in our own hell, barreling down this slick highway.

Maybe we'll crash. I hope we do. That'll show them. I shocked myself with these wicked thoughts.

God, how I hate her.

I kept crying, and Daddy's jaw remained clenched tight. *Was he crying now too?* He said nothing, just stoically drove on.

"I'm sorry," I burst out. Then I yelled the words they didn't want to hear. "But you only care about what other people will say. What about me? I want my baby. I've changed my mind. Turn around. Please. Please. Just take me back."

Mama glared at me. "We're not going back. You signed the papers. We can't change that. It's final. Billy, tell her." Her voice broke. "You did this, Laura. You. Look what you've done to all of us."

I kicked the back of the seat, shouting, "I want my baby!"

By now, Mama was hysterical. My sobs quieted again. Straightening my back, I stared ahead. Back at our old pattern, our game: I escalated until she lost control, and then I stopped crying.

Now that I had pushed her to this point of no return, I was silent.

I want her to hurt, and to hurt bad. She tricked me. She should have come inside with me when I was left at that place.

Daddy pulled the car over on the side of the highway with such force that we all slammed forward, catching ourselves. His head whipped around.

"Laura, stop this right now," he barked at me. "We talked about this. You know you can't raise that baby. For God's sake, you're a teenager." He was angry. I had intentionally upset Mama.

"But, Daddy, I need to go back. Please. Please, just take me back, and you can leave me there."

"We are not going back. Get that outta your head. We talked about this. Now, stop." He turned away. "You'll understand one day."

"No, I won't understand." Wiping at my face, I screamed, "I hate you."

"Stop, Laura." Daddy's voice boomed at me. "Look what you're doing to your mama."

"But Mama said she was going to raise him, and you stopped everything. You. It was your idea, not mine."

"Enough." Daddy glared.

I had to get the last word in. "Mama, you lied. You said you'd raise him. You lied so I would go along with the plan. You lied. You both lied."

I stopped, defeated. I could scream and cry all I wanted, but did it really matter to them? They were determined to get through and over this.

A fatigue like I had never known seeped into my bones, my body a hollow shell. My breasts ached; sticky blood pulsed out of me.

I glared at the backs of their heads. Daddy's gray crew cut, neat and precise. Mama's head barely visible over the back of the car seat, her dark hair shiny as a mink. It's a wonder the force of my furious eyes boring into them did not blast their heads aflame.

How did I let them talk me into this? Why did I not fight harder or run away? Does it make me a better person to have left my baby for a finer life with better people?

By the time we turned down the narrow road, hate, my new companion, had wrapped its ugly arms around me, squeezing any love and expectation out of me. Now, not only did I despise the two people I had once loved best in this world, I loathed myself even more.

℘

Barely waiting for Daddy to brake in our driveway, I flung myself out of the car. Warm sandy soil shifted under my feet, and I breathed in the moist, salty air. The breeze through the trees felt silken and heavy. The Gulf Coast. Home.

Grammy hurried from her fenced front yard into ours, gathering me in her arms as Daddy and Mama hoisted my things and the blue suitcase from the trunk. Her familiar scent of Jergens lotion and freshly ironed fabric, along with the warm embrace of her strong arms, soothed me.

Tommy and Michael hurried onto the front porch to watch my arrival. They stopped in their tracks. This type of emotion and breaking down in the front yard was not a common occurrence in our family. Curious but uneasy, they hung back. Mama had assured me the boys knew nothing about my pregnancy. Tommy's light brown hair had grown out into a new Beatle cut since I had last seen him. He called out to me, "Hey, Laura." I nodded, watching him settle onto the porch swing, waiting for me.

"Oh, honey, I sure missed you." Grammy's eyes peered into my swollen red ones.

"I missed you too." My little brothers watched intently as I whispered frantically in her ear, "Grammy, I made a mistake. I need to go back. I'm so sorry. But I need to go back to New Orleans. Please tell Daddy. Please."

Grammy shook her head. "Stop." She gently covered my mouth

with her soft hand, looking around to make sure no neighbors were peering out their windows. "Hush, hush. Laura, honey, don't talk about this now."

We headed toward her yard, arm in arm, heads bent together, just as Mama stepped out on the porch and called to us, "Laura, time to come in. Now. Mother, she can visit with you later."

There was no compromise in her voice.

"Oh, there she goes." Grammy huffed. "Your mama has been miserable and hard to take this whole time. You better go on home. I don't want her making another scene. Come visit later, honey, when everything dies down." She shook her head, scowling back at Mama, who stood planted on the front porch, face swollen and hands on her hips.

These two women would be at war even if the world was coming to an end.

Defeated, I gave Grammy one last hug and headed up the steps to the porch. Everything looked the same. How could this be? I was different now, but nothing here had changed.

On the front porch, Tommy perched on the old swing, his eyes narrow, a smirk on his face. He watched my every move.

"You're lucky you got to stay with Gramma Effie, Laura." Nine-year-old Michael ran alongside me, words tumbling out. "Guess what? I had a party for my birthday. You should have been here."

"Oh, I'm sorry I missed it." I smiled at my baby brother.

"Mama got you a surprise in your room. A new blue bedspread."

Her favorite color, not mine.

Ungrateful and angry at Mama, I resolved I would hate any gift she ever gave me again.

Reaching over to tousle Michael's soft blond hair, I promised, "I'll tell you about Grandma Effie's later, and you can tell me about your baseball team. Okay?" Behind thick eyeglasses, far too serious for his little boy face, his green eyes peered adoringly into mine. He followed me to my room chattering away, glad his big sister was back.

Chapter 32

Somehow in my fantasies I had thought that because I'd given in to their wishes, all would be easier for me and my parents once we were back together. I had envisioned sitting together around the dining room table, Daddy and Mama drinking coffee, concerned looks on their faces. I would tell them how it killed me to walk away from Jamie. Perhaps they would take me back to get him.

I planned on conversations with Grammy. In my mind, we would sit with our hot tea, just like in the old days. She would hug me and pat my back, as she had my whole life, telling me she loved me and that I was forgiven. In those daydreams, I would pour my heart out about Jamie, admit I had made a mistake, and I had learned my lesson. She would agree and tell Daddy he had to take me back over to New Orleans. Ultimately, we would bring Jamie home and be a family again.

Those fantasies were just that.

That first week, I seldom left my room. My appetite was nonexistent. It didn't matter, because I was afraid to eat. My clothes felt tight and uncomfortable. I began a private campaign to starve myself as I worried hourly that I might be dying because I continued to bleed. *How much bleeding is too much bleeding?* Most days, feverish and miserable, I never left my bed, rolled in a ball, sleeping the hours away.

That first week, I wrote letters to my friends at the Home begging for news of Jamie. Lizzie was still there, and I missed her miserably. I cried as I listened to my tiny transistor radio, positive the lyrics to every sad song had been written for me alone.

I would sing along softly with the Mamas & the Papas' "Dedicated to the One I Love," tears streaming. I couldn't remember laughter and joy. I doubted I'd ever laugh again. I was hollow and dead inside.

Staring at my four walls, hating myself, my parents, Clay, and his parents, I sulked and schemed. I needed to find a way to escape as far away from all of them as soon as possible. Maybe I could hitchhike to New York, or maybe California. But when the thought flitted through my head, I'd envision every gruesome detail of being kidnapped by some lunatic and murdered on a backcountry road far from home.

The new blue bedspread disgusted me. That was supposed to make me happy? I wadded it up in a ball, pushing it deep into a far dark corner in my closet. If I did leave my room, it was to ask Mama for more Kotex. Eventually giving in to hunger pains, I would rummage aimlessly through the refrigerator, never finding whatever I was searching for.

I attempted to sit with my parents in the mornings. They never mentioned my zombie-like behavior and whenever I brought up the subject of the Home or Jamie, they changed the subject or found an excuse to leave the room.

One bright, hot morning, I sat at the kitchen table, nibbling on a dry slice of toast, allowing myself only tiny bites, worried about how many calories I was consuming.

"Going to be a killer outside today. Hotter than hell itself," Daddy muttered, looking up from his newspaper.

"I already have a headache," Mama said, listlessly stirring her coffee.

I joined in, "Days like this in New Orleans were the worst. I'd try to sit outside with the girls because I felt like the walls were closing in, but in that heat I'd feel like my head would bust open."

Silence.

"Mama, do you have those brochures they gave you at the Home?"

Daddy remained silent, and without taking her eyes away from her own newspaper, Mama said, "Laura, I didn't keep anything from that place."

Daddy stood to leave. Mama walked him to the front door. I dropped the toast and slipped into my room, resenting how they stuck together, ignoring me and the subject of Jamie.

They don't care. I hate them.

During my afternoon visits with Grammy, we talked about anything and everything except what had happened to me. I told her I still felt sick and weak. She told me that was normal. I told her I was still bleeding heavily. She assured me that would end. Then she would change the subject just like Mama and Daddy. She constantly warned me that I must be vigilant and "not ever slip and tell a soul" what had happened to me.

"And I mean *nobody*, honey. Your reputation will never recover if you tell. Don't trust anyone."

"Grammy, I'm so sad. I can't stop thinking about my baby. I miss him. I hate that I did this. I have no one to talk to," I cried.

"Laura, that baby is not your baby. Some other family is raising him. He is their baby now. You must get over this. Your reputation is at stake. And all we have is our reputation."

"Don't worry. I'm not ever telling anyone."

"My garden club was planning to sponsor you for the Miss Camellia Queen contest, and then—poof—you were gone. That caused a bit of talk."

I shook my head and said in a voice so low, I hoped she didn't hear, "Grammy. I don't care about any Camellia Queen pageant or what the garden club ladies think."

"Well, I care. I was a nervous wreck. I almost quit going to garden club. After all, I'm not a liar, Laura. This almost killed me."

She sipped her tea, her eyes shiny with unshed tears. I realized I was holding my breath. This was the closest I had ever come to doubting Grammy's love for me.

"It's important you go to church with me next Sunday. It'll be good for you. Your daddy and mama should go, but I know they won't. Looks like they've stopped going, and that doesn't look good either. If you go with me, you'll stop idle gossip just by acting like everything's fine. Tell you what: We'll go to lunch with Miss Latil after church. We can go to Morrison's cafeteria in Mobile. We'll make a day of it. Would you like that?"

"I'm not ready for that, Grammy. I doubt I'll ever feel ready for church again." I hoped I never saw the inside of our old church again, and I never wanted to see the good reverend again. The Home had been his idea.

"Oh, dear, that's ridiculous. Why are you being difficult? You must go back. That's that."

My tea remained untouched. I sat chewing on my thumbnail.

"Honey, why do you bite your nails? It's such a nasty habit. Remember, you can always tell a lady by her hands. Here, let's get you some of my clear polish." Grammy left to retrieve the magical nail polish that would make me a lady. I wanted to laugh out loud. Instead, I cried.

∾

Mama stayed hidden in her bedroom most days. Never much for alcohol, Daddy surprised us and came home tipsy a few times after stopping at the neighborhood bar after work. I cringed as I listened to Mama cry and berate him through the night. It was another thing for me to feel guilty about—we all knew why he was drinking.

My brother Bill was working a summer job and off with friends whenever he wasn't working. My younger brothers took off in different directions every day, enjoying their summer. The house was as silent and disorganized as ever, with haphazard meals. We had countless bologna-and-mayonnaise sandwiches on white Sunbeam bread for supper, with glasses of milk or cherry Kool-Aid, when Mama couldn't get out of bed. Grammy brought over casseroles, taking pity on us kids.

We all went our separate ways, fending for ourselves and avoiding each other. Laundry for a household of six went undone. Numb and too ill to care, I was guilty of doing nothing to help the matter. The constant roar of the window fans moved humid air around; dishes piled up on the countertops; newspapers and odds and ends were scattered across tables and furniture. The hateful Teddy barked and growled constantly. Grammy visibly shuddered when she stepped into our house, causing more tension between her and Mama.

I was suffocating.

∾

"Um, Mama?" I knocked on her bedroom door.

"Come in."

"When does this stop? I need more pads." I walked into her bedroom and sat at the foot of her bed. She lay turned toward the wall with her books and magazines, a glass of ice water sweating a ring on her nightstand.

"Take that box from my bathroom; then you can wait until I go shopping." She sounded weary.

With no energy to push the matter, I went back to my room, closed the door, and broke down.

One afternoon, Nancy came to visit with a surprise in her oversize handbag: a pint-size bottle of cheap vodka and a pack of Newport cigarettes. We sipped the harsh alcohol in my bedroom, giggling. The burning sensation spread through me, warming me from top to bottom. I felt tension leaving my body as we sprawled across the unmade bed, whispering.

"I'm numb and I like it." I grinned. "Thanks, Nanner."

"Want to go for a ride or something?" Nancy looked around my disheveled bedroom.

"No. I don't feel up to it. Plus, Mama won't let me leave. Stay here with me."

"Okay, but you gotta leave your house sometime." Nancy shrugged and stayed awhile, but even she couldn't last long around the depressed person I had become. She left the cigarettes and remainder of the vodka for me, promising she'd call later.

I'd wait each night, and when everyone was in bed, I'd light up. The caustic smoke burned my throat. I kind of hated it, but I continued to do it, rebelliously exhaling out my open bedroom window. This became my nightly ritual, reading until 4:00 or 5:00 a.m. and smoking. If I'd gotten caught, Mama would have had a fit. In her opinion, cigarettes were for trashy women. Blatantly smoking in her house made me the ultimate disrespectful, trashy daughter.

My visits to Grammy's ceased. I didn't want to hear her ranting about church. The simple act of bathing and getting dressed became daunting, so I wore the same clothes day after day. I remained sluggish and feverish. My hair hung limp, and my pale complexion took on a waxy hue. As I gazed at myself in the full-length mirror in my room, critically observing each flaw, I was sure it would never matter how I looked again. I figured there was nothing to look forward to. Those days were long gone.

Chapter 33

A loud, rapid knock on my door startled me one hot, sticky afternoon as I sat at my desk, mindlessly doodling the name Jamie intertwined in flowers and hearts, hidden in the drawings. Always hidden.

"Hey, hon." Mama's best friend, Lena Mae, pushed into my bedroom, trailing the scent of coffee, along with Ivory soap. Witty and always full of life, Miss Lena Mae had been like family since I could remember. I adored her. A crown of short reddish-brown hair bounced on her head. Her glasses covered concerned eyes. Inching the door closed behind her, she winked at me, popping her Juicy Fruit gum.

"Aw, hon, how ya doin'? You okay?" She wrapped me in her arms for a long hug. Melting into that embrace, I burst out crying.

"Oh, hon, I'm so sorry." She patted my back.

My head jerked back. She knew. I fumed, betrayed all over again. *Who else has Mama told?*

"I'm fine," I lied, clenching my jaw.

Lena Mae sat down on the bed, patting the spot next to her.

"Your mama says you never come out of your room and your light is on all night long. She smells cigarette smoke coming from under your door. She's worried about you."

"That's a bald-faced lie, Miss Lena Mae. She's not worried."

"Oh, honey, don't say that. Your mama loves you. She *is* worried. She's so sad for you, and she's hurting too. She says you won't even talk to her."

"Me? It's the other way around. She won't talk to me. I've tried," I argued. "She hates me for what I did."

"Now, listen, hon, she's not mad, just sad. She doesn't hate you. You are her baby girl. Just talk to her."

"I'm so confused. I feel awful. My head hurts all the time, and I can't think." I was strangling, trying to explain. "Miss Lena Mae, I had a baby boy and I want him back. They ignore me when I beg them to take me to the Home. Please tell Mama I need to go back." I slumped forward, turning my face away from her.

"I know, darlin'. I know. Oh, Sugar, it's okay. You go right ahead and cry. My heart's breaking for all of y'all. This about did your mama in. She's worried to death about what's gonna happen to you. Oh, and that precious baby. Well, she's a mess over this whole thing."

Finally, someone was listening to me, someone who understood. Miss Lena Mae assured me I needed to talk to Mama and that it would help both of us. Clear-headed for the first time in ages, a calm, peaceful sensation came over me after she left my room.

Maybe it is all me. Maybe Mama really does want to talk.

I would try again. I would tell her how sorry I was. I'd explain that I bet Jamie was still in New Orleans. I would ask her to take me back, and maybe together we could explain that I had made a mistake.

Screwing up my courage, I pushed open the door and peeked into my parents' bedroom. The drapes were closed tight against the heat outside the tall windows. A fan whirred softly in the darkness.

I tiptoed in. Mama was rummaging in her crammed walk-in closet, her back to me.

"Mama, can I come in?"

"What now, Laura?"

"What are you doing?" I started off, keeping my voice light.

"Looking for something. What are you doing?"

Taking a deep breath, I began, "Mama, we need to talk. First off, I'm sorry. You must know I am." Sweat pooled under my blouse, and I trembled. "I wish I could take back the awful things I screamed at you and Daddy. I should have apologized sooner. Um, can I ask you some questions?"

"What is it?" Her voice was weary as she turned around, her face closed.

"I feel sick all the time, and I'm still bleeding bad. Is that normal? I hurt down there. Do you think I have an infection? Do you think I should see a doctor?" My face flushed as I embarrassed myself by asking these questions.

She didn't say anything and turned back to sorting through clothes.

I became braver. "I guess what I'm asking you is, do you think something's wrong? And, Mama"—I started talking fast, hoping to get it out before she stopped me—"I know this is all my fault, but I wanted to keep my baby. I'm so sad, and I was wondering, can we go back and . . ." I gulped, the words stuck in my throat.

Mama turned to me. I expected her to reach out to me. After all, Miss Lena Mae had said Mama was as sad as I was.

"I don't know what to tell you. You signed the papers. There is no baby." She caught her breath and her eyes were hard. "You did this, and now we all have to live with it."

"Mama," I wailed, "I'm hurting bad. I think something must be wrong with me."

"Well, Laura, what do you expect?" She turned cold, matter-of-fact. "When you sleep around with a bunch of men and act like a whore, this is what happens. You get an infection or, worse, you get pregnant. God knows what you might have picked up. Maybe some sex disease. How would I know what you should do?" She glared at me, adding, "I thought you were smarter than that."

Did I hear her right? Did my own mother just call me a whore?

Losing my cool, I yelled in her face, "Mama, I didn't sleep with a bunch of men. How can you say that? A whore? I'm not a whore. How dare you? I'm your daughter. I just left my baby, and I'm dying here. It's killing me. I'm sick." Spent, out of breath, and ready to collapse, I stood my ground, my hands shaking, I wanted so badly to slap her face.

She straightened her five-foot frame, holding her head high, squaring off and staring up into my eyes. "Don't come around asking me what to do now. It's too late. This has almost killed your daddy and me. You selfish girl. You get what you deserve." She turned her back to me.

I rushed from her room with a promise to myself that I would never ask her for anything again. I was a fool to have believed Miss Lena Mae and thought that Mama would let her guard down and help me. Would she always make this whole sorry story about herself? She was the victim and I was the disappointment, the sinful daughter. As I fled from her bedroom, I heard the lock click behind me.

In my room, I pushed items off my dresser. Knocking my books out of their shelves and onto the floor, I stomped on them. I was furious with myself for crying. I stared in my mirror, snot and tears running down my face.

I can't stay here.

I ripped my ridiculous pink princess phone out of the wall and threw it across the room, watching it bash into the door. Only a year ago, Mama had given it to me. How happy I had been. How dumb. A phone meant nothing. I flung myself on the bed, my ears ringing.

I'll show them. No one in my family cares.

One painful thought flashed in my mind: *Jamie is two weeks old today.*

Chapter 34

"**M**ama and Daddy will kill me," Billy argued.

"Please, Billy. They'll never know," I pleaded with my younger brother. Even though he had never said a word to me about it, he must have known what had happened to me.

I'd tossed and turned all night, forming a plan. If Billy would help me out, we could drive to New Orleans in the morning and be back by late afternoon. I had begged him to drive me. I was desperate. I had no car. Consumed with the thought of seeing Jamie, I worried constantly that he was already adopted and that I would never see him, yet I was also afraid he lay in the nursery, unwanted by any new parents. I had to find a way to return to the Home.

I stared into Billy's eyes, forcing my most pathetic face.

He sighed. "Okay, okay . . . God, you're such a pain. You got an address, right? We'll just go straight there and head right back. Understand?"

I loved Billy more in that second than I ever had.

"You're such a good brother!" I squealed.

I hugged him awkwardly, and he pushed me away, shaking his head. I felt his eyes following me as I sprinted up the steps to our front porch. Every day I felt stronger, and the thought of seeing Jamie made me feel like I was taking on the world. If someone had said I could fly, I would have believed it in that minute.

"Mama!" I yelled as I ran into the house, the screen door slamming. "Billy's taking me on a drive along the beach. We'll be back soon."

I grabbed my handbag and ran a brush through my hair, and within minutes I was seated on the passenger side of Billy's fire engine–red '59 Chevy Impala.

"Let's go." I grinned from ear to ear.

There was a primal pull within me to return and see my son. This might not work—it might get me in more trouble—yet I had no control over this overpowering feeling. I had to see Jamie, regardless of the consequences. If Mama found out, I didn't care.

I had no plan B. What if Jamie wasn't there? I didn't remember anyone coming back to the Home after she had had her baby. I doubted the staff allowed it. I had signed the papers. He was not mine to go see, according to Mama and Grammy.

These three weeks had felt like three years. My arms ached to hold him. A crippling vacuum held me prisoner, and nothing made it better. I had been in private mourning since the day I had left New Orleans. Now, blood surged through my veins again. I felt like I could conquer anything. I was going to Jamie.

Billy drove the endless route to New Orleans while I nattered about random things and turned on the radio. The Beatles crooned "All You Need Is Love," Aretha belted out "Respect," and I sang along, happier than I had been in an awfully long time. Billy seemed glad to have his big sister back.

The reason we were on this trip to New Orleans never entered our conversation. When I had pleaded with him that I desperately needed a ride, I had not said why, and he'd never asked.

Once there I directed Billy to park on a side street. A stew of emotions flooded through me, an odd mix of joy, along with dread and trepidation. The month before, these gnarled old oaks had sheltered us as I'd walked these streets with my unwed sisters, all in various stages of pregnancy, all with different stories, yet the same old story, to tell.

We had lived together, worked together, laughed and cried together, and had one by one given up our babies in this redbrick building.

"Okay, wait here."

Bill nodded, scanning the building and lighting a cigarette, obviously relieved that he didn't have to go inside.

Remembering how some of the babies seemed to wait longer before they were adopted had troubled me for weeks. Those babies grew fast, their eyes lighting up when we reached for them. They recognized us, and I worried about whether they remembered us and missed us, their caretakers, when they were handed over to new parents. I knew the average age for adoption had been six to ten weeks. Jamie was only three weeks. I longed to see him but also hoped that he had been adopted and wasn't here.

That Sunday afternoon was a scorcher, with jungle-level humidity. The back of my blouse stuck to my back, dripping from the ride in the unair-conditioned car.

Be brave. Be brave.

The cool, dark lobby was empty and silent, and goose bumps covered my arms after I pushed open the front door. Wasting no time, I hurried straight through into the narrow hallway leading to the nursery. Hesitating at the viewing window, my heart in my throat, I forced myself to look in.

The nursery was dim and seemed empty. Only a couple of bassinets were visible as I peered through the glass. My eyes adjusted to the dark, and I held my breath.

He's not here. Was he already adopted?

Delli rounded the corner. When she saw me, her dark eyebrows shot right up to her hairline and her face split into a shimmering smile of surprise. I grinned and waved enthusiastically. Hurrying over to unlock the door, she peered down the hall, grabbed my arm, and drew me into the nursery, those huge liquid eyes so close to mine, I could have counted each dense eyelash.

"Laura, look at you."

"I never got to say goodbye, Delli. My daddy and mama came for me . . ."

"Hush, hush, honey. I understand. It's so good to see you, Laura."

She looked behind me, worry creasing her forehead.

"Is he here?" I gulped. "I have to see Jamie. Please," I begged.

"He's here. He's such a good baby. You wash up. I'll get him for you." She scurried away.

I knew the drill. My hands trembled as I scrubbed my hands and arms hard, all the way to my elbows. I grabbed a sterilized smock and smiled as I wrapped it over my clothes. Delli shut the blinds over the observation window, glancing out first to be sure no one stood there. She headed to the rear of the nursery. I followed.

My shoulders relaxed. I remembered so well the familiar peaceful grunts and baby noises, along with the white-sound serenity that filled this room. Inhaling the familiar scent of sterilized cotton sheets and blankets, along with the milky smell of formula, I sighed.

I stopped in my tracks. There stood Delli with Jamie, wrapped snugly like a cocoon. My heart ramped up to a frantic pounding and the familiar solid lump blocked my throat. Leading me to the rockers, she gently placed my son in my arms.

Hot tears wet my cheeks as the weight of that precious bundle warmed my body and healed my aching chest. I audibly exhaled. What was this? He had changed. He was heavier, his oval face had filled out, and the fuzzy down on his baby head was thinner. I studied his closed eyes, feather-soft eyelashes set flat against his baby cheeks, breathing in the soft, clean scent of him. His tiny fingers wrapped around my own and held tight. His body fit my arms perfectly as I rocked him, surges of fierce love flooding through me. I wanted to feel this way always.

"Delli, he seems to sleep all the time. Is he okay?" I swallowed and gently tickled his warm toes.

"He's full. Already took five ounces. Such a good eater, and a good sleeper too. Your boy's one of them no-trouble babies, Sugar. Don't you worry. He's a fine, healthy boy. He was awake for sure before you got here. He lets you know when he's hungry, all right. Ooh-wee." Delli chuckled.

∾

I have no idea how long I held him. After a while, I was aware of the tension signaling Delli's anxiety.

Could she lose her job? Am I being selfish?

"Honey, you have to put him back. You need to leave real soon."

At first, I ignored her. She had always been gentle and kind. But, glancing up at her, I felt her fear. She was risking it all to give me this gift of holding my precious boy.

"I know, I know," I whimpered, hugging Jamie close to me, kissing his velvety head. "I wish I could take him with me right now."

Delli's eyes widened. "Now, don't say that and don't be thinking that. This is for the best. You know that, Laura."

Reluctantly I got up but quickly sank back into the rocker. "Delli, I can't leave him." A wretched, raw sob burst from my core. Jamie's eyes fluttered open for a second and then closed again.

She rose, trying to take him from me. I held on tight. "Not yet. Please."

I could walk out the door with him. What would happen if I did? Where could I go? Would they send police? I'm his real mama, no matter what.

My eyes pleaded with Delli, and her sad eyes pleaded back.

"I know, honey. I know. But you must leave. Now, Laura. Maybe this wasn't a good idea."

I clung to Jamie, studying his face, and then walked him back, robot-like, to his bassinet. My lips lingered on his sweet head, and I squeezed him one last time. He squirmed as I laid him down.

This is your son, my conscience screamed at me.

Delli peered nervously between the window blinds and motioned for me to hurry.

"I love you, Jamie. I'm so sorry. Please don't forget your mama loves you," I whispered, paralyzed at his bassinet and willing myself once again to memorize my infant son's soft features. My eyes flickered up to the tiny cardboard birth card on the bassinet. I peeled it off and stuffed it in my pocket.

Laying my hand across his tiny body, I closed my eyes, praying that God would watch over my baby and silently begging Jamie to forgive me. Then I turned and walked away without looking back.

My body rolled into itself, and I stopped at the door and reached for Delli's smooth, well-worn hand, taking it in mine. I had never held her hand, now I held it for dear life.

"You've been so good to me. I will never forget you, Delli."

Delli smiled shyly and said, "You're a good girl, Laura. Your little Jamie's gonna be fine. Almighty Jesus is watching over both of you. Don't you forget that. You gotta have faith in our Lord God. You go on now, girl. Pray for your boy, but try to go on with your life, honey. You go on, now."

My vision blurring, I squared my shoulders and walked quickly down the hall, through the lobby, and out the front door. In my heart, I knew I would never come back here. I was leaving my firstborn son for the second time.

Will I regret this for the rest of my life?

ᘖ

Billy was outside his car, slouched against the driver's door, surveying the neighborhood with hooded eyes. He had walked across the street and bought a root beer. "Everything okay?"

"Yes," I mumbled, as I slunk into his car like a criminal. "Let's get out of here."

We silently wove through the Irish Channel traffic toward the highway and began making our way back to the Gulf Coast.

My mind numb, my voice gone, I stared out the passenger window as pine trees and waterways flew by. Low clouds were forming in the dark sky. I don't recall a word that we said during those hours driving home, but I do remember songs on the radio that played over and over in my mind my entire life, anytime I drove from the coast to New Orleans. The Beatles' "All You Need Is Love," the Mamas & the Papas' "Dedicated to the One I Love," the Troggs' "Love Is All Around," and on and on. It was the summer of love, and I thought I would never love again.

Chapter 35

That night reality didn't simply hit me, it sucker-punched me. Jamie was mine alone. My secret. When would I get it through my thick skull? No one wanted to talk about him. I firmly faced the fact that that would never change and that I had no one and nowhere to turn for comfort.

After I hid the tiny birth card in a flat wooden box in the back of my closet, I sat in my room, alone with the dark fog of my grief. At last I could mourn him and the life that would never be.

I also mourned the old me. Who was I now? I was a mother, but I wasn't a mother. I could never claim Jamie. I could never speak of him. Seeing him had been the worst thing I could do, but the best thing too. He deserved better than what I had to offer. Something was broken inside me, but I knew I would push on. I might never be the old me again, but I would survive.

～

Nancy picked up on the first ring. "You okay?"

"Yeah, but I need to figure stuff out. I need a job, and I really need to get away from here. I can't live here anymore."

"You'll figure it out. I'd say come here, but with Aaron and me getting married, it's just not the right time."

"Oh, no, no, that's okay. I would never butt in on you at this time," I assured her.

It was up to me. I couldn't hide in my room or in this house forever. I would find a job. I would hitchhike if I had to, but I knew one thing: I would get as far away from Mississippi as I could. If I never saw an oak tree or a front-porch swing again, I would be happy. My animosity toward my parents and my old life clawed at me daily. It had to stop, or it would eat me alive. I couldn't live where I was constantly silenced by a look or an action. I would leave here, or this lie staring me in the face every day would kill me.

For the next couple of days, I scoured the local newspaper, searching the help-wanted ads. Sitting at my desk with a lukewarm cup of coffee, I felt like a grown-up painstakingly writing a list. I wasn't sure what to do, but I knew I had to start somewhere. In red ink, I wrote:

1. Job.

2. Place to live.

3. Save $$.

4. Find an apartment. How much $$ do I need?

5. Roommate? Who?

The only job I could see myself doing was clerking. I knew how to type, but I wasn't fast. Childcare? No, I didn't want to go down that road again. I had never had a real job, except the nursery. Who would I write down for references? I couldn't put down the nursery experience or the summer fiasco with the young military mother, and I had no high school diploma.

I saw an ad for a clerk at Penney's, and an opening at the phone company. Grammy had always said I should get a nice job at the phone company after I graduated. "Look how well Miss Latil's niece did working there," she would remind me. "Now, *that* is a real career."

I had starved myself, and it had paid off. My prepregnancy clothes hung on me. I was delighted when Grammy warned me I looked too thin. "It's unattractive. All those young girls in the magazines you admire are too skinny, and that black goop circling their eyes makes them look sad. It's downright unappealing. You need to smile more, Laura."

Many evenings as the house settled down, everyone in bed, I would go to my closet, take out the little box, and open it. There it was: the birth card, proof of my son. Carefully unfolding it, I'd pray to God that Jamie was healthy and had a new mama and daddy to love him the way he deserved to be loved. Jealousy filled me when I thought about his new parents, but I always quickly asked God to forgive my meanness and please watch over my boy.

I wondered daily what he was doing. *Was he eating baby food? What does he look like now? Was he teething?* I always imagined him with dark blond hair and blue eyes, a carbon copy of Clay. My fantasy baby was always smiling; then he would change and morph into a little kid resembling my baby brother, Michael. With a heavy heart, I would tuck his birth card back into the slim wooden box and hide it in my closet.

Chapter 36

"I need to do something. I've been home a month. I might as well start looking for a job," I stammered, trying to sound nonchalant.

I had slowly worked up the courage to ask Mama if I could use her car to go apply for jobs. Her reaction surprised me. She agreed.

For the first time in ages, I made up my face, parted my hair down the middle, and smoothed it straight on each side. Glancing in the mirror, I was satisfied that I looked like any ordinary girl job hunting, not like a desperate, fallen woman.

Mama was sitting at the dining room table, paying bills, her checkbook open in front of her. Loose papers, stacked magazines, and lunch makings were spread across the table. Michael was building a ham sandwich, and Tommy was slurping Cocoa Puffs cereal and milk out of a coffee mug.

"I won't be long." I tousled Michael's hair. He looked up, giving me his sweet smile. Tommy pointedly ignored me.

"You should fix your hair," Mama said.

"I did fix my hair," I huffed.

"You look like Geronimo." She was deadpan as she reached into her handbag and handed me her keys.

Tommy howled, spitting milk.

"I like your hair," Little Michael chimed in, always the peacemaker.

I pecked Michael's round cheek, glaring at Tommy, snatched the car keys, and walked outside, furious once again, purposely revving the motor when I started her car.

Penney's was a ten-minute drive away. The gray building sat in the middle of downtown, looming in front of me. I had been there hundreds of times, shopping for fabric with Grammy, but it felt foreign to me as I pushed through the back door, air-conditioning hitting my face. The smell of floor wax and dusty bolts of fabric tickled my nose.

Quivering inside, I asked an older clerk with a blue-tinted perm where to apply for the job opening. She sweetly pointed out where to go, and I immediately recognized an old classmate standing at the hiring counter.

"There ain't no applications to fill out," a condescending Betty Jeannette Townly informed me as she popped her gum, refusing to make eye contact. "Job was filled last week."

Betty Jeannette and I had never been friendly at school. When I smiled and said thank you, she looked me up and down, sniffed, and turned away as if she had no idea who I was.

Humiliated, I hurried out to the car in the back lot, and there, leaning on the hood of the car, slumped my old friend Wayne, "bad boy" written all over him. Immediately I was transported back to the months after Clay left, when Wayne had convinced me to drink beer with him after football games. I had partied with him and his rough crowd and regretted it now. What had I seen in this guy? My skin crawled as I remembered his advances. I wanted nothing more to do with him. If I was honest, hadn't he always given me the creeps?

Once I had realized I was pregnant, I had stopped answering his calls, thinking I would never see him again. Fear sent sweat dripping down my chest, yet, maintaining a cool demeanor, I strolled up to Mama's car and opened the door.

"Hey, girl, where you been? I thought I'd never see you again."

"I was living in Mandeville, at my Grandma's." Sweat trickled down my back. Red-flag warnings screeched in my head. My gut said, *Run.* "I'm late. My mama will be mad. Gotta go," I stuttered. I had not talked to a boy in eight months. Fear clawed at me. *Do I look different? Can he tell?*

I slid into the car. In less than the time it took to start the engine, he came over to the passenger side, whipped open the door, and planted himself in the seat next to me. His shaggy reddish hair was oily and slicked back. He reeked of stale cigarettes, moldy clothes, and old sweat. His wrinkled white T-shirt and tight jeans looked slept in. He gave me a devilish smirk, nonchalantly lit a cigarette, and tossed the match out the window.

"What are you doing? Get out." I struggled to sound braver than I was.

His eyebrows flew up in surprise.

"This is my mama's car. No smoking in here. She'll kill me. You gotta get out now."

He tossed out the cigarette and continued to look at me with an evil glint in his steely dark eyes. "You disappeared on me, girl. You don't like me no more?"

Other girls might have liked that malicious pout, but I was petrified.

Reaching over, he grabbed a lock of my hair and tugged.

"Stop." I pulled back, batting him away with my hand.

"Hey, calm down, girl. I missed ya when you were gone. Why did you leave, again? Don't make sense you'd go live with your old grandma in Sleaze-iana. I think I heard some rumors."

"Get out of my car. I'm serious." My face burned, and I started the engine.

"Humph, I remember when you liked me. What do ya say we drive to the river, get a six-pack? You need to calm down some. You act mad as a wet hen." He grinned again.

"Get out, Wayne. I'm serious. I'm gonna scream." There were no other cars in the dusty old lot. My heart began to pound.

"Man, you sure turned into an uppity bitch. You always was a prick tease." He climbed out of my car and spat on the ground. "You're not the sweet little girl you used to be. You think you're Miss High and Mighty 'cause you lived in Louisiana?" He slunk away, glancing over his shoulder, lighting another cigarette.

The entire drive, humiliation burned my cheeks. He knew.

A few days later, I pulled myself together. Dressing carefully, I wound my hair into a prim bun, feeling confident that I looked older and almost sophisticated. The phone company receptionist handed me an application. "Good luck, now, honey. Ya never know." She smiled brightly and winked at me.

Leaving the building, I was elated. Maybe this would all work out. I bet I could get a job here. That receptionist had been so pleasant. I drove past our old high school hangout, the Burger Drive-In, and made an illegal U-turn to head back there.

Seated in the car in the back parking lot, taking deep breaths, I decided I would go inside and buy a chocolate shake, just like the old days. If I ran into any friends and they asked where I had been, I'd repeat my well-rehearsed lie, change the subject, and laugh as if I was happy.

"I thought that was you."

Startled, I turned quickly, and there stood Wayne. *Again?*

"Hey, girl, I drove up behind ya. Never noticed before how scrawny your neck is." He cackled and swaggered closer, grabbing at the car door.

My heart hammered. "Damn it! You scared me, Wayne!"

"Yeah, your neck's so skinny I could put one hand around it and squeeze the life right outta you." Wayne leered and spat on the pavement.

Restarting my car, I backed out as he hung on to the window, glaring at me. The smell of stale beer and unwashed clothes radiated from him as I growled, "Get away from me."

"Stupid bitch. I know you want it. I know who you are!" he yelled, as he jumped away from the car, flipping me off.

He knows. Why else would he be doing this to me? Who else knows? Fear quickly replaced my revulsion and fury.

❧

From that day forward, I avoided everyone. Billy's friends stopped by the house, and whereas at one time I would have laughed and flirted with them, now I made myself scarce. I was a hermit in my room, daydreaming of escape. I stayed up most nights reading book after book. Mama never said a word.

Things seemed to settle a bit back into whatever was normal for our family. My little brothers often poked their heads into my room, and I half listened to their stories. They were excited school was starting soon. Billy was consumed with getting ready for his senior year of high school, and we never spoke. Mama seemed calmer and oddly happy that I had become a shut-in.

Daddy remained on the outskirts, leaving for work before I woke up and arriving back home at 4:00 pm on the dot, sitting down to an almost silent supper, then settling in for a distant night of crossword puzzles and his sci-fi books, seldom speaking a word.

Grammy continued her campaign to get wayward me back to church. All that had been a huge part of my life now made me angry and annoyed. My cousin Mark visited me, and even he didn't bring up the subject of New Orleans. He was excited about returning to school in the fall, and as I sat nodding my head, listening to his stories of being a college student with a smile on my face, there was a jealous gash in my heart.

Had he forgotten about Jamie? Had everyone?

Chapter 37

Mississippi heat blasted us in August. We kept the drapes closed tight to keep out the brutal sun. Window fans swirled stale, humid air through the house. The television and the newspapers screamed out that our president, Lyndon B. Johnson, was sending forty-five thousand more American troops to Vietnam, and that income taxes were increasing. I read that the median household income was seven thousand dollars per year. I couldn't even imagine that kind of money. The news blasted that the Summer of Love was here and everything was going to hell in a handbasket. I couldn't relate to free love and young people fleeing to California as I sat staring at the fig tree outside my bedroom window, listening to Scott McKenzie sing about going to San Francisco and wearing flowers in your hair.

California was as far away as Mars, for all I knew. Was my life always going to be here in my messy room, where I would wither away and die? I was a prisoner living completely in my own head.

I daydreamed about Jamie, sketching an amateur drawing in charcoal of my baby boy and then crying for hours, realizing I didn't even know what he looked like and never would. Some nights I dreamed of a toddler, his arms outstretched to me. His hair was red this time, and his little face scrunched up as he cried. Waking up with a jolt, I worried:

Jamie is only six weeks old. The baby in the dream can't be him but maybe this means he needs me.

I lived vicariously on the phone and through letters. Lizzie wrote regularly. In true Lizzie fashion, she had given birth to a baby girl and named her Ruby. Then, just as she had predicted, she had left the Home with her baby, and she and Bobby Lee were planning a wedding. I was thrilled for her, envious, and sorry for myself at the same time.

Oh, Laura, she wrote, *you have to see her. Ruby is the most beautiful little girl in the world. Why, she looks just like Bobby Lee. She's the best baby. You would love her.*

Lizzie had pulled it off. My chest filled with love and pride for her.

♺

Pepper's family was vacationing on the coast in August before she headed off to college. Her call to tell me she was in town brightened my world. It felt good to finally have someone with whom to compare feelings about the Home, but we tiptoed around that subject.

"Hey, there's a party at the beach tonight. Y'all want to go?" Billy had found us whispering and giggling in my room. Billy never invited me to parties. He was probably just interested in taking Pepper out, and the thought of going to a party terrified me.

"Come on. Let's go. It'll be fun." Pepper grinned at Billy and then playfully pushed my shoulder. She had just lectured me about starting to live again.

I surprised myself. "Okay. Why not?"

We began the timeworn discussion of what to wear and instantly, a familiar tingling of anticipation pulsed through my body. As day turned into early evening, Billy drove us to the beach. I gulped in the salty, warm gulf breeze. Gritty sand glowed pristine in the golden air of dusk. The sound of water washing ashore in lazy laps was a balm to my ears. An enormous bonfire already blazed, flames licking skyward. Music and boisterous voices filled the air as kids milled about, loose and carefree.

My heart began to bang in my chest, my throat closed.

"I'm not sure. I need to go back," I rasped at Pepper's back.

She and Billy continued weaving through the crowd, not wanting to hear me. I stumbled trying to keep up with them, warm sand filling my sandals.

Stopping to slide off my shoes, I straightened up and looked directly into the face of a young man playing the guitar. His hair was glossy, a curly light brown. Thick eyelashes framed his penetrating hazel eyes. His face was serious as he quietly strummed his guitar. An unexpected moment of recognition caught me off guard as we locked eyes.

Some clean-cut young guys, beers in their hands, hope on their faces, circled around the guitar player.

Billy nodded toward them. "Those are air force guys from the base. They're cool. I've met a few of them at other parties."

The guitar player looked me up and down. My face burned.

Did I sense that this young man, so far from home and lonely, was looking for a girl to love him? How could I have known he was damaged in ways I would never understand? Or that I was broken in ways he could never know? He pulled his eyes away from me and nodded to Pepper. Smiling wide at her he said, "Hi, my name is Nick." I pretended to ignore him.

༄

The stars were aligned that night. Fate was making her moves. Within five months, Nick and I would be married. Nine months after that wedding, we would have a son. Within eighteen months of meeting, we would permanently move to his home state of California. My

escape from the pain of Mississippi would be thrown into unstop-
pable motion.

Part Two

Chapter 38
July 1977, La Mesa, California

Out of breath. My chest exploding. Evil red talons grasping at my back. My legs pumped harder. I was running for my life. A scream traveled up my throat, but regardless of how terrified I was, no sound came out.

My eyes flew open. Sweat drenched my body; my heart thudded. Catching my breath, I took in the dark room. Moonlight glowed through the shimmery drapes, silhouetting tree branches against the night sky. All was calm. Still, adrenaline pumped through my veins.

What did it mean? This same nightmare had haunted me across the years.

I shuddered, breathed deeply, and listened to the soft puffs of breath from the baby boy lying next to me. Dark lashes rested on his ivory cheeks. Staring at him, I felt my heart expand as my hand reached ever so softly to stroke the downy face of my youngest son, Ian.

Remembering another velvety cheek on a different baby boy made my contentment morph into an ache. *What happened to him? Where is Jamie?*

Ten busy years had flown by, filled with difficulties and adjustments but just as many joys and thrills. I held tight my treasures: the three sons I gave birth to after Jamie. Before each birth, I was fraught with worry that something would go wrong. Would I be punished?

But fickle destiny had been kind, and all three boys were born whole and healthy. In an eight-year span, I became the mother of four sons. Raising three, all the while mourning the first one.

∾

Less than five months after that fateful evening when Nick and I met on the beach in 1967, we married for all the wrong reasons. He was a lonely California boy stationed at an Air Force base in the Deep South, looking for love in all the wrong places. I was damaged by grief and the loss of my firstborn son, desperate to escape the life that suffocated me. Nick was my ticket out. I was the perfect woman for him: lacking self-esteem, eager to please, and willing to do whatever it took to get away from my hometown and my grief.

Our start was dubious, to say the least. Those courting months were not filled with laughter and adoration. Part of me knew from day one that his self-important, spoiled nature was wrong, at least for me. Early on, my patience wearied of his tactics and his need to be sarcastic and cynical, always the center of attention. I fooled myself by saying that his caustic behavior was a sign of his intelligence, his moodiness dark and romantic. After all, he was another musician.

That December, on Christmas Eve, my daddy walked me down the aisle of our chilly family church. A small group of close friends and family clustered on the pews. I looked up to see Nick standing at the front altar, surrounded by wedding-white poinsettias, and my gut lurched. I stumbled. Daddy peered down at me, a question in his eyes. I gulped but kept walking. I had made my bed. I had to follow through with this. The photo of Nick and me standing with Reverend Riken is so telling: the minister, his chin stern; Nick, nervous and grim; and me looking like a frightened little girl playing bride—no smile, just a vacant, startled look on my face, wondering, *What have I done?*

❧

Now, a decade later, I knew what I had done. I had married a man with little empathy, a man whom I would never quite understand, whose values and concerns were alien to me. Hadn't I known it that night a month before our wedding when tears streamed down my face, as I hoped for compassion and sympathy? I had finally discovered the strength to tell him about Jamie. My conscience demanded that I be honest and start off our marriage the right way.

As I confessed my deepest secret and heartache, he silenced me, shutting me down immediately. Through gritted teeth, he warned me, "Why are you telling me this? Never—I repeat, never—talk about this again. I don't want my parents to find out about this kid, or about what you did."

"I promise," I wept, reaching for him.

Shrugging off my hand, he faced away from me. The air between us was silent, frigid. My heart hammered. *What have I done?* I became frantic. "I-I wanted you to know in case that made you not want me anymore," I grasped, falling apart. "Nick, I had to tell you."

He turned back to me, his eyes hard. "I just want to know one thing. Are you going to love me as much as you love this Jamie?"

My gut told me it was wrong when he offered no kindness, not an ounce of concern. I had bared my soul to him. Why didn't I run the other way? I felt only relief when he said he would still marry me knowing my truth. After all, I was damaged goods, a liar, and a misfit.

❧

I had spent ten long years trying to prove that yes, I loved him as much as I loved Jamie. That I loved our sons beyond measure. I worked hard at being the best mom I could be, the most reliable wife possible.

Years of condescending remarks and emotional abuse toward me and his own sons had lessened my love for him. True, we had days, even months, of peace living our day-to-day lives. We camped in the mountains with the boys, there were soccer games, beach days, and vacations. Weekly dinners with his kind parents were a highlight. I adored my gentle in-laws.

We had a small circle of close friends and an engaging social life. There would be harmony for months when things were going well. But always there was that cloudy, mysterious sadness of living the secret that our marriage, which appeared perfect to the outside world, was privately hollow.

No matter what I did, I never seemed able to completely please him or was never enough. Still, I plugged on. Eventually I realized I was caught in the same web I had been in with Mama, catering to his whims and moods, uneasy each day and night. Grasping for crumbs of his affection.

∾

I was six months pregnant with Dustin when Nick lashed out and hit me. His excuse? He was drunk, and I infuriated him when I laughed at him. My glasses sliced a bloody path across my nose and cheek, flew across the room, and shattered on the floor. As I cowered, tears, snot, and blood running down my face, I panicked. We would be moving to California soon. Was this my life from now on?

I was blind as a bat without my glasses, but Nick told me we couldn't afford new ones. With a slashed cheek and swollen nose, I reached out to my parents, asking them if they could help me replace my glasses. They never questioned my bruised, sliced face. They paid for a new pair without a word.

Why did I stay with Nick after that? I stayed because I knew I had nowhere to turn. I stayed because I couldn't admit to Mama and

Daddy, "Once again, I've screwed up my life. Once again, I have made the worst decision."

After a miserable eight-year anniversary, I had high hopes in marriage counseling. I read books with titles like *Can This Marriage Be Saved?* and *The Total Woman*, a blockbuster evangelist book published in 1973, which explained that the reason marital strife exists is that the male and female egos are at odds. Wives simply need to surrender their own egos and bend to the authority of their husbands and submit, serve, and obey. Basically, if you do your job well and do whatever pleases your husband, he will treat you well, but even if he walks all over you and treats you like dirt, it's your job as a "total woman" to live with it and service him with a smile on your face and a song in your heart.

I tried all the tricks.

I endured Nick and he endured me. The best and maybe only good thing in our marriage remained the three beautiful human beings we had created. They were worth far more than any problems we had.

Often I worried that Nick thought our sons were a burden; he seemed invested in them only when it was self-serving. I worried what kind of example we set for our kids, never seeing eye to eye with each other. The coldness, the walking on eggshells—would I never feel equal, loved?

Still I stayed.

∿

The years played on behind my closed eyes. Torturing myself, I let thoughts of Jamie drift in. I allowed myself to feel the distant ache that never left.

After marriage and our move cross-country, life settled down. I remembered my son Dustin's birth, a short fifteen months after Jamie's. Dustin had been my salvation. Was Jamie like him? Or maybe Jamie resembled Marc, my third son. My longing to know about Jamie always remained tucked in a corner of my heart, ready to spring up and haunt me late in the night.

Sure, sometimes when I was crazy busy and life was good, it softened, took a back seat, but not on this night. There I was, and there was Jamie, before Nick, before California.

The bedroom door squeaked open.

"Mom, I'm scared." Marc, his soft curls a tumble, slipped quietly into the bedroom and crawled under the covers alongside Ian, giving his baby brother a gentle hug.

"It's okay, sweetie. Come here," I whispered, reaching for him and rubbing his thin back.

Before long, Dustin entered the room, scooching in on the other side. Nick was working tonight; normally, this was his side of the bed.

"Mom, Marc woke me up," Dustin grumbled, snuggling next to me, falling back to sleep in minutes. I gently kissed his freckled cheek, brushing his ginger hair with my fingertips, inhaling his little-boy smell of Johnson & Johnson baby shampoo, cotton pajamas, and freshly mown grass.

This is my world now. My sons. I thank God for them daily. The same God I ask to watch over Jamie.

July 8, 1977

The next day brought devil heat, and my little boys bounded out of bed bright-eyed and bushy-tailed. After breakfast they ran through the lawn sprinklers while I stole upstairs to my bedroom closet. There it was, the hidden, tiny brown box that held one of my dearest treasures, also my deepest secret.

The Eagles busted loose with "Lyin' Eyes" on the stereo downstairs as my boys squealed and laughed outside the window. I looked at the tiny birth card. It had traveled with me from New Orleans, across the country, and to every apartment or house we had lived in for these ten turbulent years. Always hidden away, it was my rock. It was my own truth. Proof Jamie did exist. As my chest exploded, tears slid down my face. Jamie was ten years old today.

Tonight, I would call Mama. We would chat about my boys and she would gossip about family. She'd sit in her recliner, her window air conditioner roaring so loudly, I would be able to hear it over the line two thousand miles away. We would both avoid the subject of Jamie. After all these years, I was still a coward, and I hated myself for it, but I couldn't rock the boat. Finally, our relationship was better. Still difficult, but better. I wanted her to love my boys. I wanted her to forgive me, and I still had the hope, the dream, that someday she and I could speak Jamie's name out loud. I wanted her to miss him as much as I did.

"Why are you calling so late, Laura?"

"I can't sleep. Do you know what day it is, Mama?"

"Of course I know what day it is." She laughed. "It's Friday."

Does she not remember, or has she pushed that memory so far down?

She changed the subject, launching into a lighthearted story about Daddy. Soon we both were laughing and I marveled at how I still longed for the sound of her voice. We were having a normal mother-daughter conversation, rare for us. The distance between California and Mississippi had enabled us to relax, to be less critical. Phone calls were always much easier than face to face. Tonight's conversation was exceptional and ended any thought of mine to mention the true reason for my call. I couldn't destroy this moment. I never uttered a word about the past. All this time, and still my throat was paralyzed about the shameful skeleton in my closet: my son, her first grandson.

Chapter 39

Nick raged at me, "I'm leaving. I met a woman in Northern California when I was there with the band. Ya know, it made me fuckin' realize something. How you don't love me. You love the boys more than me. You're consumed with the boys. Good luck finding some guy who wants a woman like you, with these kids hanging all over you."

I saw red. When would this end?

Soon after that hellish shouting match in the fall of 1977, our fate was sealed. That was it. Something deep inside me ruptured. Although I felt used up at the age of twenty-eight, I was ready to face whatever lay ahead, if only for the peace of being away from the constant tension. My disgust at what I had settled for finally trumped my insecurity and fear of being alone.

Nick made short order of phoning Mama and Daddy before I could, breaking the news that our ten years of marriage were a failure, thanks to their worthless daughter. That call left my parents shocked and speechless, but after they recovered, they called me. Mama was incredulous that I had not told them what was happening to my marriage. Daddy demanded that I come back to Mississippi where I belonged and offered to drive to California and help me move.

Nick moved in with his parents, leaving the boys and me alone in our house, along with the mortgage. I had been a stay-at-home mom for ten years, with no means of my own, living thousands of miles away from family, and I was too naive to realize the tough times in store for me.

Friends worried when word got out that Nick had left me.

"What are you going to do? You'll never make it on your own," naysayers predicted out loud.

"You'll have to move back to Mississippi." Grammy and Mama finally agreed on something.

An odd peace settled over me. Enjoying the calm before the storm, I didn't worry about how I'd live through this. A far worse thing, losing Jamie, had happened to me, and I had continued to breathe.

But I struggled emotionally and was close to destitute within no time. As my small bank account dwindled, reality smacked me in the face. I had no way to feed my children. Our house was slipping into foreclosure, and Nick never sent a dime. I stretched the money left in the bank, buying milk, eggs, and bread. Simply buying gas at sixty-eight cents per gallon became a feat. Panic began to slip in, especially late at night when I sat awake for hours, the boys tucked in bed. Other women found jobs and raised children without men. I could do this. Couldn't I?

∿

"You need to sign here." The disgruntled social services clerk pushed papers toward me. I glanced at the faces of my little boys, taking in their wide, anxious eyes as all three huddled together on the metal chair beside me. Baby Ian, fussy and exhausted, his arms reaching for me, sat on nine-year-old Dustin's lap. I squeezed his little hand to comfort him and turned back to sign the papers, feeling like the most worthless mother in the world.

Food stamps. How did I get here?

"Thank you." I smiled at the distracted clerk. No smile back.

He pushed the food coupon booklet towards me. "You'll get more in the mail. Don't forget, you can't buy alcohol or cigarettes with these." He sneered. "Only food."

What kind of mother does he think I am? I'm desperate to feed my boys, not to buy cigarettes or booze.

There was no kindness in his cold eyes as he frowned at my sons. I saw fear on seven-year-old Marc's face and grabbed his hand. It had been a rough three-hour wait for these sons of mine. They had reached their limit. And so had I.

Herding the boys into my yellow Volkswagen bug, furious and embarrassed at this state I was in, I drove straight to a grocery store and traded the vouchers for much-needed groceries. I splurged on ice cream for my sons, hoping the vouchers covered that too. *I don't care what I have to do—I'll never ask for a handout again.* Now more than ever, I was determined to find a job and make this work.

℘

I found that except for being close to penniless, I rarely missed Nick. The boys and I lived peacefully without his moods and anger. He seemed to have slipped easily back into the single life, seldom calling or picking up the kids for visitation. When he did, he would drop them off with his heartbroken parents. I was thankful that at least my sons began seeing their beloved grandparents again. They had always showered the boys and me with so much love.

Setting out on a job hunt and searching for childcare landed me a job at a large insurance company within a month of the food-stamp debacle. As a junior file clerk, I worked for hours pulling manila claims folders from floor-to-ceiling shelves and hurrying them back to the main office, filled with forty demanding, mostly male, claims adjusters. At twenty-eight years old, I was the old lady of the entry-level job, working mostly with eighteen- and nineteen-year-old women. Exhausted each night, I drove home to my boys with dinner to make, their schoolwork to help with, and baths to give, while my coworkers raced out to happy hour. I made $2.65 per hour. Although the two older boys were in school and aftercare, daycare for Ian took over half of my take-home pay.

I hatched a plan to head to Mississippi after the school year ended and begin a new life with my boys. I would have family to help with the kids. My cousin Mark had written begging me to come to New Orleans and promising to help me find a good job. Nancy called and said I could live with her and her son, Shane, on the coast. My parents offered to help me with the move. It began to look like the only way to go. Still, part of me felt unsure. After all, could I handle Mama's judgment now that I had been away from it for ten years? On the other hand, maybe we would finally talk about Jamie. Maybe I could find him. This move would be a good thing for all of us, I reasoned.

Chapter 40

A nother routine Saturday, running late, racing kids to soccer games. I never seemed to have an extra minute to spare. Weekends were filled with homework, sports, and mountains of laundry. I staggered my bill payments, watched every penny, and miraculously scraped by.

Working and learning how to be a single mom gave me renewed self-confidence, and I realized the last thing on earth I wanted was another man in my life dictating who I should be. A fierce fire began to burn inside me as I maneuvered the freeways of Southern California in my battered car, singing along with Helen Reddy's hit "I Am Woman." A strength was growing in me. *I can do this.*

෨

That chilly, clear morning, I could feel fall in the air. I held my hand above my eyes, shielding them from the glare as Dustin and Marc raced across the soccer field, their legs fast and furious. Ian clapped, grinning at me with his pearly white toddler smile. We called out together, "Go, boys, go!"

Nick had shown up at the game and was standing on the other side of the field. Divorce imminent, we were sanctimoniously polite with each other. Sitting on a tattered quilt with Ian on the sidelines, I avoided the clique of soccer moms I had once been part of. One hair-sprayed mom had embarrassed me in front of all the parents when she brayed, "My God, Laura, Marc needs new cleats. I'm shocked you let him play in those. Poor kid."

If only she knew. I had resorted to buying powdered milk for the boys and stretched our groceries to remarkable levels, often skipping meals for myself. I borrowed clothes from my best friend so I would have appropriate clothes to work in. How could I afford new cleats?

As the game ended, Nick strode across the field, a stranger at his side.

All charm and smiles, Nick surprised me. "Hey, Laura, this is an old neighbor of mine. We went to elementary school together. He's the opposing team's coach. Thought I'd introduce you."

Immediately on guard, I grumbled under my breath, "I don't want to meet any of your friends." But when I looked up from the ground, a pair of soulful dark eyes and a warm, kind smile startled me.

"Hi, I'm Gene." The old neighbor spoke in a soft, calm voice that put me at ease yet sent an electric sizzle down my spine. I recall most the laugh lines at the corners of his eyes that lit up his face.

I stumbled over the words, "Uh, glad to meet you" and turned away quickly. I ignored their small talk and simply gathered the boys together, sneaking a quick look at Nick and this guy, Gene, parting ways with a handshake.

Surreptitiously, I took in Gene's long dark hair and the way he walked. His shoulders were broad, his back straight. He wrapped his arms around two children's shoulders, a curly-haired tall boy and a small blond girl, her braids askew.

From that day on, Gene seemed to be at every game. He would seek me out and sit on the ground next to me on the tattered quilt, and we quickly became soccer-parent friends. Always soft-spoken, he seemed innocent enough. We shared tidbits about our lives, and I discovered he had been a single dad for a few years.

Once, I confessed I didn't know how I could combine work and raising the kids without failing at each.

He looked surprised. "Really? I think you're the kind of woman who can do just about anything you set your mind to. You're strong, Laura. I see it in you."

Flattered, I smiled at him. "Anything?"

"Anything."

What is it about him? Why this quirky déjà vu feeling? He seems to listen to every word I say, but do I really know him?

∾

A month later, Gene showed up at my house uninvited. My little boys were running in circles in our front yard alongside our white dog, Blue. I stood watching them when an avocado-green Toyota truck drove up and parked in front of our house. The boys stopped racing and stood still as none other than the coach from the soccer field stepped out of the truck and hopped over our white rail fence. Blue wagged his tail eagerly at the stranger.

Oh no. Why would he show up like this? I was both irritated and intrigued.

I looked down at my wrinkled top and cringed. I hadn't bothered to brush my hair that morning and felt it sliding out of a two-day-old ponytail.

I heard one quick rap on the front door and took a deep breath. Leaning against the door frame, Gene loomed over me, grinning from ear to ear. His arms were overloaded with brown grocery bags, but all I saw was his shiny hair and those dark eyes. My stomach clenched.

"What are you doing here?" I demanded, my hands on my hips.

"Hi, sorry to drop by unannounced. Your address was on the soccer roster. I brought you a little something. Well, really something for the boys."

As I opened the door wider, he stepped in, walking confidently toward the kitchen, my sons trailing behind him.

Removing an enormous jar from a bag, he handed it to me. The weight of the jar startled me.

"It's peanut butter." He laughed. "Nine pounds of it, to be exact. My company sells these to restaurants and schools. I thought you could use it for the boys' lunches."

"What's in the bags?" Dustin and Marc demanded.

"Shh . . . Be polite," I warned them, as Ian wrapped his arms around my legs, almost tripping me.

Gene dumped dozens of snack-size bags of chips across the table. "Do you guys like chips?"

They cheered, turning to me. "Yes! Mom, can we have some?" There had been no room for potato chips in our budget.

Gene said he knew how tough being a single parent could be and that he simply thought I could use a little extra help. He turned and headed toward the door, explaining that he had to run and didn't want to wear out his welcome.

"Wait, wait. Ian, stay with your big brothers." I ran behind him as my wild sons bickered over who got which chips.

"Wait!" I scrawled my phone number on a slip of paper and shoved it toward him, then spontaneously stood on my tiptoes and gave him a quick peck on his cheek. I breathed in fresh air, sunshine, and soap. "Thank you for the peanut butter."

Jumping back, a startled look on his face, Gene quickly waved goodbye. It seemed he couldn't get away fast enough as he raced to his truck, not looking back once.

Why did I kiss him? He'll think I'm easy. Desperate. He'll never call me now.

Going about my Sunday chores, preparing for the week ahead, I was unable to shake thoughts of Gene from my mind. I was mortified I had kissed him, but no one had ever asked me if I had enough food for my children. This man had cared enough to make a gift of food to the boys and ask nothing in return. I felt humbled and grateful for such a friend.

Apparently, Gene wasn't scared off, because the phone rang that night and we talked into the wee hours of the morning. I had not laughed that much in an entire year. My world suddenly seemed brighter as I lay awake the rest of the night, running our conversation through my mind, a smile never leaving my face.

∾

The next week found me in a neighborhood coffee shop with Gene. I was giddy with excitement to meet him away from the soccer field. It felt illicit and titillating.

We had talked on the phone every night that week, but I had never mentioned my plans to head back to the South because I didn't want to break the magical spell I felt every time I heard his voice. I began to daydream about the two of us, fantasies always tinged with lust.

You're acting like a teenager, I admonished myself.

Now here we were. After an hour of fun bantering, our coffee grown cold, he reached across the table and gently laid his hand on mine. His warm fingers sent shivers through me, but when words came out of his mouth, he caught me completely off guard.

"Laura, I'm leaving next week. I'm moving up to Lake Tahoe for a while. I planned this sabbatical a year ago, long before we met. I thought I should let you know I like you a lot, but I don't want or need a relationship. I just need alone time to think about my life."

Why was I so crestfallen? I didn't want a relationship either. I had told myself a hundred times the last thing I needed was a man complicating my life. I nodded, plastering a fake smile on my face.

I plan to go home to Mississippi, so why am I holding my breath, and why does my heart feel like it has been ripped apart?

"We'll write to each other." His hand tightened over my limp one. His smile was kind, oblivious to the knife he had shoved in my chest.

Another jerk.

Chapter 41
July 1987, El Cajon, California

Summer's warm breath pushed in through the open windows. Birdsong and rustling eucalyptus leaves were music to my ears. I faintly detected the sounds of twelve-year-old Ian stirring around in the kitchen with our golden retriever, Peaches. Muffled hip-hop beats thumped behind the walls of sixteen-year-old Marc's bedroom.

"Morning, beautiful."

I turned my sleepy face to peer into the warm, gentle eyes of the person I loved most in this world: my husband, my knight in shining armor, my soul mate, and all the other corny love names I can think of. I had never felt safer or more cherished. I snuggled close, nipping at his broad shoulder. "Mmm, Gene, I love you." I couldn't keep my hands off him, and he felt the same about me. After seven years of marriage, we adored each other, were utterly in love, and lustier than ever.

His embrace was strong and he nibbled at my throat just as the jarring sound of splintering glass instantly ruined the mood.

"Mom," Ian called at our bedroom door, and reality started our day.

ॐ

Helping Ian clean up the broken glass and orange juice on the floor in front of the fridge, I looked up at the calendar I kept there, along with random coupons. Red ink indicated doctor appointments, kids' stuff, and work commitments across the squares. Today's date glared loud and clear. No red circle needed.

July 8.

Jamie is twenty years old today. How is that possible?

ॐ

Gene had left for his office. Running late, as usual, I rushed back into my bedroom to dress for work, stopping to lock the door. I retrieved the secret box from a shelf in my closet. I hesitated before opening it, knowing that it always triggered a physical reaction. My body stiff with grief, I once again experienced the pain that inevitably washed over me each time I removed the tiny card from inside. Instantly, I recalled that baby boy's face.

I know he's a young man now, but I can't imagine his features. Is he a college student? A military recruit? Does he wonder about me? Is he happy?

Rubbing my finger over the name on the birth card, remembering the day I stuffed it in my pocket, I held it to my lips and whispered, "I'll never forget you, Jamie."

The rattling bedroom doorknob startled me. "Mom? Why is your door locked?"

"Be there in a minute, Ian."

I lightly kissed the card and tucked it back into its hiding spot.

ॐ

That evening, I was stuck in rush-hour traffic, listening to the Bee Gees singing about not getting too much heaven anymore. The crammed freeway was miserably hot and sticky. I knew Gene and the kids were waiting at home and they'd greet me with, "What's for dinner, Mom?" How I simultaneously loved and hated those words after inching along on the freeway for an hour.

Instead of thinking about what to cook, I let the Bee Gees take me back to that time Gene moved to Tahoe. I had struggled with the challenges of being a single mom. I wasn't perfect, and I didn't fit the glossy-magazine idea of what a '70s mom should be, but for once I was doing it my way. Entry-level work at a vast insurance company was tough. Going home exhausted to three sons under the age of nine and trying to be the mother I wanted to be, instead of a burned-out mess, was tough. Having virtually no bank account was tough. I had never felt such fatigue, yet somehow, I pushed through each day. The boys grew, and I did too, right alongside them.

True to his word, Gene sent weekly letters. His descriptions of his days in solitude in the majestic snowy mountains lightened my heart. I loved reading his deepest thoughts about life. I in turn wrote to him, describing my days, my hopes, and my fears. In those dispatches, we poured out our hearts and soon knew each other in ways we never would have without the sincere words that flowed from our pens and our hearts.

❧

In the spring of 1978, my life was about to change course again. Gene, who had "never wanted to be in another relationship," arrived back in San Diego, and nothing could keep us apart. Moving back to Mississippi was no longer an option. Our love had grown and blossomed over those long months and winter letters, and I wanted to be with this man for the rest of my life.

Soon I felt compelled to tell Gene my darkest secret. Intuitively I knew I could trust him, but it was a risk. He often said he thought

I was a wonderful mother. Would he still feel that way if he knew the truth? One rare evening alone, no kids or distractions, I finally screwed up enough courage.

"I need to tell you something about me. Something no one knows."

He was intrigued but quickly puzzled because I started trembling as I blurted out the entire story of my time in New Orleans, the tale of Jamie. I watched his eyes go from confusion to disbelief and then to empathy and concern. He reached for me, gathering me in his arms.

"Laura, I can't believe you went through that. I'm so sorry. God, I can't imagine."

Years of pent-up shame and grief slowly began to release, and my body eased against him as my tears lessened.

"Do you want me to help you find him?" He hugged me tightly.

This man. He had already stolen my heart, but now he had sealed the deal.

Our love story grew stronger yet, and eventually Dustin, Marc, Ian, and I moved in with Gene and his two children, Erick and Carly. Our 1970s blended family, complete with a magnitude of growing pains, was not always a piece of cake. Ours was a loud and rowdy bunch, from age twelve down to five years. There was never a dull moment, between our time-consuming careers, the kids' various schools and sports, and always the other parents: Nick, never involved; Gene's ex, overly involved.

Somehow, we took it in stride, argued often, laughed often, dealt with daily drama, and laughed some more. We told our friends, "*The Brady Bunch* is a lie."

Still, Gene balked at marriage. "We'll live together. We don't need a piece of paper to prove our love for each other, Laura." He was firm.

I was firmer. "I love you, Gene, but I'll not be your live-in girl-friend for life. I want my sons to see an example of two people who respect and love each other enough to commit to marriage. Call me old-fashioned. If you can't commit, I'm moving back to Mississippi."

"I don't have to be married to be committed."

"I do." I shrugged and meant it.

December 28, 1980

Three years after meeting on that soccer field, we gathered, along with family and close friends, at Presidio Park, overlooking beautiful San Diego Bay. I was overjoyed in a cream-and-lavender Victorian-style dress, with lavender flowers and French braids; Gene, handsome in a three-piece beige suit and tie. Along with my best friend, Dorothy, our five children stood with us. Carly was in lavender too, holding a bouquet that was a miniature twin of mine, and our four sons were resplendent in their first-ever leisure suits, complete with vests and ties—gifts from Nick's wonderful mother, who, thankfully, was still in my life. Gathering my handsome children together, I gloried in their eager young faces. I had never felt more pride as I did under the arbor in that simple family wedding.

Promising to "love, honor, and cherish each other until death do us part" was the very best thing we had ever done. Gene brought me healing and the confidence of being well loved. I brought him optimism and a forever love he had not thought possible.

Chapter 42
July 8, 1997

Another ten years gone, and there I sat alone, the tiny box in my lap. Jamie was thirty years old today. I stared at the card. *How can it seem like yesterday yet also a hundred years ago?*

That young girl was gone, and in her place sat a forty-eight-year-old career woman, fulfilled and content. She and the love of her life had raised five healthy and marvelous children. Fortune had smiled on her with many bright, colorful patches of joy and success.

❧

Although I had suffered dark, melancholy patches too, my sunny days outnumbered the blue days in this period. My strengths outweighed my insecurities. With experiences, the wisdom of age, and Gene's belief in me, I had grown and blossomed. I welcomed this thing we called middle age.

Two of my darkest days in the past decade had been losing my beloved Grammy and my cherished cousin Mark within a year of each other. Grammy died at eighty-one; Mark at a mere forty-one years old. Losing two of the most important loves of my life left me untethered. I battled an aching sadness, privately admonishing myself for not being stronger. For years I closed my eyes at night and saw Grammy lying in her plush coffin, her beautiful hazel-blue eyes permanently closed. Her funeral had cracked my heart wide open. Had I told her enough how much I loved her?

At Grammy's burial in Biloxi on a sweltering day in May, Mark stood next to me, his arms holding me protectively as I sobbed. We were Grammy's adored first grandchildren. There was no doubt in our minds that she had loved us best. Later that night, Mama shamed me for "making such a display of emotions" at the funeral. She looked disgusted.

"Why didn't you get better control of yourself? I was afraid you were going to collapse," she sniped at me. "And instead of going off with Mark to that dinner tonight, you should stay here with me and your daddy. It's only right." She started crying. "You head back to California tomorrow, and when will we see you again?"

Out of guilt and duty, I stayed home with them, telling Mark I would have to miss the after-funeral dinner. That decision would weigh on me forever, because that would have been the last time I would have seen my dear cousin alive.

ॐ

In 1988, we had read headlines and news stories about AIDS, but the general public knew little about this mysterious plague that seemed to attack primarily homosexuals.

Mark called me months after Grammy died. "Laura, I've gotten myself into a fix. I don't know how to tell you this, but I . . . I have AIDS." He broke down. "I'm afraid. So many of my friends have died. I think I'm dying too. Please come soon."

My blood ran cold, and I stopped in my tracks. Not Mark. I quickly assured him that this would all be okay. He was young, healthy. I promised I would always be there for him.

He was calling from New Orleans, alone in bed in his lovingly renovated three-story Victorian house, in a neighborhood ridiculously close to the old Home where I had left Jamie all those years before.

Those months we spoke often on the phone. My life was filled with raising kids and advancing in my career. I kept assuring Mark that as soon as I could, I would come visit him.

One evening in October, he called. "Laura, when are you coming?"

"I promise I'll be there soon, Mark. Work is crazy busy now, and the kids . . . well, it never stops. Honey, can I call you back tomorrow? Gene and I are out the door, headed to a Halloween party. You should see us."

He perked up. "Tell me about your costumes."

"Well, I rented this great flapper outfit. It's all red sequins and I'm wearing fishnets. I feel gorgeous."

"Perfect. Red is your color."

"Thanks. Oh, and Gene is a 1920s gangster. Our friend throws this party every year. You would love all the costumes."

He asked me to tell him more. Who had we dressed up as last year? How had I done my hair tonight? I patiently talked to him while Gene waited, sticking his head in the door a few times, giving me that look. I shooed him away, shrugging my shoulders, letting him know I simply couldn't hang up on Mark.

Finally I said, "Listen, honey, I really have to go—we're running so late. Story of my life." I chuckled and added, "Try to stay strong. I promise I'll fly to you as soon as I can. I love you, Mark."

A week later, Mark died. For the rest of my life, I would regret not having flown back to New Orleans soon enough. I had lost forever my adored cousin, one of the dearest champions of my life.

❧

Today, Jamie's birthday, easily turned cheerless and heart-rending as I clasped the tiny card that still filled me with yearning for my secret son. Never-ending guilt and shame burned my face as I embraced the hurt. I did not discuss this pushed-down pain with Gene. Why bother him dredging up the sorrow I seemed determined not to forget? This part of me stayed private.

Holding the card to my heart, I talked to the son who hadn't heard my voice in thirty years.

"Happy birthday, Jamie," I whispered to the empty room. Gauzy curtains fluttered in the soft summer breeze. Our golden retriever, Angelbaby, curled at my feet and Eric Clapton's "Tears from Heaven" played softly in the background as emptiness filled me.

∾

Alone in my home office, I spent furtive hours scrolling through reunion sites on my newfangled computer. I composed clandestine emails and sent them to various adoption/birth parent sites, hoping to find him. My eyes burned as I read the endless names and dates in minuscule fonts. Reality hit me smack in the face: *This is not only my story.* There were hundreds of thousands of birth mothers like me, searching along with biological fathers, half siblings, and relinquished children desperate to find their birth parents I found no record of a baby boy born on July 8, 1967, in New Orleans.

I read articles about closed adoptions in the '50s and '60s. I was stunned when I saw a graph showing that from 1945 to 1973, approximately 2.5 million women surrendered their newborns, the majority because there was no ring on their finger.

No, this is not only my story. There are millions of us.

The thought *I'll never find him* stabbed at me as I shut down my computer and headed to bed.

Lying next to my sleeping husband, I prayed: *Dear God, please watch over my sons. All* four *of them.*

∾

My adult sons had moved out and were seeking their fortunes in various ways. Through the dramas and traumas of raising five kids, financial ups and downs, petty hurts, and sporadic hair-raising arguments, Gene and I had kept our heads and, most important, our hearts. After seventeen years of marriage, there was still no one I would rather have had by my side.

My long-distance relationship with Mama had mellowed. Perhaps time truly does soften everything. I was more tolerant, and she seemed less critical. I cherished the fact that Daddy and I had started adding "I love you" at the end of every long-distance call. Still, infrequent visits back to Mississippi continued to be taxing. Those visits inevitably ended on a sour note: Daddy would gently remind me not to upset Mama, and I would hurry back to California with hurt feelings due to her cool reception and ugly comments.

They had recently celebrated their fiftieth wedding anniversary, and Gene and I had flown my parents out to California. In the photos from that day, their faces were happy as my smiling adult children gathered around them, the centerpiece a huge, elaborate pink-and-white cake. There was no celebration planned in Mississippi, so I invited them here, unable to let such a milestone go by without celebration. One truth had held steady over all those years: Theirs was a love story for sure.

❧

Mama seldom initiated our phone calls, but she surprised me one bright morning, a giddy quiver in her voice. I settled into a chair at the kitchen table with the phone, mentally noting that the ferns hanging above the sink needed watering, sipped my coffee, and listened to her laughter.

"Hon, you're not gonna believe this."

"Tell me." I smiled.

"Well, we're gonna be great-grandparents. Tammy's pregnant! She was so worried, but we said, 'Tammy, honey, we're family, we'll get through this.'"

She's actually giggling.

My cloudy coffee turned to acid as I listened to Mama.

Has she forgotten? She refused to utter a word about Jamie for thirty years, and now she's raving about her unwed granddaughter's pregnancy.

I didn't comprehend a word she was saying as she pattered on, just felt smug and righteous at the sound of her voice.

"Is she getting married?" I asked, sounding more sanctimonious than I felt. That fact certainly didn't matter to me. I couldn't have cared less if Tammy was married or not.

"Oh, no. But, Laura, times have changed. Aren't you happy for me? My first great-grandchild."

Yes, times had changed. Over the past decades, I had observed society's new tolerance for unmarried mothers. It had become accepted, commonplace. Federally and state funded programs were now available for unwed young mothers who proudly kept their babies without a whiff of scandal. I agreed and supported any assistance given to young women faced with an unexpected pregnancy. *Why am I enraged? Why does her happiness hurt me?*

Mama prattled on, oblivious to my terse silence.

"I have to go." A toxic balloon expanded in my chest as I hung up the phone, and jealous tears flooded my eyes. I knew I was irrational, acting ridiculous.

Am I too sensitive? Why can't I be happy for Mama and her first great-grandchild?

All that day, I tried to shake it off. When Gene arrived home that night, I had already knocked back two glasses of chardonnay and quickly blurted out Mama's "news" complete with imitations of her squeals and giggles.

"Maybe your mom resorts to denial to get through the memories of that time, Laura," he reasoned with me.

I poured another glass of wine and glared at him. "No. She's punishing me again. She's hateful."

He shrugged, weary from a rough day at the office. Then he held me close.

Has she forgotten the way she treated me, her scandalous, unwed daughter? Has she forgotten her first grandchild?

Chapter 43
July 8, 2007

O ne of my clients flattered me: "Your son Dustin is thirty-eight years old? Impossible. I'd never have guessed that." I thanked her, telling her she'd made my day as I thought, *What would she think of me if she knew I had an even older, secret son?*

∾

On Jamie's fortieth birthday, the slim box sat in front of me on my desk once again. I held his birth card, questioning how dreamlike it felt: *Baby Boy Jamie.*

Has he really lived half a lifetime without ever hearing my voice or feeling my arms around him? I have missed his entire life. He has never known mine.

Dry-eyed and hollow, I placed the card carefully in its hiding place in my closet just as the patio door burst open in the family room.

"Grammy, we're hungry!" our grandchildren, Jake and Paige hollered as they raced inside, their bathing suits dripping on the hardwood floors.

PaPa Gene followed, calling out, "Grammy, let's make lunch for these two."

Relishing our new roles, Gene and I were eager babysitters and my favorite thing was being called Grammy.

The ups and downs of raising our own children had passed and given way to the joys of helping to raise our grandchildren. As I put together grilled cheese sandwiches and sliced fruit, we bantered happily with our grands and I couldn't help but think of Dustin's four little ones in Wisconsin: Noah, Ashlyn, Gabe, and Baby Kreagen. Long-distance grandparenting was difficult, but I cherished all six of our grandchildren, hoping they felt half the love for me that I had for my own grandmother.

∾

We had also lived through our children's weddings and a couple of their stormy divorces. Ian was home from the army and thriving in San Diego. Marc had married Virginia, a lovely young artist, and was pursuing his music. Carly was building her business and lived with her partner, David. Erick and Trish were busy parenting and working. Dustin, a single dad, was working and raising his children in the Midwest.

"We're so lucky," Gene and I often agreed.

Is Jamie married? I wondered each time we proudly watched our glowing children dance at their weddings.

∾

Gene and I traveled back to the South more frequently during this decade.

Two years earlier, in 2005, my parents lost our old family home and everything in it to the devastating hurricane Katrina. For three days, I couldn't get through to anyone back there. Watching the overwhelming news reports, I grew weaker each hour.

Eventually we learned the horrific details of how Mama and Daddy had survived by standing on their kitchen countertop as the house filled with six feet of water, watching helplessly as ferocious winds ripped off parts of the roof, water poured inside, walls imploded around them, and their refrigerator floated across the kitchen, with Mama's critically necessary insulin locked inside.

Nothing mattered to me except finding them alive. Any anger that had ever lingered vanished. My hometown was destroyed, and my childhood home, built by my great-grandfather, sat smack in the middle of the destruction. My father had been born in that house.

I had to see my parents and hold them in my arms. Gene and I flew back to them within days.

ॐ

As I got older, and my parents became more feeble, a fierce magnetic force within me and an overpowering desire to help pulled me toward them. Gene and I purchased a house in Mississippi and moved my homeless parents into it. I went to church with Daddy each time I visited. "Praise Father, Son, and Holy Ghost," we sang side by side.

Mama, who suffered from Type 2 diabetes, was chronically ill and in the beginning stages of dementia. I looked into her eyes, and they seemed empty, blank. Daddy, always a dedicated and loving caregiver, was worn out and frail. He and I had developed a habit of exchanging daily calls and emails. His emails, often lengthy dispatches, told the stories of his life. I treasured them.

Daddy never spoke of Jamie, and neither did I. I held tight this cherished closeness with my father, not willing or able to rock the boat.

ॐ

It was also in this decade that one morning I opened another email from Daddy, expecting more lighthearted news of his simple days caring for Mama, his volunteer work, or babysitting great-grandchildren. There was no text, simply an attachment: a scanned photo of a short, simple obituary, cut neatly from a newspaper.

Clay. Dead at the age of fifty-four. Cancer.

My heart stopped.

I reread the obit a couple of times.

A few years back, Nancy had told me that Clay had moved back to the Gulf Coast. She mentioned that he had divorced and that she had actually dated him a few times. She had added that he never asked about me. I was stunned silent.

Clay and I had never spoken after our last, miserable conversation on the phone before Daddy hauled me to Georgia for the shotgun wedding that never happened. In my mind once again, I was that stricken, heartbroken teenager crumpled in the back seat in her wrinkled white dress, scraggly longleaf pine trees and the rolling green hills of Alabama flying past the car window.

Did Clay never think of me? Did he ever wonder about the baby?

For a long time, I sat staring at that screen. Numb.

Chapter 44
October 2015

"**Y**ou'll miss us," my clients and coworkers warned.

Gene worried. "You're going to get bored."

"Mom, I hope you have something to do. I've read people get depressed and die when they retire because they have no purpose."

Laughing, I assured Ian that I would always wake up with purpose and did not plan on dying anytime soon.

After over thirty-five years of working in the demanding field of title insurance, I was retiring. I told my friends and clients, "I want a chapter before the final chapter." I had decided to write a family history for my sons as one of my projects and had become obsessed with the website Ancestry.com, tracking our genealogy back to the 1200s. I planned to intertwine my research with the old family stories that Grammy and Daddy had repeated to me all those years ago.

Embracing all my newfound freedom, I worked on projects I had never had time for before. I planned another trip to the UK for Gene's and my anniversary. I signed up for classes. One, Julia Cameron's *The Artist's Way*, had me working on a timeline of my life.

I write in my journal religiously every day, spilling my guts out on the page. Hesitantly, for the first time ever, I began to write about Jamie, using the code *NO* (*New Orleans*), still leery of someone reading my words. I thought this tactic would keep my secret secure.

During this decade, in June 2011, Mama died of renal failure and

Daddy followed four short days later. Their deaths broke me in half. For months afterward, I was a shell, crippled with grief. Daddy's death certificate read, *Failure to thrive* as his cause of death. I googled it and found that the term applied to unexplained infant deaths, as well as geriatric deaths when no terminal illness or physical reason existed for the individual to die. This haunted me, and still does to this day. I can only imagine my father died from a broken heart. He and Mama had been married for sixty-five years, and he had stood by her side always. I don't think he wanted to live without her.

Would I die without ever seeing my son Jamie?

ᐁ

The month before Mama died, I flew back to Mississippi several times. Both parents were ill, Daddy with pneumonia, Mama placed in a rehabilitation hospital. At the end of one visit I stopped at the hospital to say goodbye to Mama on my way to the airport. She broke my heart as she begged me to take her with me. I explained she was too ill to fly now but promised that maybe when she and Daddy were better, we could do just that.

There she sat, slumped in a wheelchair, looking abandoned. Kneeling, I straightened her blouse, kissed her cheek, and patted her shoulder. I tucked a fluffy white teddy bear, an impulse gift, in her arms and she clasped it close to her chest. It held a red heart, *I love you, Mama* embroidered across it.

She had been vacant and confused this whole visit. I often wondered if she even recognized me. I kissed her cheek again, hugged her fragile body, and told her I loved her. Jerking back, she peered into my eyes, a weak smile brightening her face. She seemed alert for the first time in days. Her eyes registered acknowledgment, and in a clear, strong voice she said, "Laura, I love you."

I could not remember the last time I had heard those words from

Mama. A week later, she was gone. I have always known that one of the most amazing gifts I have ever received from the universe was hearing that final "I love you" from my mama.

I flew back again upon the news of her death. I hurried straight from the airport to Daddy's hospice room with my brother Bill. I knew the minute I saw my father lying in his bed, tragically thin, deathly pale, and drained of life, that it would be our last time together. I straightened his blankets and held his hand, fighting back tears, forcing myself to be brave in front of him.

"I'm here now, Daddy. Everything's going to be okay. All is set for Mama's funeral, just like you wanted." I tried to sound calm and positive as anguish filled my chest.

He motioned for me to come closer, gently kissing my cheek, repeating that sweet gesture several times. As I felt my heart splintering, I knew it was now or never.

Is this the right time? Dear God, if not now, when?

I pulled in a long breath. Leaning in close to him, I quietly asked, "Daddy, did a man ever come looking for me?"

"What kind of man, hon?" His voice was a raspy whisper now.

"You remember the baby boy? My baby?" I choked on the words. "Daddy, he's a man now."

He looked puzzled at first; then recognition flooded his face. "Of course I remember." He swallowed, his lips parched. I held a long sponge swab to his mouth, patting his arm as he sighed from the relief that the cool moisture provided.

Looking straight into my eyes, with no confusion, he said, "No, hon. And if he had, don't worry. Your mama wouldn't have told him where to find you."

He closed his eyes and exhaled loudly. I was speechless, shocked silent at his words.

As I wiped his forehead with a wet cloth, tears rolled down my face. Before I left his side that night, I hugged him close, my chest aching. "Good night, Daddy. You can rest now. I love you so much. Always have."

Would they really have not told my son where to find me? Did they think that was what I wanted all these years?

Daddy died before dawn the next day.

∾

I miss my father more than I ever could have imagined. We spoke every day for the final five years of his life, yet still so much was left unsaid. My parents' deaths and their double funeral linger in my mind and heart each day. The concealment of our family secret and the inability to speak our truths will haunt me forever.

April 2016

My friend Jill and I had been walking buddies for thirty years. One chilly spring day, we decided to head to Seaport Village for our stroll. We started off at a quick clip, and, as if a higher power had taken control of my voice, I heard myself say, "Let's sit. I have something to tell you." I pointed to a public bench overlooking the harbor.

Tourists chattered and hurried past us on the windy sidewalk as they took in the beauty of San Diego Bay. This was totally unplanned, but I could not stop myself as I cautiously began to tell my friend the story of Jamie.

She reached out to me, comforting me, listening to the secret I had held so close, as tears flowed down my cheeks. "I'm so sorry you had to go through that, Laura. Why didn't you tell me? Please let me help. Do you want to try to find him? I'll help."

I was incredulous. "You don't think less of me?"

"What? Of course not. I think more of you."

I broke inside.

I had spoken the words out loud. I had said Jamie's name and confessed that I had left my firstborn son, and this dear friend of mine continued to care for me. Her unconditional love brought with it a massive, cathartic relief. A powerful physical reaction followed, and almost instantly I experienced sharp, violent cramping, reminiscent of labor pains, which made it difficult to walk back to our parked car.

On waking the next day, I discovered a fiery red rash circling my mouth. It lasted for weeks and resulted in visits to my baffled dermatologist. The toxic secret was leaving me, ravishing me both physically and emotionally.

Soon, surprising things began to happen. I started to write about long-buried memories that were bubbling to the surface. In class the teacher asked us to write a list of the things we would do if we had nothing stopping us. I wrote the words *Find Jamie* every day at the top of my list. In writing about finding Jamie, I began to find myself.

Understanding, along with profound forgiveness for Mama and Daddy, Grammy, Nick, and even Clay, seeped into my very being. Decades-old wounds began to mend. Many nights I woke from sleep, cheeks wet and salty, unearthed hurts from fifty years before vivid and raw. I allowed myself the pain of remembering. In my dreams, the girls' faces at the Home loomed behind my eyelids for the first time in almost fifty years. Delli, the doctors, the nurses, Miss Felton— all were still there, along with the healing love of Nancy, Pepper, and Mark. I called Nancy, and we talked for hours, trying to unravel the meaning of that time. I began to reveal more to Gene and to open up about the deep hurt that I had hidden even from myself. Together we daydreamed about Jamie. I was finding a voice for that broken and silenced seventeen-year-old girl.

One morning, I laid a sheet of my most special stationery on my desk. The heavy cream paper has scalloped edges and lovely red roses embossed on the margins. I addressed an envelope to seventeen-year-old Laura in 1967 from sixty-seven-year-old Laura in 2016.

April 2016

Dear Laura,

I know that you are facing one of the worst chapters in your life, and I have come back to you from the future to let you know, my dear girl, that this too shall pass. You're a survivor. Hold your head high. You have nothing to be ashamed of. You are a beautiful spirit and a gifted human being with so much to give. Know that your dreams are still possible and that your life ahead will be fulfilling beyond your wildest dreams.

Although today you think you are unworthy, soon you will move away from the South. You will move across the country and reinvent yourself. You will become the mother of three more amazing sons and two marvelous "extra" children through an incredible marriage to the love of your life, your knight in shining armor, your soul mate.

Eventually you will become Grammy to six adored grandchildren. You will be the backbone that a good mother and grandmother is for her family.

So many lovely surprises will come your way, and, once again, you will love your parents and come to terms with the way this loss of your son happened. You will one day understand the grief and loss that they too endured.

Yes, you will always mourn your secret son. Not a day will pass that you do not, but one day you will be able to talk about him and write his and your story, and then you will see that, yes, you are still loved. And, most importantly, you will learn to love yourself again.

Have faith and stay strong, because in the end you will experience more love than you can even imagine today.
You deserve this. I adore you.

Your older self,
Laura

Sealing the envelope, I tucked the letter into a drawer in my desk. A quietness settled over me as I peered into a mirror. She was still there. Although silver strands adorned her hair and wrinkles circled her eyes, there she was. At once I embraced myself entirely and forgave her with all my heart. After all, I am her.

Part Three

Chapter 45
October 9, 2016

Our day had been remarkably ordinary. Gene and I had enjoyed an entertaining afternoon with a group of friends and had settled down for a quiet evening. I was thinking about the book I was reading and my to-do list for the next day as we relaxed. The presidential debate monopolized all the television networks, and we watched the first twenty minutes of it. I found it unnerving and couldn't bear to see another second.

"Honey, I'm taking the girls out and then heading to bed to read." I stood and stretched.

"Okay, I'll be in there soon. Be sure and take your phone. It's dark out there."

Pecking him on his cheek, I grabbed my phone, heading out the door with Atlee and Annabelle, our chocolate Lab and golden retriever. The "girls," as we lovingly called them, bounded ahead of me down to the lower end of our property.

All was well in our world. It was another typical fall evening in San Diego, crisp and cool, with twinkling stars scattered in a clear cobalt-blue sky. A chilly breeze filled the night, and as I hurried the dogs along, immense gratitude flowed through me.

My iPhone pinged. I glanced at it: *Email from Ancestry.com.*

I decided to ignore it. I didn't plan to sit at my computer all night, scrolling through the extensive family tree I had created.

Gene and I had sent in our DNA samples the year before and had also purchased kits for all five of our kids. It had been fun seeing everyone's expected ethnicities, and a few surprises as well. I had secretly wondered if Jamie could be in this database but figured I would only be setting myself up for more disappointment if I thought too long and hard on that. After all, it had been almost fifty years.

But what if . . . Glancing down at my phone, I clicked open the email.

It read, *Parent/Child Match.*

I skidded to a stop. My knees buckled, and I caught myself, gasping.

Heart pounding erratically, I stared at the screen. Fight-or-flight adrenaline surged through my body. Where seconds earlier my checks had felt chilled, heat instantly scorched my face. I couldn't catch my breath and soon experienced the mother of all anxiety attacks. As my body physically shifted in the most powerful and radical way, I feared I was experiencing cardiac arrest.

Forgetting the dogs, I rushed into the house. Gene looked shocked at my stricken face. He called out to me, "What? What happened?"

I had lost the ability to string words together and desperately shook my head, hurrying into our home office. Trembling uncontrollably, I flung my body into the chair at my desk, logging on to the Ancestry website and my private DNA results page.

There it was again: *Parent/Child Match.* Beneath those words, listed along with the names of my three sons, a fourth and unknown name appeared.

I sat paralyzed, staring at the screen.

Is this really happening? My God, could this be Jamie? Who else could it be? It has to be him. Richard? A name I never would have chosen for him. They named him Richard?

Gene hurried into the office after he rescued our baffled pups.

"Laura, what is it? What's wrong?"

"Listen to this, honey," I cried and began reading aloud:

I just received my DNA profile, and Ancestry.com says we are a parent/child match. I was adopted and I am looking for more information.

We sat side by side, unable to speak, simply staring at the screen. As I folded into myself, deep, wrenching sobs bubbled up from a deep well of long-held hurt.

Tears sprang into Gene's eyes, and he hugged me, saying, "I knew this would happen one day, Laura. Do you think it's really him?"

My eyes met his, and I stammered, "I don't know. Maybe? Wait, yes. Oh God. Yes, I do know. I know it's him."

Who was this man? Was he friendly? Hostile? Would he hate me for giving him up, or would he forgive me?

"Who else could it be?"

"Just go slow," Gene cautioned, worry replacing the shock on his face.

Here was something I had wanted so badly yet feared as well. All those long years praying I would find him, and now he had found me on the internet. It was something I could never have dreamed possible in 1967, when no one could have imagined such a thing as the internet.

Why am I so afraid? The huge secret that I had held so close in my heart, the secret that had changed the direction of my life, was now spilling out in front of me on the computer screen. I realized I had never thought past finding Jamie.

If this is my Jamie, why am I not jumping for joy? Why am I gripped with fear?

Once again, I was that seventeen-year-old girl dropped off at the Home, humiliated, broken, and ashamed. Here I was, fifty years later, brought to my knees by the painful memories of that time. In a second, my life had changed once again.

If this is Jamie, how will this affect our lives? My family? His family?

"What are you going to do?" Gene searched my wet face, his hand on my shoulder. "What will you say?"

"I don't know. I don't want to scare him by acting too emotional. What if he doesn't write back? What if he hates me? What if he thinks I just left him?"

"He won't hate you," my adoring husband gently assured me. "Think before you reply. Stay calm."

"Okay, here goes—I'm writing to him." I braced myself.

"I'll make you a cup of tea." Gene left the office.

I typed, *My heart is doing flip-flops, but can you please tell me the date of your birth and the place you were born?*

Now we will wait and see. I exhaled, sitting back, staring at the screen. *This may take a while. Don't get too excited.*

But my wait was only a minute. I jumped as the answer popped up: *July 8, 1967 . . . New Orleans, Louisiana.*

I stared hard at those words, reading them again and again.

It's him.

I cried out to Gene. "It has to be him. It is him. Gene, it's Jamie!"

I knew with all my soul that this was my son, who now signed his name Richard. Fragile and shaken to the core, I felt my hands trembling so badly I could barely type, but type I did, and nonstop for hours.

Jamie (Richard) and I immediately began emailing each other, sidestepping cautiously, asking simple questions, trying to come to terms with the miracle taking place.

I learned that Richard had had a good life with loving adoptive parents who had raised him a mere four-hour drive from my home-town. They had adopted him at five weeks, and with that information I was instantly relieved. I had worried needlessly for years remembering babies left at the Home for months.

He emailed that he was happily married and had three children.

I was stunned again. *We have three new grandchildren?*

I learned that his wife was the director of a private school and he was an assistant attorney general for the state of Louisiana. Their lives were busy and full.

Richard wrote that his mother had died eighteen years earlier and his father was eighty-two years old and in ill health. I learned his parents had been close to my parents' ages when they adopted him— another fact I had never imagined.

As thrilled as I was in that moment, overwhelming guilt and sorrow still tore at my heart and soul. My conscience screamed at me. Why couldn't I have been raising this boy, along with my other three sons? Though I was grateful he had loving parents, I felt that old twinge of jealousy. Bittersweet elation filled me as I read and reread his words.

I knew I had not been given a choice when it came to surrendering Jamie to adoption, but my heart questioned whether I could have fought more to keep him.

In my next email, I felt brave enough to let my emotions show. I quickly typed, *I am overcome.*

He wrote back immediately, saying he was too, and that he was shocked at his own reaction. He said he had never had the inclination to find me. That hurt, but I swallowed my feelings. He went on to say he only searched at his wife's urging. She was primarily concerned about the health history of his biological parents. Now that he had found me, he was surprised that he found himself paralyzed with emotions.

Our emails soon changed from one or two hesitant sentences to lengthy missives in which we poured our hearts out to each other. In a couple of hours, I knew more about Richard than I ever could have dreamed I would. All those years of fear and doubt melted as my fingers flew across my keyboard. My voice broke as I read each of his emails aloud to Gene.

I wrote that I never had wanted to give him up. That I had lived with heartache since I had left New Orleans and had grieved as if he were dead. I told him the fact that I had never known where he lived had left me with never-ending sorrow and that as much as I had longed to find him, I had been afraid he would reject me. I had feared he would hate me.

I never hated you, he wrote. *I can only imagine what you went through. A young unwed teenager in the Deep South in the 1960s.*

He continued telling me that from the time he could remember, his parents had always told him he was adopted and that they had never put a negative twist on the adoption or me. Just when I thought I had no more tears, copious amounts flowed as I read those kind words. This was a balm I had never believed I deserved.

Thank you, God. Thank you for his parents.

My phone pinged, and I stared at the face of the son I had thought I would never see. His smile filled the screen. The resemblance to me and my family was striking. A strangled gasp escaped from my throat. It was as if I were looking into my own eyes. A powerful cocktail of shock and euphoria pulsed throughout my body. I could not study the man in the photo enough.

This man is my son Jamie, all grown up.

He looked as if he had sprung from me alone—no resemblance to Clay. Here was a robust, dark-haired, handsome forty-nine-year-old with my skin, chin, mouth, nose, and eyes, dressed in a suit and tie. In him I saw my other sons. My baby brother, Michael, had died years before, and I saw a glimmer of him as well. Mama was there too. DNA shouted out from this photo. No longer a fantasy, this was the truth. This was happening.

I will call you tonight, at 7 p.m. your time. Is that OK? he wrote.

Of course, of course! I answered.

The wait began, and I watched the clock as if my life depended on it.

What would Mama and Daddy think if they were still alive? I want to believe they would be happy for me. What will my children say? How will I explain a fourth son, a secret half brother?

Magically, within moments, my whole being shifted from years of shame and worry about what others would think of me to the cavalier notion: *I don't give a damn what anyone says or thinks. I can face anything.*

All the years of holding this secret inside me were melting with each breath I took. I wanted to shout from the rooftops, "My son has found me!" I couldn't get the smile off my face.

I fluctuated from falling apart one minute and grinning like a fool the next as the afternoon dragged on. Gene seemed perplexed yet eager to see what was about to unfold. We began making plans about how to tell our children.

"It's your story, Laura," he said. "You need to be the one to tell it. It's much too important and personal for me to tell, and I don't want to mess it up."

Now, here we were: Jamie was in our lives overnight. The list on my yellow legal pad grew longer and longer as I wrote names of family and our circle of friends who needed to know about my secret son.

ॐ

As promised, that night the phone rang precisely at seven o'clock.

I grabbed it and squeaked, "Hello, is it you?"

"Yes, it's me."

Can this be? I know his voice.

He said it before I could: "I know your voice."

The joy from hearing those simple words was indescribable.

After some nervous laughter, we tiptoed, making polite small talk. With a lump in my throat, I hesitantly worked up the courage to ask Richard about his life. It felt awkward and forward, but I had to know. He willingly told me about his boyhood, his adoptive parents, and growing up in Louisiana. He had graduated from LSU, become a psychologist, and later graduated from law school.

He described his children and wife with deep affection, proud of each of them. He worried about his elderly father. I asked when I could thank his father for loving him and giving him a wonderful life.

I listened spellbound, reeling from this surreal day and this story of my son's experience. I secretly couldn't shake the battle between my selfish jealousy toward his parents and my simultaneous thanks to God for them. They had given him a life I never could have.

Yet even though it would have been different, wouldn't I have given him a good life as well?

He wanted to know about my life and asked cautiously about his father.

"He was my boyfriend. We were so young, so immature. The times were extremely different back then. When I got pregnant, it was as if I had committed a crime. That was just the way it was. Your father and I were both teenagers. He had started college that summer, and we had broken up and gotten back together time and time again. Then he joined the army that fall after I told him I was pregnant. I am sorry, but he moved on from me and his family wanted no part of me. Of us."

Sorrowfully, I explained that Clay had died young, from cancer, and that I knew this only because my daddy had emailed me the obituary. I told him I never talked to his father after I returned home and knew essentially nothing about his life since I had last talked to him. I was no longer angry at Clay. When you are young, you cannot imagine this, but life does have a way of softening just about anything that happened in your past.

I told him how it had been drilled into us girls at the Home to go back to our hometowns and forget that our pregnancies had ever happened, as if we had given away a pair of shoes that didn't fit.

"I moved to California a year after you were born. I never wanted to see the South again. I tried to forget everything that had happened that summer. But I never could."

"Did you ever come back here to the South?" he asked.

"Oh, of course—over the years, many, many times to visit my family and friends. But it took several years for me to feel comfortable enough to go back to Mississippi.

There was a long pause. I worried. What could he be thinking? I quickly added, "You have three half brothers."

"Really?"

"Yes! They are wonderful sons, and I'm proud of each of them."

Then I told him about Dustin, born the year after his own birth, and about Marc and Ian.

"My children are the best part of me. Raising them has been the most important thing in my life. No success at work or in life mattered as much as they did. But there was always a sadness because no matter how busy or fulfilled I was, there was always a part missing—you. Truly a day did not pass that I didn't think of you."

That night there were tears and cautious laughter. Simply listening to the cadence of his voice, with its Southern accent, filled me up. He was intelligent and respectful. His voice was soft, and in it, didn't I hear a vague remembrance of Clay's voice, or did I simply imagine that?

I told Jamie/Richard about my family—his family. I talked about Mama and Daddy, my brothers, and my life in Mississippi as a girl. I told him how I felt as if I had escaped to California back then, yet I had not been able to escape myself. We laughed as we compared similar likes and dislikes. I kept pinching myself. Was this really happening?

How do you cram into brief sentences this tremendous gift we call life? We tried. We had so much to say to each other.

It's like talking to a friend, but much more. I could talk to him forever. After all, he's only eighteen years younger than I am. I have friends his age.

I glanced at the clock, shocked to see that it was after midnight in

Louisiana. In those five hours, I had learned more about my firstborn son than I had ever dreamed. Tender and precious time flew by.

I laughed. "I need to let you go. You have work tomorrow, right? Shouldn't we call it a night? We can talk now anytime. I might drive you crazy calling you."

He laughed. "I hate to hang up. I could talk to you forever."

∾

I floated down the hall to bed and didn't sleep a wink, playing that incredible conversation in my head all night. I was infatuated. *Is this too good to be true? Please let this be real. This feeling. This feeling.*

Let me try to describe that feeling. It was that same delirious happiness a new mother feels after she gives birth and kisses the velvety head of her newborn, ecstatically counting his tiny fingers and toes. It was comparable to the amazing bliss of looking at that perfect and wondrous human being and proudly thinking, *I did this. This child is part of me.*

But best yet, there was the joy a mother feels when she first brings her new infant home, only richer and more layered because she has seen that baby's future. She now knows that he has had a wonderful childhood and loving parents and an excellent life.

Instantly, I was that young girl who had become his mother all those years ago, while at the same time I was this older, experienced woman rebirthing the son I had never forgotten.

I was in love.

Chapter 46

The next morning, drained yet filled with anticipation and eager for the day, I got out of bed early. As the sun rose over the mountains, I sat at our kitchen table with toast and a cup of tea working on my ever-growing list of people to tell about Jamie. I was eager to get this show on the road, bursting to tell the world my son had found me.

My children were my priority. They deserved to hear this story before anyone else, and it was time to break my silence, time for the truth. Starting with Ian, I spent hours on the phone, explaining the story of Jamie to each of them.

Gene and I often discussed how different our five kids were, individuals with minds of their own and diverse not only in appearance but in personality as well. These important phone calls only proved that more than ever, as their responses were all over the board.

All five had the same first reaction: shock and puzzlement. Their mother had kept an astonishing event in her life from them, a secret that would change their lives. After the news of a secret brother had settled in, the questions began. Erick was full of them. Carly was astonished but happy for me. Ian was excited and supportive, sincerely pleased for both Richard and me. Marc, always sensitive, was a bit skeptical yet positive and reassuring.

Dustin's response stopped me midstream in the telling.

"Wait, wait, Mom. Is this a book or a movie?"

"Dustin, you're not listening. This is my story. This happened to me. *Me*, your mom."

He was speechless for a heartbeat, then asked, "Mom, are you telling me I'm not the oldest anymore?"

His spontaneous question lightened the intensity of the moment, and we both laughed a little. Then I cried again. Then he comforted me with words that warmed me to my core: "Mom, seriously, I'm happy for you. I hope this heals the hole that must have been in your heart this entire time."

☙

Gene, ever my cheerleader, watched over me throughout the day, insisting I take breaks between calls. Always concerned I would burn myself out, he was vehement that I pace myself.

Richard's texts continued bolstering me during the day: *What are the kids saying? Are they okay? Are you?*

I texted back: *They are all wonderful. You'll see when you meet them. I'm good. Never happier in my life.*

☙

That evening found me soaking in the bathtub with bubbles and a glass of cabernet, alternately crying one minute and laughing the next. I ached all over, as if I had run a marathon. My conversations with my children ran through my head. One moment I felt fulfilled, almost self-assured: *This is a miracle.* The next moment, I was sucked dry and empty. *Are the kids really okay with this?* Their approval of and love for me were vital to my entire being.

Climbing into bed, scooting close to Gene, I marveled, "Honey, can you believe this? All these years, I've been afraid of what the kids would say or think of me if they knew. Today they were all kind and understanding. I'm so proud of the adults they've grown up to be. Is this really happening?"

He reached for me, holding me tight. It really was.

❧

The support and love that poured from my family and friends as I made my way down the list boosted me for the next two days. I couldn't sleep. Incredible energy soared through me. There were not enough hours in the day to tell everyone.

Richard and I compared notes.

"I'm telling everyone about you. They're overjoyed that we found each other," I told him.

"Me too. People didn't know I was adopted. They're thrilled for me. Our kids are beyond excited. The girls want to know what to call you."

"All the grandkids call me Grammy." My own grammy flicked through my mind.

"Can my kids call you Grammy too?"

"Of course. They're my grandbabies too."

We both laughed. This lovefest felt like a gigantic group hug across the miles, warm and comforting.

On the third day after our initial connection, I sat in a restaurant in Mission Valley with one of my dearest friends, Terri. After we ordered lunch, I began, "Terri, I have to tell you something. Please don't think less of me."

I began sharing my story, and we cried together. She reached for my hand when I got to the part about Richard finding me.

"Terri, wait until you see his picture." I handed her my phone.

"Oh, my. Oh, Laura, this truly is a miracle. He looks like you. I see Ian too." She was peering at the photos, when she frowned. "Oh, wait. Someone is texting you. I think it's him."

She held the phone out towards me. I grabbed it.

Hi, do you mind if I fly out there and meet you tomorrow?

"Oh! Terri, he wants to come out here. Tomorrow. Oh, my. Oh, wow."

Mind? Of course not. Please come! Please!

His reply was immediate: *Booking a flight now.*

I hugged my dear friend, whose face was radiant with joy and tears, and raced home, stopping by Trader Joe's. *What will I cook? I don't even know what kind of food he likes. So much to do in twenty-four hours. I need to prepare the guest room. I'll make a* WELCOME HOME, JAMIE *sign.*

I grinned the whole drive.

Chapter 47

The next afternoon, Gene and I waited anxiously, peering out the living room windows. We had decided it would be best if only the three of us were here for the initial meeting. Family and friends knew what was happening and had sent encouraging texts all morning. *Take photos!* was the prevailing message.

It was a magnificent golden San Diego fall day. The temps were perfect, and there wasn't a cloud in the sky; still, I shivered, queasy one minute, filled with unbridled joy the next.

Richard had dutifully texted when his plane landed. That had been almost an hour ago.

"He should be here by now. It's taking too long."

Gene reasoned with me. "Laura, he had to go to baggage claim. It's an unknown airport for him, so it'll take a little while. Plus, we're at least a thirty-minute drive to the airport with no traffic. Calm down."

"You're right." I sighed. "Now, honey, remember the plan. I'll open the door, and then you video Richard coming into the house. I want to have our first meeting on video forever."

"I know, I know. Don't worry."

"Wait, maybe you should open the door when he knocks, Gene."

"Whatever you want. I can open it, but maybe you should."

"You're right. Of course. What am I thinking?"

Our nerves on edge, we continued debating the best way to greet this person whom I had not seen since he was a tiny seven-pound infant sleeping in my arms. Soon an Uber driver barreled down the driveway and a dark-haired man got out of the back seat with a small suitcase, looked around, and headed toward our house.

All plans flew out the window as I pushed past Gene in the entry-way and wrenched open the front door as Richard stepped onto the threshold. Throwing my arms around him, I held on for dear life. So much for not appearing emotional.

I stepped back and studied his face, trying to see that tiny baby in his features.

"Oh my God. Oh my God," I kept repeating, as relief surged through my body.

"We thought you got lost," I teased, looking up into his smiling adult eyes.

Turning to Gene, I said, "Honey, this is Jamie. He grew up." It sounded so silly, but that was exactly what I blurted out. All three of us laughed, tears glittering in our eyes. That sound was splendid. This was finally happening. This was my son.

Taller than I had imagined, handsome and charming, he supported me with his strong and sturdy arms. Our embrace felt strangely familiar. He was solid. He was real. It was that glorious feeling you have when you touch your child and it feels as if you are touching yourself.

I remember thinking, *Please let him like me. I so want him to like me.* I was as insecure as a teenager.

ᕰ

That first afternoon of Jamie/Richard's visit raced by in a surreal blur. I could feel his eyes scrutinizing me, and I found myself blatantly checking him out. We were discovering each other, observing each other's every move. I tried to hold back—I didn't want to overwhelm him, have him think me overly emotional—yet I couldn't prevent myself from often reaching toward him and simply touching his arm, patting his shoulder.

Gene and Richard hit if off immediately, amusing each other with fishing stories and LSU football talk—guy stuff that held no interest for me but sent shivers of happiness through me as I watched the two of them together.

I plied Jamie/Richard with more questions about growing up, his adoptive parents, his wife, his children. He had a younger adopted sister. I was enthralled with his stories about his boyhood.

As dusk closed in, we moved from the family room to the backyard deck, lighting a fire in the fire pit. Gene's eyes were dark and shiny with unshed tears as he smiled at me. In this magical moment, we nodded to each other, our love stronger than ever.

∾

I had been entirely off all those years imagining that Jamie resembled Clay. *All along, you were all me.*

"You are Mattie," Richard stated flatly. He sounded dumbfounded.

I laughed. I had seen photos of his daughter Mattie, and she did resemble me more than any of my other grandchildren. It had been another delightful surprise.

"No, really. She looks like you in photos but wait until you meet her. You'll see. It's incredible." Soon we were making plans for me to fly back to Louisiana to meet his family.

"I don't even like to fly. This unplanned trip was so unlike me," Richard told us while we ate dinner. "I never do things like this, but once I knew who you were, I just had to see you in person. Like I told you, I never thought I wanted to find you, but once I heard your voice, I couldn't stay away. This is mind-boggling. Here I am, sitting in California with . . . well, my mom and her husband. All those years,

I thought you lived somewhere in New Orleans. I still can't believe this."

A chilly, dry breeze wrapped around us. Queen palms gently swayed high above us in the night sky and we talked for hours. I memorized my son's face in the light of the glowing embers of the fire pit.

Richard had brought photos of his wife and children. There were some of him as a baby and a little boy, along with an old baby book. The one that intrigued me most was of him at five weeks old, when he was adopted. I had held him in my arms for the last time just two weeks before, when I had visited him secretly. My hand shook as I held that photo.

He also showed me a yellowed, creased letter written by his adoring mother. It appeared to have been written to a caseworker after the adoption. I studied the handwriting of this woman who had been Jamie's mother, who had loved and cared for the baby I couldn't keep.

> I can't tell you how delighted we are with Baby Richard. My husband and I would never have believed we could love him this much. So fast. We have always felt that we were living full lives. Now we realize just how much we were missing.

They had loved him from the start.

My chest ached as I looked long and hard at the photographs of Richard with his parents and his younger sister. The images were typical Instamatic shots from the '60s and '70s, some blurry, with that golden glow characteristic of pictures from that time. I studied his mama with curiosity, amazed at how different she was from me. She had been almost twenty years older than I was when I gave birth to Richard. Her blondish-red hair was neatly styled; she dressed primly in each photo and always had a smile on her face. And here was my baby boy, dressed in a blue bonnet and sweater, held by a woman I would never have the chance to know or thank.

Over the years, how many hours had I spent imagining Jamie's new family, concerned about whether he was happy and loved? Here they were, an all-American family, happy, living a normal and loving life. Jamie's face looked wide-eyed into the camera, innocent and brand new.

In one picture, my first son was standing in his crib, a proud smile lighting his face just like his half brother Marc's smile would look a few years later. Another snapshot was of a year-old Jamie about the same time I was giving birth to his younger brother Dustin. There was one with a football helmet, crooked atop his little-boy head. I had taken an almost identical photo of two-year-old Ian seven years later.

Richard's first haircut; riding his first two-wheeler, that same smile on his face. Here he was in a high school cap and gown for graduation. So many highlights that I had never shared.

Didn't I have these same photographs of my other sons growing up, so similar, yet two thousand miles apart? Devilish grins, lopsided and adorable; Buster Brown '70s bangs; cowboy hats; Easter suits. I remembered the "mother love" that I had felt as I snapped those images, and I knew that Richard had been loved with that same fierce feeling by his adoptive mom.

Richard and I sat up late that night after Gene had turned in. I showed him pictures of his brothers and old home movies. We looked at the family tree I had created, and I lovingly told him more stories about Mama and Daddy, Grammy, and my family in Mississippi.

I proudly showed him two old photos of Clay and me. In one, we sat on the white-sand beach while Clay strummed his guitar, our young teenage bodies sleek and strong, our faces fresh, smiling. Together we read a few ancient notes his father had written to me. At once, I was glad I had been too sentimental to toss the photos and notes years ago.

I will love you forever, Clay had written to the young girl I had been, and I had believed him.

∾

The next day dawned, adrenaline still surging. Richard's visit was almost over.

At noon we sat on a patio overlooking the bay and the gorgeous downtown skyline in one of our favorite Coronado Island restaurants. I looked up to see my youngest son, Ian, confidently striding over to our table with a smile that lit up his face. No one in that restaurant could have guessed these two half brothers were meeting for the first time. Richard rose from his seat, hand out; Ian grabbed his hand and shook it, then gave him a big man hug.

"What took you so long?" Ian asked Richard. We all burst out laughing, with tears in our eyes.

Making his way around the table, Ian grabbed Gene's hand and bent to kiss me on the cheek, whispering, "Mom, he looks like Nanny."

I could never have imagined this scene before now. Watching my oldest and youngest sons at lunch together was as close to a slice of heaven as I ever could have dreamed.

∾

The next morning arrived too soon. We still had so much to learn about each other, so many words still unspoken. At the airport, we assured each other we would stay in touch. I reached up to hug Richard, his starched shirt scratching my cheek, and we held on tight. I worried, *Is this too good to be true?*

Shifting from lost to found was difficult. For half a century, I had thought of myself as the mother of a lost son. Now he was found. Shaking off the skin of a secret mother, I began to carefully pull on the skin of a mother whose children were all accounted for and present in her life. The new skin felt awkward and uncertain. It kept me awake at night. Would I grow into it? Could I erase this shameful guilt from the past and live each day now with hope and gratitude?

Chapter 48
Two Months Later: December 28, 2016

G ene and I had returned from our preplanned and much antic-
ipated three-week trip to the UK in the middle of December.
Christmas markets from London to Dublin had made for a magical
adventure, but the knowledge that my son had found me was mostly
what put a spring in my step and a smile on my face.

While exploring the tiny village of Chiddingstone, England, on
a freezing, wet day, Gene and I took shelter in an empty medieval
church where my ancestors had prayed. My phone had not received
a signal all day, and when it pinged I was surprised to see a text.
Richard's eighty-three-year-old adoptive father had died of heart
failure. His dad's death was made even sadder by the knowledge that
I would never meet or thank the man who had loved and raised my
firstborn son.

∾

Anxiety blossomed as I sat in the clouds. Relaxing or concentrating
was out of the question. Sleep was impossible. My hands clammy, my
stomach unsettled, I opened my Kindle and read the same paragraph
over and over. Giving up on trying to focus, I simply sat staring out
the window during my nonstop flight to New Orleans.

Four hours into it, the pilot cheerfully announced. "Ladies and gentlemen, we're approaching the Crescent City." Quickly taking in the faces of my fellow passengers, I wondered what stories they would tell if asked why they were flying to New Orleans today.

I bet I have the best story.

I thought of Gene. Even though today was our thirty-sixth wedding anniversary, he would never have begrudged me this trip. His hug had been long and tight when we said our goodbyes at Lindbergh Field.

"You call me the minute you land, okay? You're sure they'll be there to pick you up?"

"Of course they'll be there. Honey, please stop worrying."

I laughed and tried to appear brave, but a tiny prickle of reservation pinched at me. Even though Richard and I texted and had called each other many times in the past two months, I was a virtual stranger planning to invade his family's home for five days.

The plan was for Richard's wife, Lauren, to pick me up at the outside loading area because he had a deposition. After landing, I quickly made my way through bustling Louis Armstrong Airport, heading toward the baggage claim, my heart pounding, my ears ringing. In the stampede of travelers, the cacophony of airport noises was thunderous, but in that chaos I thought I heard, "Grammy, Grammy." Turning toward the voices, risking being trampled by the folks behind me, I heard it again—an unmistakable "Grammeeee..."

Two small girls, rosy cheeked and bright eyed, with cascades of glossy curls, stood side by side, almost hidden in the crowd. They held signs decorated with pink and red crayon hearts, flowers, and ladybugs. The words *Love* and *Welcome Grammy* were written in endearing, childish print, complete with curlicues.

Time stood still as the rest of the world dissolved. Tears clouding my vision, heart battering in my chest, I dropped my backpack and rushed toward them. Without hesitation, I knelt to their level and swept them into my arms.

I studied those sweet, innocent faces. Here were two new grand-daughters whom I had never held as babies, never cuddled, whose hair I had never combed. This was Temple, age six, and Mattie, eight years old. They were exquisite, charming, and brave enough to offer hugs to a new grandmother they had not known existed three months before. I felt their small hands patting my back as I held them close.

I was mesmerized by Mattie's face. Her brown eyes framed with glasses, so like mine, startled me. It was as if the child I had been was staring back at me.

"Welcome, Laura." My new daughter-in-law, Lauren—blond, striking, with a smile that could light up a room—broke the spell.

"I thought you'd be taller. You almost walked right past us," she called out in her charming Southern accent. She wrapped her arms around me as if she had known me forever.

"I'm sorry. I wasn't expecting this." I wiped my eyes as the girls reached for my hands. "You really didn't have to come all the way inside the airport. I told Richard I would meet you at the pickup curb."

"I'm sure. I'm not about to tell Richard I drove by and picked up his mama on the curb. He'd kill me!"

His mama.

We all laughed, with tears in our eyes, as the airport throng milled around us, oblivious to this marvelous event taking place.

Chapter 49

I sat on Richard's front porch swing, once again back in the Deep South, ancient oak trees lining the neighborhood streets, my first-born son at my side. Neither of us at a loss for words, we talked for hours. Richard proudly showed me his home and his family, letting me enter without a hitch. We were only an hour away from the oaks that had lined the streets in the New Orleans neighborhood where I had last held him as an infant.

Later that evening, I met Richard's son, Alexander. Seeing this intelligent, gentle eighteen-year-old and looking into his warm brown eyes for the first time filled me with awe. Here was my oldest grandson, whom I had never known about all these years.

As we gathered around the fireplace to celebrate our first-ever Christmas season, Richard's gift to me was a print from a splendid painting that his artist father had painted. His brown toddler eyes looked out from the portrait, sweet and innocent. My heart swelled.

Then I gave my special gift to Richard.

∾

Weeks before my visit, I had lamented about to what to give him, wanting this first Christmas present from me to be sentimental, something worthy of our reunion.

"I know what you should give him," Gene offered shyly. "Give him the birth card."

"Oh, no. It's mine," I answered, without skipping a beat. "It has been my only connection with him all these years. I can't part with it."

"But, honey, now you have him. Do you really need the card anymore? I think it would mean a lot to him. Think about it."

The seed was planted. If I parted with the birth card and gave it to Richard, I would be giving him something that had kept me anchored for almost fifty years. All those birthdays, Christmases, and holidays, I had pressed it to my lips and hoped that his life was good, that he was healthy and loved. I had prayed that one day I would meet him and tell him I had missed him every day of my life after leaving him. How many times had that tiny card been my sanity?

In a small wooden display box with a shadowbox frame, I placed the card, along with a small scanned photo that Richard had given me of himself, a five-week-old Jamie. I also included the only picture I had of myself taken soon after his birth. It wasn't my best—my face was somber, my eyes knowing.

When he unwrapped it and read the birth card, he covered his face with his hand, overcome. He came across the room and held me close. That powerful link was now passed to him. My prayers had been answered.

With no reservation, I tumbled into the welcoming arms of Richard and his family. My family.

Chapter 50
Spring–Summer 2017

The gift of having Richard back in my life once again took me on a different path. Technicolor days brought joy and excitement that left my old expectations looking dim and gray by comparison. I looked over my shoulder often that first year, frightened that this would all end tomorrow. I frequently worried that my other children were feeling slighted and left out by my new, nonstop involvement with this lost son. There were a few bumps along the way. This was all new to them, as well as to me. Gene and I tried to tamp down our enthusiasm at times. But in the end, our adult children were champions and readily shared their mom with their new sibling, realizing there was room in my heart for all six of them.

Spring 2017 saw Gene and me flying to New Orleans for a visit with Richard and his family. Trying to make up for lost time, Gene and I attended Grandparents' Day with the girls. We enjoyed a fun-filled crawfish boil at Lauren's parents' home and basked in the love this family showered on us.

I repeatedly found myself studying my son and his children, looking for clues to our family connection. Mattie the bookworm, so like the little girl I had been. Temple, a passionate miniature drama queen, reminded me why Mama and Grammy had nicknamed me Sarah Bernhardt.

One day when Gene and Richard were occupied on a fishing trip,

Lauren and I headed to New Orleans. Brunch at the famous Court of Two Sisters, pedicures, and spa massages made for an unforgettable girls' day of bonding with my new daughter-in-law.

"I've never been back to the Home in that old neighborhood," I mentioned to Lauren as we sat side by side after our massages.

"I'll take you there."

"You will?"

"Of course I will. I'd love to see it too." She smiled at me.

On that beautiful spring day in May 2017, we headed to the old neighborhood in the Irish Channel of New Orleans where exactly fifty years before I had walked the sidewalks, living, laughing, and crying with a sisterhood of brave young women.

The sidewalk was crumbling in places where bulky tree roots pushed up through the concrete, just as they had all those years ago. Magnificent old oak trees still shaded the neighborhood of hundred-year-old houses, some in obvious stages of decline, others beautifully preserved. Children playing in the street called out to each other, and a warm breeze ruffled our hair as we approached the redbrick building. My body coursed with adrenaline, making my breath short and my heart pound. Once again, I was that frightened young girl seeing this place for the first time.

Tears sprang to my eyes, and I became more anxious with each step we took. I gulped down a hollow sob that threatened to escape from my throat. Lauren reached out for my hand and held it. I squeezed hers back even more tightly.

"It's just like I remembered it." My voice was high, thin. "The street. The houses. This building."

All was right in my world. Why this anxiety, these tears?

We walked up the steps to the front door. The building was locked; a sign on the door read CLOSED DUE TO REMODELING AND CONSTRUCTION. A plaque inset in the brick entryway read that this had been an Institution of Mercy, established in 1886, and that the building had been rebuilt in the 1950s. The final wording assured that this establishment had been SUPPORTED BY THE CHURCH . . . THAT THEY MIGHT HAVE LIFE.

I placed my hand on that plaque. My heartbeat slowed, and calmness washed over me. Turning and taking in the neighborhood, I closed my eyes and inhaled an extra-long breath, centering myself. Exhaling slowly, I opened my eyes. The smells, the sounds, and the warm, moist breeze immediately took me back to 1967.

"There. Look, Lauren." I pointed to the small mom-and-pop corner store. "It's the little store I described to you and Richard. That's where we girls bought our candy and Cokes. And cigarettes."

There, floating across the street, were the ghosts of all of us girls, giggling, gossiping, determined to still act like the normal teenagers we had left behind when entering this place.

I'm back.

Sadness fell over me as we explored the run-down building, peeking through the windows at empty corridors and rooms. I told Lauren about my friends and our daily outings as we walked blocks and blocks. I pointed out the window where my room had been and what had been the patio area in the courtyard where so many of our dramas had taken place. I could almost hear the Beatles crooning "Penny Lane," along with static on the transistor radio. We walked across the street to the tiny store, closed on this Sunday afternoon. Security bars crossed over the door and windows now.

The hour drive back to Baton Rouge was reflective, and when Gene and Richard returned from fishing, the four of us spent hours talking about the Home. I felt vindicated because my memory had served me well. The old neighborhood had been through fifty years of changes yet remained the same.

"Next time you come to visit, I'll go there with you," Richard promised.

I could finally show him the place where I had said goodbye to him so long ago.

July 7, 2017

Two months later, I found myself, along with Ian and his fiancée, Isabel, on another flight headed to New Orleans. The next day would be Richard's fiftieth birthday. We were excited to surprise him, and what could be more perfect than to spend this first birthday with him? After a night at a local hotel, the three of us drove to Richard's house, parked a block away, and made our way to his front door, decked out in party hats, carrying noisemakers.

Richard and the girls swung open the door. The looks on their faces were priceless. What had been a difficult and sad day for me for five decades instantly became one of celebration and joy.

Later that weekend, as I sat across from Lauren and Isabel and my oldest and youngest sons, I watched the miracle of my children enjoying each other's company. I marveled at that remarkable invisible bond that binds us as families, even if we are strangers. I was content to be the old grammy, quietly tucked in the corner of the living room in her comfy chair, while they bantered. Their boisterous laughter as they got to know each other washed over me, filling my soul with pure wonder.

December 2017

This would be a Christmas of firsts. Richard was flying his family out to California to spend the holiday with us for the first time, something I had never allowed myself to imagine. We planned outings to Universal Studios and Legoland for the grandchildren, along with a party, inviting many of our closest friends to meet the newest additions to our family: Jamie, now known as Richard, and his wife and children.

Most of our other children would also be meeting their half sibling for the first time. Dustin, back in Kansas City, would be the only one missing, along with his four children, for that Christmas of firsts.

ॐ

Finally, the long-awaited Christmas Eve arrived. Gene and I had always made it a priority to make Christmas the best celebration possible for our children. Our family had experienced just about every kind of Christmas. There were several broke Christmases in our younger days. Stressful Christmases with teenagers mingled with storybook Christmas memories from years past. Family feud Christmases fraught with in-law issues and ex-spouse issues were recollections we chose not to dwell on. And there had been many lavish Christmases as we and the children aged and prospered in life. Most of all, every Christmas had been overlaid with affection.

Christmas season had always held a secret sorrow for me too, though: *Where is Jamie? Is he happy?* Amid family celebrations, traditional foods, and countless gifts, thoughts of him were never far from my mind. But there would be no time for sadness this Christmas—simply gratitude and heart-melting love.

As the kids began arriving that afternoon, I found myself analyzing every word and moment while they introduced themselves to Richard. I knew this could be awkward and difficult.

Gene, sensing my discomfort, quietly walked me into the laundry room, away from the chaos, and said, "Honey, let this all unfold the way it's meant to. Stop worrying, okay?"

I shrugged. "I can't help but worry. They don't seem to be talking to each other."

"Stop." He hugged me. "I promise you. It will be okay."

ॐ

All my worries that Christmas Eve and any concern that our family celebration might seem corny and not up to par was soon replaced with delicious contentment. Among the glittering tree, gifts, twinkling lights, candles, seafood gumbo, and holiday cookies, I sighed with relief. The house was soon loud and filled with laughter. Marc brought out his guitar after dinner and played our piano with Mattie. As presents were exchanged and exclaimed over, Gene's and my eyes met across the room. Watching our children and grandchildren together was our best gift of all.

"Tonight was wonderful." Richard hugged me tightly after everyone headed home that night. "It was exactly how I always thought Christmas should be. Y'all made us feel so welcomed. Ian and Marc are simply great—well, all of the kids are—and I love the way y'all sing songs and enjoy each other so much. It was amazing, Mom."

As I wrapped my arms around my oldest son, I thanked God for this miracle. The simple pleasure of baking Christmas cookies with my granddaughters, sharing a glass of ruby cabernet with my new daughter-in-law, and watching Richard unwrap the blanket I had crocheted for him in his beloved LSU colors had delighted me to no end. I had been enchanted listening in on the endless chatter of our children, finally together and here with me. Earlier in the day, Richard had helped me make my daddy's gumbo, something neither Daddy nor I ever could have imagined. Gathering for the annual Christmas photo of the family, which I always cherished, was extra precious this year. Watching our grown sons singing "Feliz Navidad" together as Marc strummed his guitar . . . Well, there was nothing like that.

Have I ever been prouder of my grown children? They had accepted Richard and his family with extraordinary care and open arms. The ordinary family love that I had taken for granted was extraordinary that night.

Be it cliché or not, I believe it with all my heart: The best gift of all is the unconditional love of family.

Chapter 51

All those years, my son Jamie had never been far from my mind, and now he was miraculously in my life. The trauma of losing him had changed me. It had taken me thousands of miles from my roots. It had colored my choices in life and affected the people I loved. It had been an invisible cloud that hung perpetually over my head, a secret rip in my heart that never completely healed.

I didn't know it then, but the future held endless conversations on Richard's front porch, surrounded by those beautiful old oak trees, their emerald branches majestically canopying the street. I would come to know Alexander, my oldest grandson, for the fine young man he was. Mattie and Temple would take countless walks with me along those uneven sidewalks, the fragrance and softness of the warm, humid air forever reminding me of the Home in New Orleans.

Time truly does have a way of healing, and once we open our minds and hearts, the universe imparts wisdom that eventually lays peace upon us. One of the most valuable lessons life has taught me is the power of forgiveness. As time passed, I was awed in recalling the love and support Mark, Nancy, Pepper, and Delli gave me during my darkest hours. I realized I had forgiven Mama, Daddy, and Grammy long ago. I had forgiven a society that had forced upon me the trauma of leaving my son all those years earlier. I had forgiven Clay and Nick and anyone who hurt me, sometimes without even knowing they had.

319

Most important, I forgave the seventeen-year-old girl who still lived within me. I had never forgotten her. I never would. The pain of separation and the shame of leaving my son would continue to rear their ugly heads occasionally, each time piercing my heart, but I was determined to grow into this new role. I would embrace any surprises and changes, no matter the outcome, because wasn't I the luckiest of women? Of mothers? I had finally found peace with forgiveness.

Richard and I had managed to live our lives without each other for forty-nine years. Now, we would never be apart. Two thousand miles would not get in the way of our knowing that with faith and love, dreams do come true. My secret son had always had a mother who never forgot him and always loved him beyond measure.

Epilogue
July 2021

Two days before it happened, Richard sounded happier than I had heard him in many months, less stressed, not as anxious. It had been a typical Sunday afternoon catch-up call. We had talked on the phone that beautiful spring day for forty-five minutes, mostly about future plans. Gene and I told Richard now that the Covid restrictions were lifting and we were vaccinated, we would travel back to Louisiana soon to visit him and the kids. It had been a year since we had seen him. Gene and he talked about another fishing trip. At the end of our conversation, Richard said, "Mom, you're the best thing that ever happened to me." My heart swelled.

I remember turning to Gene and saying, "He sounds better, not as depressed." He agreed. 2021 was looking brighter already.

Two days later my twenty-three-year-old grandson called. It was a call no one ever wants to get. A call that rocked our world and stopped my heart. Richard was gone. He had taken his own life. Four and a half years after our miraculous reunion, Richard was forever lost to me. The first loss of my infant son had changed the course of my life and had wounded me for decades. The second tragic and final loss of Richard paralyzed me and crushed me with a pain like no other.

They say time heals all. Maybe it softens the pain, but time never takes it completely away. I cherish the short years Richard and I had together and the fact that I came to know my son intimately, learning about his life that I had not been able to be part of for forty-nine years. Our conversations and laughter will color my days for the rest of my life, and I am forever grateful for the gift of three glorious grandchildren he left for us to love. There is so much to be thankful for, but I am changed. I am a mother who lost her first-born son, twice.

Acknowledgments

For fifty years, I never spoke about my time in New Orleans. Few people on Earth knew about my secret son. Exactly one day after Richard found me, that changed. I wanted to tell the world about my son and the truth about that dark time in my life. The joy and complete relief I felt upon Richard's and my reunion outweighed any guilt or shame I still carried.

Three months after this miracle took place, I signed up for my first memoir class, at San Diego Writers Ink, with writing coaches Marni Freedman and Tracy J. Jones. Within two months, the story of my stay at the unwed mothers' Home in New Orleans poured out of me onto my computer screen.

I have learned during the past five years that just as it takes a village to birth and raise a child, it also takes a village to write and birth a book. As I began the most grueling learning curve of my life, I met some of the finest writers and best human beings I have ever known. My talented teachers and mentors, Marni and Tracy, supported me, critiqued my pages, edited countless drafts, and instilled confidence in me that I was indeed a writer. I can never thank them enough.

I would be remiss not to mention here that I owe a debt to my writing sisters, authors Deborah Reed and Lisa Shapiro, who were the first to hold my hand and believe in my ability to tell my story long before I believed it myself. They gave me advice and introduced me to the International Women's Writing Guild (IWWG), and I can honestly say this group of outstanding women writers changed the direction of my life.

At IWWG conferences, I met a powerful group of women who nourished my love of writing and gave me strength to write about my most harrowing experiences. Kelly Dumar, Judy Huge, and Maureen Murdock, to name a few, led me in directions I could only have stumbled toward without their guidance. Suzanne Westhues, Diana Eden, Roberta Kuriloff, Cathleen O'Connor, and so many other IWWG sisters inspired me with their advice, read my pages, critiqued my work, and shared their own books and writing with me.

To my beta readers: Thank you for your honest appraisals, your questions, and your advice. Nina Little, Roberta Kuriloff, Bernice Palumbo, Madonna Treadway, Jim Edwards, and Nancy Campbell, I am forever grateful to all of you for reading my manuscript.

Another group of writers who inspired and shared knowledge with me was my excellent Read and Critique Group. Joining that group three years ago was the smartest thing I ever did. Tracy J. Jones, Francine Lehmann, Kathleen McCabe, Saadia Esmail, Deb Rudell, Lauren Cross, Jen Gasner, Kathryn McLane, Suzi Gold and Stephanie Weaver: Thank you for reading my work and taking time to critique and advise me. All of you are dear to me. I could not have done it without you.

I am ever grateful to the amazing community of San Diego Writers Ink, particularly Judy Reeves. I am lucky to have the gifted Jeniffer Thompson, first my website creator, now my dear friend, inspire me to be the best I could be.

Also very close to my heart is our fabulous organization, the San Diego Memoir Writers Association (SDMWA). SDMWA was instrumental in providing workshops and presentations that broadened my writing life in all the right ways. I adore this community, and it was in one of our meetings that I met the brilliant Brooke Warner, who four years later would be publishing my book. I am forever thankful to Brooke and She Writes Press (SWP) for having faith in my story.

I want to thank my SWP project manager, Samantha Strom, and I am ever grateful to the talented Annie Tucker, editor extraordinaire, for polishing my final draft. To incredibly talented author and human being, Dani Shapiro: Thank you for interviewing me on your podcast, *Family Secrets*, and helping me to find an audience for my book.

Often when an older, retired person embarks on a project with which she has no experience and no knowledge of the industry she is attempting to break into, family and friends shake their heads and wonder why. Fortunately, I have been blessed with an excellent support network of friends who cheered me on when I did just that. You know who you are. Girls of '67 in Mississippi: They say our oldest friends are golden, and you all are. I am fortunate to have reconnected with many of the alumni from the unwed mothers' Home, who gave me advice, discussed our stay there in the 1960s, and helped me with research. My cherished sister-friend Nancy Mills, who was part of this story and loved the idea, encouraged me until the end of her life. My book club, the Finches, and other circles of friends: I appreciate all of you so much. I give special mention here to two longtime friends who embraced the idea of my writing a book with such enthusiasm that I felt I simply must keep writing and not let them down. Jill Chaffin and Terri Pontzious believed in me, and for that I will forever be thankful.

Last but by no means least, I owe gratitude to my family in California and my family in the South. To my children—Richard, Erick, Dustin, Marc, Carly, and Ian—and your loving partners, plus our grandchildren, who patiently listened to my nonstop chatter about my research, my writing, and this book over the years: Thank you for believing in your mom and grammy.

I saved the best for the last. To my beloved husband, Gene Engel, who looked across a table many years ago and said to me, "Laura, this is your story." Honey, thank you for always believing in me, never complaining about all the hours I spent writing, lifting me up when I was ready to throw in the towel, and encouraging me to keep going and take my book to the finish line. You are my greatest cheerleader and the love of my life, and with you by my side, I always feel like I can climb the highest mountains.

About the Author

© Chad Thompson Photography

Laura L. Engel, originally from Mississippi, migrated to San Diego more than fifty years ago. She is married, with six grown children and ten cherished grandchildren.

Her first memoir, *You'll Forget This Ever Happened: Secrets, Shame, and Adoption in the 1960s* is the story of a secret Laura had planned to take to her grave.

She has had three essays from her memoir published in *Shaking the Tree* anthologies. Two of those essays were performed live onstage in San Diego. Laura is now dabbling in playwriting and has had a skit performed onstage, as well as a monologue from her memoir.

Laura serves as president of the San Diego Memoir Writers Association. She is a member of San Diego Writers Ink, the San Diego Writers and Editors Guild, and the International Women Writers Guild.

In spring 2019, Dani Shapiro interviewed Laura for her *Family Secrets* podcast, and thousands of people listened to the episode, "Secret Son."

Please check out Laura's website at www.lauralengel.com.

SELECTED TITLES FROM SHE WRITES PRESS

She Writes Press is an independent publishing company founded to serve women writers everywhere. Visit us at www.shewritespress.com.

Home Free: Adventures of a Child of the Sixties by Rifka Kreiter
$16.95, 978-1-63152-176-8
A memoir of a young woman's passionate quest for liberation—one that leads her out of the darkness of a fraught childhood and through Manhattan nightclubs, broken love affairs, and virtually all the political and spiritual movements of the sixties.

All the Sweeter: Families Share Their Stories of Adopting from Foster Care by Jean Minton $16.95, 978-1-63152-495-0
The stories of twelve families who have adopted one or more children from the US foster care system, accompanied by topical chapters that explore the common challenges these families face, including the complications that accompany transracial adoptions, helping children understand adoption, relationships with birth parents, and raising a traumatized child.

You Can't Buy Love Like That: Growing Up Gay in the Sixties by Carol E. Anderson $16.95, 978-1631523144
A young lesbian girl grows beyond fear to fearlessness as she comes of age in the '60s amid religious, social, and legal barriers.

Hippie Chick: Coming of Age in the '60s by Ilene English
$16.95, 978-1-63152-586-5
After sixteen-year-old Ilene English, the youngest of six, finds her mother dead in the bathroom, she flies alone from New Jersey to San Francisco, embarking upon a journey that takes her through the earliest days of the counterculture, psychedelics, and free love, on into single parenthood, and eventually to a place of fully owning her own strengths and abilities.

Fatherless, Fearless, Female: A Memoir by Mary Charity Kruger Stein
$16.95, 978-1-63152-755-5
In this tale of single mothers and fatherless children, a Rust Belt farm girl escapes poverty, weds, has a son, is widowed by her first husband, and then falls in love with a Jewish man whose mother opposes their relationship—just before she moves halfway around the world.